SMP AS/A2 M

# Core 4

## for AQA

CAMBRIDGE
UNIVERSITY PRESS

The School Mathematics Project

**SMP AS/A2 Mathematics writing team** Spencer Instone, John Ling, Paul Scruton, Susan Shilton, Heather West

**SMP design and administration** Melanic Bull, Pam Keetch, Nicky Lake, Cathy Syred, Ann White

The authors thank Sue Glover for the technical advice she gave when this AS/A2 project began and for her detailed editorial contribution to this book. The authors are also very grateful to those teachers who advised on the book at the planning stage and commented in detail on draft chapters.

CAMBRIDGE UNIVERSITY PRESS
Cambridge, New York, Melbourne, Madrid, Cape Town, Singapore, São Paulo, Delhi, Mexico City

Cambridge University Press
The Edinburgh Building, Cambridge CB2 8RU, UK

www.cambridge.org
Information on this title: www.cambridge.org/9780521605304

© The School Mathematics Project 2005

First published 2005
7th printing 2012

Printed and bound in the United Kingdom by the MPG Books Group

*A catalogue record for this publication is available from the British Library*

ISBN 978-0-521-60530-4 Paperback

Typesetting and technical illustrations by The School Mathematics Project

The authors and publisher are grateful to the Assessment and Qualifications Alliance for permission to reproduce questions from past examination papers. Individual questions are marked AQA.

# Using this book

Each chapter begins with a **summary** of what the student is expected to learn.

The chapter then has sections lettered A, B, C, … (see the contents overleaf). In most cases a section consists of development material, worked examples and an exercise.

The **development material** interweaves explanation with questions that involve the student in making sense of ideas and techniques. Development questions are labelled according to their section letter (A1, A2, …, B1, B2, …) and answers to them are provided.

**D** Some development questions are particularly suitable for discussion – either by the whole class or by smaller groups – because they have the potential to bring out a key issue or clarify a technique. Such **discussion questions** are marked with a bar, as here.

**K** **Key points** established in the development material are marked with a bar as here, so the student may readily refer to them during later work or revision. Each chapter's key points are also gathered together in a panel after the last lettered section.

The **worked examples** have been chosen to clarify ideas and techniques, and as models for students to follow in setting out their own work. Guidance for the student is in italic.

The **exercise** at the end of each lettered section is designed to consolidate the skills and understanding acquired earlier in the section. Unlike those in the development material, questions in the exercise are denoted by a number only.

**Starred questions** are more demanding.

After the lettered sections and the key points panel there may be a set of **mixed questions**, combining ideas from several sections in the chapter; these may also involve topics from earlier chapters.

Every chapter ends with a selection of **questions for self-assessment** ('Test yourself').

Included in the mixed questions and 'Test yourself' are **past AQA exam questions**, to give the student an idea of the style and standard that may be expected, and to build confidence.

# Contents

# 1 Rational expressions 1

In this chapter you will learn how to
- simplify rational expressions
- add, subtract, multiply and divide rational expressions

## A Simplifying (answers p 138)

An expression that consists of one polynomial divided by another is called a **rational expression** or **algebraic fraction**.

**A1** A function is defined by $f(n) = \dfrac{n+3}{n^2 + 4n + 3}$ where $n$ is an integer such that $n \geq 0$.

    (a) Evaluate each of these in its simplest fractional form.

        (i) $f(1)$          (ii) $f(4)$          (iii) $f(10)$

    (b) (i) Without calculating, what do you think is the value of $f(100)$ in its simplest form?

        (ii) Check your result.

    (c) (i) What do you think is the value of $f(k)$ in its simplest fractional form?

        (ii) Prove your conjecture.

    (d) Show that $f(n) \leq \frac{1}{2}$ for all positive integer values of $n$.

**A2** A function is defined by $f(n) = \dfrac{n^2 + 6n + 5}{n^2 + 7n + 10}$ where $n$ is an integer such that $n \geq 0$.

    (a) Evaluate each of these in its simplest fractional form.

        (i) $f(0)$          (ii) $f(3)$          (iii) $f(20)$

    (b) (i) What do you think is the value of $f(k)$ in its simplest fractional form?

        (ii) Prove your conjecture.

    (c) Hence show that the equation $f(n) = \frac{8}{11}$ has no integer solution.

**A3** Prove that, when $x$ is a multiple of 5, the value of the expression $\dfrac{5x+10}{x^2 + 2x}$ can be written as a unit fraction (with 1 as its numerator).

When simplifying rational expressions, it is usually beneficial to factorise whenever possible.

---

**Example 1**

Simplify $\dfrac{3x-12}{x^2-4x}$.

**Solution**

*Factorise.*
$$\frac{3x-12}{x^2-4x} = \frac{3(x-4)}{x(x-4)}$$

*Divide numerator and denominator by $(x-4)$.*
$$= \frac{3}{x}$$

---

## Example 2

Simplify $\dfrac{n^2 + 2n - 15}{2n + 1} \times \dfrac{1}{n + 5}$ .

**Solution**

$$\dfrac{n^2 + 2n - 15}{2n + 1} \times \dfrac{1}{n + 5} = \dfrac{n^2 + 2n - 15}{(2n + 1)(n + 5)}$$

*Factorise.*

$$= \dfrac{(n + 5)(n - 3)}{(2n + 1)(n + 5)}$$

*Divide numerator and denominator by $(n + 5)$.*

$$= \dfrac{n - 3}{2n - 1}$$

---

You may need to revise dividing by a fraction.

For example, $\dfrac{3}{4} \div \dfrac{5}{2} = \dfrac{\frac{3}{4}}{\frac{5}{2}} = \dfrac{\frac{3}{4} \times \frac{2}{5}}{\frac{5}{2} \times \frac{2}{5}} = \dfrac{\frac{3}{4} \times \frac{2}{5}}{1} = \dfrac{3}{4} \times \dfrac{2}{5}$ .

In general, dividing by a fraction is equivalent to multiplying by its reciprocal.

This rule applies to all rational expressions: $\dfrac{a}{b} \div \dfrac{c}{d} = \dfrac{a}{b} \times \dfrac{d}{c}$ .

---

## Example 3

Simplify $\dfrac{4n + 4}{n^2 - 9} \div \dfrac{8}{2n^2 + 5n - 3}$ .

**Solution**

*Use the rule for dividing.*

$$\dfrac{4n + 4}{n^2 - 9} \div \dfrac{8}{2n^2 + 5n - 3} = \dfrac{4n + 4}{n^2 - 9} \times \dfrac{2n^2 + 5n - 3}{8}$$

*Factorise.*

$$= \dfrac{4(n + 1)}{(n + 3)(n - 3)} \times \dfrac{(2n - 1)(n + 3)}{8}$$

*Divide numerator and denominator by 4 and $(n + 3)$.*

$$= \dfrac{(n + 1)(2n - 1)}{2(n - 3)}$$

---

## Exercise A (answers p 138)

**1** Simplify each of these.

(a) $\dfrac{x^2 + 6x}{2x + 12}$
(b) $\dfrac{x^2 - 3x}{x^2 + x}$
(c) $\dfrac{3x + 6}{2 + x}$
(d) $\dfrac{x - 3}{5x - 15}$
(e) $\dfrac{6n^2 + 4n}{4n^2 + 2n}$

**2** (a) Show that $\dfrac{14x - 4x^2}{2x - 7}$ is equivalent to $-2x$.

(b) Simplify each of these.

(i) $\dfrac{15n - 10}{2 - 3n}$
(ii) $\dfrac{n^2 - 7n}{7 - n}$

**3** Simplify each of these.

(a) $\dfrac{x^2 + 5x + 6}{x + 2}$ (b) $\dfrac{x^2 + 2x - 3}{2x + 6}$ (c) $\dfrac{x - 4}{x^2 - 2x - 8}$ (d) $\dfrac{x^2 + 5x}{x^2 - 25}$ (e) $\dfrac{3n^2 - n}{9n^2 - 1}$

**4** A function is defined by $g(n) = \dfrac{2n + 18}{n^2 + 10n + 9}$ where $n$ is a positive integer.

(a) Evaluate $g(3)$ and $g(4)$ in their simplest fractional form.

(b) When $n$ is odd, prove that in its simplest form $g(n)$ is a unit fraction.

(c) Find the value of $n$ such that $g(n) = \frac{2}{9}$.

**5** Simplify each of these.

(a) $\dfrac{n^2 + 9n + 20}{n^2 + 11n + 30}$ (b) $\dfrac{n^2 + 5n - 14}{n^2 - 7n + 10}$ (c) $\dfrac{2n^2 - 10n - 12}{n^2 + 6n + 5}$ (d) $\dfrac{3n^2 - 16n + 5}{n^2 - 3n - 10}$

(e) $\dfrac{2n^2 + n - 3}{2n^2 + 7n + 6}$ (f) $\dfrac{2n^2 + 7n - 4}{3n^2 - 48}$ (g) $\dfrac{n^2 + n}{n^3 - n}$ (h) $\dfrac{n^2 + 5n - 24}{n^3 - 9n}$

**6** Simplify each of these.

(a) $\dfrac{2x - 10}{x + 1} \times \dfrac{3x + 3}{x - 5}$ (b) $\dfrac{x^2 - 16}{x - 4} \times \dfrac{2x}{x + 4}$

(c) $\dfrac{x^2 + 7x + 12}{x + 2} \times \dfrac{5}{x + 3}$ (d) $\dfrac{6x - 12}{3x + 15} \times \dfrac{x^2 + 10x + 25}{x^2 - 4x + 4}$

(e) $\dfrac{x^2 + 2x - 3}{x^2 + 6x + 9} \times \dfrac{x^2 + 10x + 21}{x^2 - 2x + 1}$ (f) $\dfrac{4x^2 - 9}{2x^2 + 13x + 15} \times \dfrac{x^2 - 25}{2x^2 - 5x + 3}$

**7** Simplify each of these.

(a) $\dfrac{2}{x^2 + x} \div \dfrac{4}{5x + 5}$ (b) $\dfrac{x^2 - 1}{2x + 3} \div \dfrac{x^2 - x}{4x + 6}$

(c) $\dfrac{2x^2 + x - 15}{x} \div \dfrac{2x^2 - 13x + 20}{x^2 - 4x}$ (d) $\dfrac{9x^2 - 4}{2x^2 - 4x - 70} \div \dfrac{6x^2 - 7x + 2}{2x^2 + 9x - 5}$

**8** Show that $\dfrac{1}{x} \div y$ is equivalent to the single fraction $\dfrac{1}{xy}$.

**9** Simplify each of these.

(a) $\dfrac{1}{x} \div \dfrac{1}{y}$ (b) $\dfrac{1}{x} \div 3$ (c) $6x \div \dfrac{3}{y}$ (d) $\dfrac{4}{x^2} \div \dfrac{1}{2x}$ (e) $\frac{1}{5} \div 10x$

**10** Functions are defined by $f(x) = \dfrac{6}{x}$ $(x > 0)$ and $g(x) = \dfrac{2}{x - 1}$ $(x > 1)$.

(a) Evaluate $fg(7)$.

(b) Show that $fg(x) = 3(x - 1)$.

**11** Functions are defined by $f(x) = \dfrac{6x+8}{3x^2+10x+8}$ and $g(x) = \dfrac{2}{x^2+4x+4}$ where $x$ is a positive integer.

   **(a)** **(i)** Evaluate $f(2)$ and $g(2)$ in their simplest fractional form.

      **(ii)** Find $\dfrac{f(2)}{g(2)}$ in its simplest form.

   **(b)** Prove that $\dfrac{f(x)}{g(x)}$ is always an integer.

## B Adding and subtracting

Fractions can easily be added or subtracted if they are written with the same denominator. The lowest common multiple of two denominators is called the **lowest common denominator** and is usually the simplest to use.

For example, $\frac{3}{4} - \frac{2}{3} = \frac{9}{12} - \frac{8}{12} = \frac{9-8}{12} = \frac{1}{12}$.

Algebraic fractions can be dealt with in the same way.

---

### Example 4

Express $\dfrac{1}{x-2} - \dfrac{3}{5x}$ as a single fraction in its simplest form.

### Solution

*A suitable denominator is $5x(x-2)$.*
$$\frac{1}{x-2} - \frac{3}{5x} = \frac{5x}{5x(x-2)} - \frac{3(x-2)}{5x(x-2)}$$

$$= \frac{5x - 3(x-2)}{5x(x-2)}$$

*Expand the brackets in the numerator.*
$$= \frac{5x - 3x + 6}{5x(x-2)}$$

*Simplify.*
$$= \frac{2x+6}{5x(x-2)}$$

*Factorise if possible.*
$$= \frac{2(x+3)}{5x(x-2)}$$

---

### Example 5

Express $4 + \dfrac{3}{2x+1}$ as a single fraction in its simplest form.

### Solution

*Write 4 as a fraction with a denominator of $2x + 1$.*
$$4 + \frac{3}{2x+1} = \frac{4(2x+1)}{2x+1} + \frac{3}{2x+1}$$

$$= \frac{4(2x+1)+3}{2x+1}$$

*Expand the brackets and simplify.*
$$= \frac{8x+7}{2x+1}$$

---

## Example 6

Express $\dfrac{x+1}{2x-1} + \dfrac{2}{x-5}$ as a single fraction in its simplest form.

### Solution

A suitable denominator is $(2x-1)(x-5)$.
$$\frac{x+1}{2x-1} + \frac{2}{x-5} = \frac{(x+1)(x-5)+2(2x-1)}{(2x-1)(x-5)}$$

Expand the brackets on the numerator.
$$= \frac{x^2-4x-5+4x-2}{(2x-1)(x-5)}$$

Simplify.
$$= \frac{x^2-7}{(2x-1)(x-5)}$$

## Example 7

Express $\dfrac{x}{(x+2)(x+3)} - \dfrac{6}{(x+2)(x-1)}$ as a single fraction in its simplest form.

### Solution

A suitable denominator is $(x-1)(x+2)(x+3)$.
$$\frac{x}{(x+2)(x+3)} - \frac{6}{(x+2)(x-1)} = \frac{x(x-1)-6(x+3)}{(x-1)(x+2)(x+3)}$$

Expand the brackets in the numerator.
$$= \frac{x^2-x-6x-18}{(x-1)(x+2)(x+3)}$$

Simplify.
$$= \frac{x^2-7x-18}{(x-1)(x+2)(x+3)}$$

Factorise.
$$= \frac{(x-9)(x+2)}{(x-1)(x+2)(x+3)}$$

Cancel.
$$= \frac{x-9}{(x-1)(x+3)}$$

## Exercise B (answers p 139)

**1** Express each of these as a single fraction in its simplest form.

(a) $\dfrac{1}{x} + \dfrac{1}{2x+3}$  (b) $\dfrac{1}{x} - \dfrac{1}{x+5}$  (c) $\dfrac{3}{x-1} + \dfrac{4}{3x}$  (d) $\dfrac{2}{x-1} - \dfrac{2}{x}$

**2** Express each of these as a single fraction in its simplest form.

(a) $x + \dfrac{5}{x}$  (b) $\dfrac{9}{2x+1} + 3$  (c) $\dfrac{x}{x-4} - 5$  (d) $\dfrac{x}{3x-2} - x$

**3** Express each of these as a single fraction.

(a) $\dfrac{1}{a} + \dfrac{1}{b}$  (b) $\dfrac{2}{x} - \dfrac{1}{y}$  (c) $a + \dfrac{3}{b}$  (d) $\dfrac{a}{c} - b$  (e) $\dfrac{1}{2a} - \dfrac{1}{3b}$

**4** Express $\dfrac{a}{b} - \dfrac{a}{b+1}$ as a single fraction in its simplest form.

**5** Express each of these as a single fraction in its simplest form.

(a) $\dfrac{1}{x+1} + \dfrac{1}{x-1}$

(b) $\dfrac{2}{x+3} - \dfrac{1}{3x+1}$

(c) $\dfrac{x-1}{x-2} + \dfrac{6}{x-5}$

(d) $\dfrac{x}{x+4} - \dfrac{x-5}{x-1}$

(e) $\dfrac{x+1}{x+3} + \dfrac{x-4}{2x-1}$

(f) $\dfrac{x-1}{x-7} - \dfrac{x+7}{x+1}$

**6** Express each of these as a single fraction in its simplest form.

(a) $\dfrac{6}{x} + \dfrac{3}{x(x-4)}$

(b) $\dfrac{2x}{(x+3)(x-1)} - \dfrac{1}{(x-1)}$

(c) $\dfrac{x+5}{(x+7)(x+1)} + \dfrac{x-1}{(x+1)(x+4)}$

(d) $\dfrac{1}{(x-7)(2x-1)} - \dfrac{1}{(2x-1)(x+1)}$

(e) $\dfrac{1}{ab} + \dfrac{1}{bc}$

(f) $\dfrac{z}{3xy} - \dfrac{x}{4yz}$

**7** (a) Factorise the denominators in the sum $\dfrac{4}{2x^2 - x - 1} + \dfrac{12}{2x^2 + 7x + 3}$.

(b) Show that this sum is equivalent to $\dfrac{16x}{(x-1)(2x+1)(x+3)}$.

**8** Express each of these as a single fraction in its simplest form.

(a) $\dfrac{6}{x+5} + \dfrac{8}{2x^2 + 9x - 5}$

(b) $\dfrac{3}{x^2 + 2x} + \dfrac{1}{x^2 + 6x + 8}$

(c) $\dfrac{x+11}{x^2 - 9} - \dfrac{4}{x^2 + 3x}$

(d) $\dfrac{3x+5}{x^2 + 3x + 2} - \dfrac{2x+1}{x^2 + x - 2}$

**9** Express $1 - \dfrac{2}{x+5} + \dfrac{x-15}{x^2 - 25}$ as a single fraction in its simplest form.

**10** A function is defined by $f(x) = \dfrac{x+2}{x+3} + \dfrac{2x+3}{x^2 + 3x}$, $x > 0$.

(a) Evaluate $f(5)$ as a single fraction in its simplest form.

(b) Prove that $f(x) > 1$ for all positive values of $x$.

**11** Functions are defined by $g(x) = \dfrac{1}{x-1}$ $(x \ne 1)$ and $h(x) = \dfrac{3}{x-4}$ $(x \ne 4)$.

Show that $gh(x) = \dfrac{x-4}{7-x}$.

**12** (a) Express $\dfrac{1}{x} + \dfrac{1}{2}$ as a single fraction.

(b) Hence write the expression $\dfrac{1}{\dfrac{1}{x} + \dfrac{1}{2}}$ as a single fraction.

## C Extension: Leibniz's harmonic triangle (answers p 139)

This section provides an opportunity to apply the techniques of sections A and B to some fraction patterns. It also provides valuable practice in forming conjectures and proving them. The method introduced to add a series by writing each term as a difference is not part of the content for Core 4.

Gottfried Leibniz (1646–1716) was a German philosopher and mathematician who is best known for his work on calculus. The distinguished Dutch physicist and mathematician Christian Huygens (1629–1693) challenged Leibniz to calculate the infinite sum of the reciprocals of the triangle numbers:

$$\tfrac{1}{1} + \tfrac{1}{3} + \tfrac{1}{6} + \tfrac{1}{10} + \dots$$

**D**

**C1** Show that the $n$th term of this series is $\dfrac{2}{n(n+1)}$.

(You need to know that the $n$th triangle number is $\tfrac{1}{2}n(n+1)$.)

**C2** (a) Show that each term can be written as the difference $\dfrac{2}{n} - \dfrac{2}{n+1}$.

(b) Hence, show that the sum of the first $n$ terms can be written:

$$\left(\tfrac{2}{1} - \tfrac{2}{2}\right) + \left(\tfrac{2}{2} - \tfrac{2}{3}\right) + \left(\tfrac{2}{3} - \tfrac{2}{4}\right) + \left(\tfrac{2}{4} - \tfrac{2}{5}\right) + \left(\tfrac{2}{5} - \tfrac{2}{6}\right) + \dots + \left(\dfrac{2}{n} - \dfrac{2}{n+1}\right)$$

(c) Hence find a formula for the sum of the reciprocals of the first $n$ triangle numbers. Write your formula as a single fraction.

(d) Use your formula to find the sum of the reciprocals of the first five triangle numbers. Check your result by adding the appropriate fractions.

**C3** Now, think about the sum to infinity of the reciprocals of the triangle numbers. Show that, as $n$ gets larger, the sum gets closer and closer to 2.

## Exercise C (answers p 140)

In the course of his work on summing infinite series, Leibniz devised a triangle which he called the **harmonic triangle**.

Part of this triangle is

$$1$$
$$\tfrac{1}{2} \qquad \tfrac{1}{2}$$
$$\tfrac{1}{3} \qquad \tfrac{1}{6} \qquad \tfrac{1}{3}$$
$$\tfrac{1}{4} \qquad \tfrac{1}{12} \qquad \tfrac{1}{12} \qquad \tfrac{1}{4}$$
$$\tfrac{1}{5} \qquad \tfrac{1}{20} \qquad \tfrac{1}{30} \qquad \tfrac{1}{20} \qquad \tfrac{1}{5}$$

- The fractions on each edge form a sequence of unit fractions where the denominators increase by 1 each time.

- Each fraction in the triangle is the sum of the two fractions below it.

**1** Verify that the sum of $\tfrac{1}{20}$ and $\tfrac{1}{30}$ is $\tfrac{1}{12}$.

**2** In their simplest form, find the fractions in the next row of the harmonic triangle.

Consider the fractions in the diagonals of the triangle.

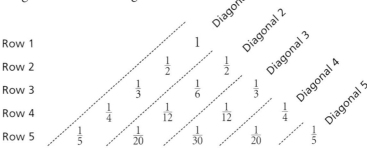

Row 1

Row 2

Row 3

Row 4

Row 5

**3** What fraction appears in row 10 and diagonal 2?

**4 (a)** Show that in diagonal 1 the $k$th fraction and its successor can be written as $\frac{1}{k}$ and $\frac{1}{k+1}$.

**(b)** Show that the sum of the first $n$ fractions in diagonal 2 can be written as

$$\left(\tfrac{1}{1} - \tfrac{1}{2}\right) + \left(\tfrac{1}{2} - \tfrac{1}{3}\right) + \left(\tfrac{1}{3} - \tfrac{1}{4}\right) + \left(\tfrac{1}{4} - \tfrac{1}{5}\right) + \left(\tfrac{1}{5} - \tfrac{1}{6}\right) + \dots + \left(\tfrac{1}{n} - \tfrac{1}{n+1}\right)$$

**(c)** Hence find a formula for the sum of the first $n$ fractions in diagonal 2. Write your formula as a single fraction.

**(d)** Use your formula to find the sum of the first four fractions in diagonal 2. Check your result by adding the appropriate fractions.

**(e)** What will happen to the sum of the first $n$ fractions in diagonal 2 as $n$ gets larger and larger? Justify your answer.

**(f)** Prove that the $k$th fraction in diagonal 2 can be written as $\frac{1}{k(k+1)}$.

**(g) (i)** Show that the fraction $\frac{1}{420}$ appears in diagonal 2.

**(ii)** In which row is $\frac{1}{420}$?

**5 (a)** Show that in diagonal 2 the $k$th fraction and its successor can be written as $\frac{1}{k(k+1)}$ and $\frac{1}{(k+1)(k+2)}$.

**(b)** Hence find a formula for the sum of the first $n$ fractions in diagonal 3.

**(c)** What will happen to the sum of the first $n$ fractions in diagonal 3 as $n$ gets larger and larger? Justify your answer.

**(d) (i)** Prove that the $k$th fraction in diagonal 3 can be written as $\frac{2}{k(k+1)(k+2)}$.

**(ii)** What is the 10th fraction in diagonal 3?

**\*6** Investigate the other diagonals in the harmonic triangle.
Can you find an expression for the $n$th fraction in diagonal $m$?
Can you find an expression for the sum of the first $n$ fractions in diagonal $m$?
What happens to the sum of the first $n$ fractions in diagonal $m$ as $n$ gets larger?

**\*7** Prove that the sum of the reciprocals of any pair of consecutive triangle numbers $T_n$ and $T_{n+1}$ is $\frac{4}{T_n + T_{n+1} - 1}$.

## D Extension: the harmonic mean (answers p 141)

This section provides an opportunity to apply the techniques of sections A and B to a new type of average, the harmonic mean. It includes some challenging work on proving statements. The harmonic mean itself is not part of the content for Core 4.

You will be familiar with the arithmetic mean of two numbers (half of the sum) and possibly their geometric mean (the square root of the product). The harmonic mean was probably so called because it can be used to produce a set of harmonious notes in music.

One of the earliest mentions of it is in a surviving fragment of the work of Archytas of Tarentum (*circa* 350 BCE) who was a contemporary of Plato. He wrote 'There are three means in music: one is arithmetic, the second is geometric, and the third is the subcontrary, which they call harmonic.'

| Consider two lengths of 4 and 12. | Add half of 4 to 4 and subtract half of 12 from 12. |
| --- | --- |
| 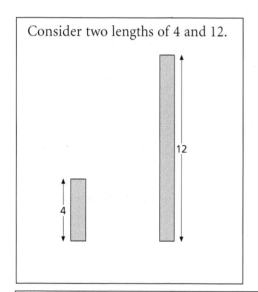 | 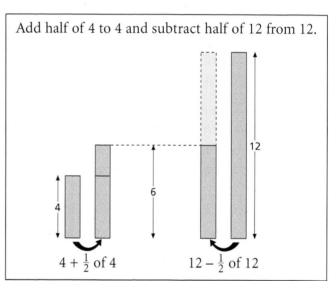 |

$4 + \left(\frac{1}{2} \text{ of } 4\right) = 6$ and $12 - \left(\frac{1}{2} \text{ of } 12\right) = 6$, so we say that the harmonic mean of 4 and 12 is 6.

For any two numbers, if you find a fraction $\frac{p}{q}$ so that

*smaller number* $+ \left(\frac{p}{q} \text{ of smaller number}\right)$ is the same as *larger number* $- \left(\frac{p}{q} \text{ of larger number}\right)$

then the value of these two expressions is the **harmonic mean** of the two numbers.

**D1** (a) Write down    (i) $6 + \left(\frac{2}{3} \text{ of } 6\right)$    (ii) $30 - \left(\frac{2}{3} \text{ of } 30\right)$

(b) Hence write down the harmonic mean of 6 and 30.

**D2** Try various fractions until you find the harmonic mean of

(a) 6 and 18    (b) 10 and 15    (c) 4 and 28

**D3** (a) If $k$ is a fraction so that $a + ka = b - kb$, find an expression for $k$ in terms of $a$ and $b$.

(b) Hence show that the harmonic mean of $a$ and $b$ can be expressed as $\dfrac{2ab}{a+b}$.

(c) Use this rule to find the harmonic mean of 10 and 90.

**D4 (a)** Show that $\dfrac{2ab}{a+b} = \dfrac{2}{\dfrac{1}{a}+\dfrac{1}{b}}$.

**(b)** Hence show that the harmonic mean of two numbers is the reciprocal of the mean of their reciprocals.

---

The harmonic mean of two numbers is usually defined as $\dfrac{2ab}{a+b}$ or $\dfrac{2}{\dfrac{1}{a}+\dfrac{1}{b}}$.

---

### Exercise D (answers p 142)

**1 (a)** In certain situations, usually where the 'average' of two rates is needed, it is appropriate to find the harmonic mean.

Suppose a car travels from Harton to Monyborough at a speed of $x$ m.p.h. It makes the return journey at a speed of $y$ m.p.h.

Show that the average speed in m.p.h. for the whole return journey is the harmonic mean of $x$ and $y$.

**(b)** Hence find the average speed for a car that makes the return journey from Harton to Monyborough at a speed of 60 m.p.h. on the way out and 30 m.p.h. on the way back.

**2 (a)** Show that 3 is the harmonic mean of 2 and 6.

**(b)** Show that the reciprocals of these three numbers, listed in order of size, form an arithmetic sequence.

**(c)** Show that if $p$, $q$ and $r$ are three numbers such that $q$ is the harmonic mean of $p$ and $r$, then $\dfrac{1}{r}$, $\dfrac{1}{q}$ and $\dfrac{1}{p}$ form an arithmetic sequence.

**\*3** A square of side $x$ is inscribed in a triangle so that one side lies along the base as shown.

Prove that $x$ is half the harmonic mean of the base of the triangle and its height (as measured from that base).

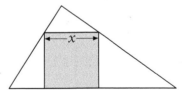

**\*4** The diagram on the right is a trapezium.

A parallel line segment is drawn through the point of intersection of the two diagonals.

Let the lengths of the three parallel lines be $a$, $b$ and $c$ as shown.

Prove that $b$ is the harmonic mean of $a$ and $c$.

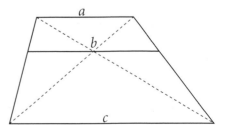

## Key points

- When working with rational expressions
  - factorise all expressions where possible
  - cancel any factors common to the numerator and denominator          (pp 6–10)

- To divide by a rational expression you can multiply by its reciprocal.          (p 7)

- To add or subtract rational expressions, write each with the same denominator.   (pp 9–10)

## Test yourself (answers p 143)

**1** Express as a single fraction in its simplest form $\dfrac{x^2 - 3x + 2}{x^2 - 4} \div \dfrac{x^2 - 2x + 1}{5x^2 + 10x}$.

**2** A function is defined by $f(x) = \dfrac{x + 5}{x^2 + 6x + 5}$ where $x$ is an integer such that $x \geq 0$.

(a) Evaluate $f(3)$ in its simplest fractional form.

(b) Prove that $f(x)$ can always be expressed as a fraction with 1 as its numerator.

**3** A function is defined by $f(x) = \dfrac{x^2 + 5x + 4}{x^2 + 4x}$, $x > 0$.

(a) Show that $f(x) = 1 + \dfrac{1}{x}$.

(b) Hence solve the inequality $f(x) > 2$.

**4** Express each of these as a single fraction, in its simplest form where appropriate.

(a) $\dfrac{2}{x} - \dfrac{1}{x + 3}$

(b) $\dfrac{2}{x + 4} + \dfrac{1}{x - 2}$

(c) $\dfrac{x}{y} + \dfrac{y}{x}$

**5** Show that $\dfrac{6}{(y - 3)(y - 1)} - \dfrac{3}{y - 3} \equiv \dfrac{3}{1 - y}$.

**6** Express $\dfrac{x + 3}{(x - 1)(x + 1)} - \dfrac{x - 1}{(x + 1)(x + 3)}$ as a single fraction in its simplest form.

**7** Express $\dfrac{2x}{(x + 1)(x + 5)} + \dfrac{x + 30}{x^2 - 25}$ as a single fraction in its simplest form.

**8** Express $\dfrac{12}{x^2 - 3x} + \dfrac{x - 19}{x^2 - 2x - 3}$ as a single fraction in its simplest form.

**9** A function is defined by $f(x) = 2x + \dfrac{1}{x - 1} - \dfrac{5}{x^2 + 3x - 4}$, $x > 1$.

Show that $f(x) = \dfrac{2x^2 + 8x + 1}{x + 4}$.

# 2 Rational expressions 2

In this chapter you will learn how to
- use the remainder theorem to help simplify algebraic fractions (rational expressions)
- divide a polynomial by a linear or quadratic expression
- add two or more algebraic fractions using the lowest common denominator
- express an algebraic fraction as the sum of simpler (partial) fractions

## A Using the remainder theorem (answers p 144)

We can use multiplication facts when we divide one integer by another.

For example, consider the division $19 \div 6$.
$19 = 3 \times 6 + 1$ so $19 \div 6 = 3$ with a remainder of 1.

We can also divide polynomials by thinking about multiplication.
For example, consider $(x^3 + 4x^2 - x + 8) \div (x - 2)$.

| | |
|---|---|
| $x^3 + 4x^2 - x + 8 = (x - 2)(x^2 \qquad ) + \ldots$ | The first term in the second bracket must be $x^2$ to give $x^3$ in the product. |

| | |
|---|---|
| $= (x - 2)(x^2 + 6x \qquad ) + \ldots$ | The second term must be $6x$ to give '$+ 4x^2$' in the product. |

| | |
|---|---|
| $= (x - 2)(x^2 + 6x + 11) + \ldots$ | The third term must be $11$ to give '$- x$' in the product. |

| | |
|---|---|
| $= (x - 2)(x^2 + 6x + 11) + 30$ | In the product $(x - 2)(x^2 + 6x + 11)$ the constant is $-22$ so we need to add $30$ to give '$+ 8$' in the cubic. |

So $(x^3 + 4x^2 - x + 8) \div (x - 2)$ is $(x^2 + 6x + 11)$ with a remainder of 30.

The remainder theorem can be useful when dividing a polynomial by a linear expression.
When a polynomial $p(x)$ is divided by $(x - a)$, the remainder is $p(a)$ (from Core 1).

So, in the above example, we can check the remainder by working out the value of $(x^3 + 4x^2 - x + 8)$ when $x = 2$.

When $x = 2$, $x^3 + 4x^2 - x + 8 = 2^3 + 4 \times 2^2 - 2 + 8$

$$= 30 \text{ (as we found above).}$$

**A1** A polynomial is defined by $g(x) = 8x^3 + 4x^2 + 6x - 11$.

(a) Use the remainder theorem to find the remainder when $g(x)$ is divided by $\left(x - \frac{1}{2}\right)$.

(b) (i) What do you think the remainder will be when $g(x)$ is divided by $(2x - 1)$?

(ii) Now divide $g(x)$ by $(2x - 1)$ and work out the remainder. Were you right?

(c) What do you notice about the remainders when $g(x)$ is divided by $\left(x - \frac{1}{2}\right)$ and $(2x - 1)$? Can you explain this?

In general, suppose that p($x$) is a polynomial in $x$ and that dividing p($x$) by $(ax - b)$ gives a quotient of q($x$) and a remainder $R$.

Then we can write
$$p(x) = (ax - b)q(x) + R$$

When $x = \dfrac{b}{a}$, $ax - b = 0$ so $\quad p\!\left(\dfrac{b}{a}\right) = 0 \times q(x) + R$

That is, $\qquad\qquad\qquad\qquad p\!\left(\dfrac{b}{a}\right) = R$

When p($x$) is divided by $(ax - b)$, the remainder is $p\!\left(\dfrac{b}{a}\right)$.

(Note that $x = \dfrac{b}{a}$ is the solution of the equation $ax - b = 0$.)

---

**Example 1**

A polynomial is given by $p(x) = 3x^3 + 10x^2 - 3x - 2$.

Find the remainder when p($x$) is divided by $(3x + 1)$ and hence simplify $\dfrac{3x^3 + 10x^2 - 3x - 2}{3x + 1}$.

**Solution**

$3x + 1 = 0 \implies x = -\frac{1}{3}$, so the remainder is the value of $p\!\left(-\frac{1}{3}\right)$.

$$p\!\left(-\tfrac{1}{3}\right) = 3 \times \left(-\tfrac{1}{3}\right)^3 + 10 \times \left(-\tfrac{1}{3}\right)^2 - 3 \times \left(-\tfrac{1}{3}\right) - 2$$
$$= 3 \times \left(-\tfrac{1}{27}\right) + 10 \times \left(\tfrac{1}{9}\right) + 1 - 2$$
$$= -\tfrac{1}{9} + 1\tfrac{1}{9} + 1 - 2 = 0$$

As the remainder is 0 we know that $(3x + 1)$ is a factor of p($x$) and so we can write p($x$) as the product of $(3x + 1)$ and a quadratic factor.

$$p(x) = (3x + 1)(x^2 + 3x - 2)$$

*The coefficient of $x^2$ must be 1, the constant term must be –2 and so the coefficient of $x$ must be 3 (to achieve $10x^2 - 3x$ in the expansion).*

Hence $\dfrac{3x^3 + 10x^2 - 3x - 2}{3x + 1} = \dfrac{(3x + 1)(x^2 + 3x - 2)}{3x + 1} = x^2 + 3x - 2$.

---

**Exercise A** (answers p 144)

**1** Work out the remainder when

(a) $x^3 + 3x^2 + x - 4$ is divided by $x - 3$     (b) $4x^3 + x^2 - x$ is divided by $x + 1$

(c) $2x^3 + 5x^2 + x + 1$ is divided by $2x - 1$     (d) $4x^3 - 4x^2 - 2x + 1$ is divided by $2x + 1$

(e) $3x^3 + 11x^2 - 3x - 1$ is divided by $3x - 1$     (f) $27x^3 + 1$ is divided by $3x + 1$

**2** The polynomials p($x$) and q($x$) are defined by
$$p(x) = x^3 + 2x^2 - 3x - 6 \quad \text{and} \quad q(x) = x^3 + 2x^2 + 5x + 10.$$

(a) Find p(–2) and q(–2) and show that p($x$) and q($x$) have a common linear factor.

(b) Hence write $\dfrac{p(x)}{q(x)}$ as a simplified algebraic fraction.

**3 (a)** Show that $2x - 1$ is a factor of $2x^3 + 7x^2 - 14x + 5$.

**(b)** Simplify $\dfrac{2x^3 + 7x^2 - 14x + 5}{2x - 1}$.

## B Further division (answers p 144)

$\frac{19}{6}$ is an improper fraction as its numerator is greater than its denominator.

We can write $\frac{19}{6}$ as $\frac{18+1}{6}$ which is equivalent to $\frac{18}{6} + \frac{1}{6} = 3 + \frac{1}{6}$, which is the sum of an integer and a proper fraction.

An algebraic fraction is 'proper' if the degree of the polynomial that is the numerator is less than the degree of the polynomial that is the denominator; otherwise it is 'improper'. Algebraic division is complete when no 'improper' fractions remain.

For example, $\dfrac{x^2 + 2}{x}$ is an improper algebraic fraction.

As the divisor is a single term, division is straightforward: $\dfrac{x^2+2}{x} = \dfrac{x^2}{x} + \dfrac{2}{x} = x + \dfrac{2}{x}$.

We have already seen examples where the divisor is a factor of the numerator.

For example, $\dfrac{x^2 + 2x - 3}{x + 3} = \dfrac{(x+3)(x-1)}{x+3} = x - 1$.

Where the divisor is not a factor of the numerator, we need different techniques.

For example, $\dfrac{x+6}{x-2} = \dfrac{x-2+8}{x-2} = \dfrac{x-2}{x-2} + \dfrac{8}{x-2} = 1 + \dfrac{8}{x-2}$.

**B1** Find an expression equivalent to $\dfrac{3x + 10}{x + 2}$ by dividing by the denominator.

An example where the numerator is a quadratic expression is $\dfrac{x^2 + 6x - 3}{x + 2}$.

| | |
|---|---|
| $x^2 + 6x - 3 = (x + 2)(\mathbf{x + 4}) + R$ | The expression in the second bracket must be $\mathbf{x + 4}$ to give $x^2 + 6x$ in the product. |

| | |
|---|---|
| $= (x + 2)(x + 4) - \mathbf{11}$ | The constant in the product $(x + 2)(x + 4)$ is 8 so $R$ must be $\mathbf{-11}$ to give '$- 3$' in the quadratic. |

So $\dfrac{x^2 + 6x - 3}{x + 2} = \dfrac{(x+2)(x+4) - 11}{x+2} = x + 4 - \dfrac{11}{x + 2}$.

We can use the remainder theorem as a check on the value of $R$.
The remainder on dividing $x^2 + 6x - 3$ by $(x + 2)$ is the value of $x^2 + 6x - 3$ when $x = -2$.
When $x = -2$, $x^2 + 6x - 3 = (-2)^2 + 6(-2) - 3$

$$= -11 \text{ (as above).}$$

**B2** Find an expression equivalent to $\dfrac{x^2 + 3x + 1}{x - 1}$ by dividing by the denominator.

An example where the numerator is a cubic expression is $\dfrac{2x^3 + 5x^2 - x + 4}{2x - 1}$.

| | |
|---|---|
| $2x^3 + 5x^2 - x + 4 = (2x - 1)(x^2 \qquad) + R$ | The first term in the second bracket must be $x^2$ to give $2x^3$ in the product. |

| | |
|---|---|
| $= (2x - 1)(x^2 + 3x \qquad) + R$ | The second term must be $3x$ to give '$+ 5x^2$' in the product. |

| | |
|---|---|
| $= (2x - 1)(x^2 + 3x + 1) + R$ | The third term must be $1$ to give '$- x$' in the product. |

| | |
|---|---|
| $= (2x - 1)(x^2 + 3x + 1) + 5$ | The constant in the product $(2x - 1)(x^2 + 3x + 1)$ is $-1$ so $R$ must be $5$ to give '$+ 4$' in the cubic. |

Alternatively we could use algebraic 'long division'.

$$\begin{array}{r} x^2 + 3x + 1 \\ 2x - 1 \overline{\smash{\big)}\ 2x^3 + 5x^2 - x + 4} \\ \underline{2x^3 - x^2\phantom{0000000}} \\ 6x^2 - x\phantom{000} \\ \underline{6x^2 - 3x\phantom{000}} \\ 2x + 4 \\ \underline{2x - 1} \\ 5 \end{array}$$

Both methods show us that $2x^3 + 5x^2 - x + 4 = (2x - 1)(x^2 + 3x + 1) + 5$.

So $\dfrac{2x^3 + 5x^2 - x + 4}{2x - 1} = \dfrac{(2x - 1)(x^2 + 3x + 1) + 5}{2x - 1} = x^2 + 3x + 1 + \dfrac{5}{2x - 1}$.

Again we can use the remainder theorem to check the value of $R$.
We are dividing by $2x - 1$ so we need to find the value of $2x^3 + 5x^2 - x + 4$ when $x = \frac{1}{2}$.

When $x = \frac{1}{2}$, $2x^3 + 5x^2 - x + 4 = 2 \times \frac{1}{2}^3 + 5 \times \frac{1}{2}^2 - \frac{1}{2} + 4$
$\phantom{00000000000000000000000} = \frac{1}{4} + \frac{5}{4} - \frac{1}{2} + 4$
$\phantom{00000000000000000000000} = 5 \ \ \text{(as above)}.$

**B3** Find an expression equivalent to $\dfrac{x^3 - 2x^2 - 16x + 1}{x - 5}$ by dividing by the denominator.

**B4** (a) Find constants $A$ and $B$ such that $x^3 + x^2 + 2x - 1 = (x^2 - 1)(x + A) + Bx$.

(b) Hence find an expression equivalent to $\dfrac{x^3 + x^2 + 2x - 1}{x^2 - 1}$.

(c) Why is it not appropriate to use the remainder theorem here?

## Example 2

Find an equivalent expression for $\dfrac{x^3 - 2x^2 + x + 5}{x^2 - 3}$ by dividing by the denominator.

### Solution

$\dfrac{x^3 - 2x^2 + x + 5}{x^2 - 3} = \dfrac{\left(x^2 - 3\right)(x - 2) + \ldots}{x^2 - 3}$

*The first term in the second bracket must be $x$ to give $x^3$ in the product, and the second term must be $-2$ to give $-2x^2$ in the product.*

$= \dfrac{\left(x^2 - 3\right)(x - 2) + 4x - 1}{x^2 - 3}$

*$(x^2 - 3)(x - 2) = x^3 - 2x^2 - 3x + 6$ so add $4x - 1$ to give $x + 5$ in the cubic.*

$= x - 2 + \dfrac{4x - 1}{x^2 - 3}$

**B5** Find an equivalent expression for $\dfrac{x^3 + 3x^2 + 4x + 1}{x^2 + 1}$ by dividing by the denominator.

An **identity** is a statement that is true for all values of $x$ for which the statement is defined.

So we can use the identity symbol '$\equiv$' in statements such as $\dfrac{2x^2 + 2x + 3}{x^2 + x} \equiv 2 + \dfrac{3}{x^2 + x}$.

## Exercise B (answers p 144)

**1** Find an equivalent expression for each of these by dividing by the denominator.

(a) $\dfrac{x + 5}{x + 2}$    (b) $\dfrac{2x^2 - 3}{x^2}$    (c) $\dfrac{2x + 5}{x + 3}$    (d) $\dfrac{3x^2 - 2}{x^2 + 1}$    (e) $\dfrac{x + 1}{2x}$

**2** Find an equivalent expression for each of these by dividing by the denominator.

(a) $\dfrac{x^2 + 3x + 5}{x + 1}$    (b) $\dfrac{x^2 - 2x - 11}{x + 2}$    (c) $\dfrac{x^2 - 9x + 21}{x - 4}$    (d) $\dfrac{x^2 - 2x - 5}{x - 2}$

(e) $\dfrac{2x^2 + x - 4}{x - 1}$    (f) $\dfrac{3x^2 + 8x}{x + 3}$    (g) $\dfrac{2x^2 - 3x + 7}{2x + 1}$    (h) $\dfrac{6x^2 - 19x + 8}{3x - 2}$

**3** Find an equivalent expression for each of these by dividing by the denominator.

(a) $\dfrac{x^3 + 3x^2 + 5x + 9}{x + 1}$    (b) $\dfrac{x^3 - 5x^2 + x - 8}{x - 5}$    (c) $\dfrac{2x^3 - 7x^2 - x + 3}{2x - 1}$

(d) $\dfrac{x^3 + x^2 + 2x + 5}{x^2 + 1}$    (e) $\dfrac{3x^2 + 4x - 10}{x^2 + x}$    (f) $\dfrac{6x^3 - 4x^2 - 3x - 5}{2x^2 - 1}$

**4** Show that $\dfrac{x^3 + 1}{x^2 - 1} \equiv x + \dfrac{1}{x - 1}$.

**5** Find an equivalent expression for each of these by dividing by the denominator.

(a) $\dfrac{x^2 + 6}{x + 1}$    (b) $\dfrac{x^3 + 5}{x - 3}$    (c) $\dfrac{x^3 + x}{x + 2}$    (d) $\dfrac{x^3}{x^2 - 5}$

**4** Find the values of the constants $A$, $B$ and $C$ in each case.

(a) $\dfrac{3x^2 + 6x - 2}{x^2 + x} \equiv A + \dfrac{B}{x} + \dfrac{C}{x+1}$

(b) $\dfrac{2x^2 - 3x + 5}{x(x-1)} \equiv A + \dfrac{B}{x} + \dfrac{C}{x-1}$

(c) $\dfrac{8x^2}{(x-3)(x+5)} \equiv A + \dfrac{B}{x-3} + \dfrac{C}{x+5}$

(d) $\dfrac{4x^2 - 7x + 1}{2x^2 - x} \equiv A + \dfrac{B}{x} + \dfrac{C}{2x-1}$

**\*5** A function f is defined as $f(n) = \dfrac{3}{1 \times 4} + \dfrac{3}{4 \times 7} + \dfrac{3}{7 \times 10} + \ldots + \dfrac{3}{(3n-2)(3n+1)}$,

where $n$ is a positive integer.

(a) Evaluate $f(3)$ and $f(4)$ as fractions in their simplest form.

(b) (i) Express $\dfrac{3}{(3n-2)(3n+1)}$ as partial fractions.

(ii) Hence show that $f(n) = 1 - \dfrac{1}{3n+1}$ and so $f(n) < 1$ for all $n$.

**\*6** A function g is defined as

$$g(n) = \dfrac{1}{1 \times 2 \times 3} + \dfrac{1}{2 \times 3 \times 4} + \dfrac{1}{3 \times 4 \times 5} + \ldots + \dfrac{1}{n(n+1)(n+2)}$$

where $n$ is a positive integer.

(a) Evaluate $g(5)$ as a fraction in its simplest form.

(b) (i) Find a formula for $g(n)$ in the form $k + f(n)$, where $k$ is a constant and $f(n)$ is a single algebraic fraction.

(ii) Hence show that, as $n$ tends to infinity, the series $g(n)$ converges to a limit of $\frac{1}{4}$.

## E Further partial fractions (answers p 147)

**E1** Express each of these as a single fraction in its simplest form.

(a) $\dfrac{1}{x} + \dfrac{1}{x^2 + 1}$

(b) $\dfrac{1}{x} - \dfrac{x-1}{x^2 + 1}$

**E2** (a) Can you find constants $A$ and $B$ such that $\dfrac{1 - 2x}{x(x^2 + 1)} \equiv \dfrac{A}{x} + \dfrac{B}{x^2 + 1}$?

What happens? Can you explain this?

(b) Can you find constants $A$, $B$ and $C$ such that $\dfrac{1 - 2x}{x(x^2 + 1)} \equiv \dfrac{A}{x} + \dfrac{Bx + C}{x^2 + 1}$?

If the denominator of an algebraic fraction is a product of expressions where one of them is a quadratic that cannot be factorised then it may not be possible to express the fraction as partial fractions where each numerator is a constant.

Algebraic fractions of this type are beyond the scope of this course.

**E3** Express $\dfrac{1}{x+3} - \dfrac{1}{(x+3)^2}$ as a single fraction in its simplest form.

**E4** Explain why you cannot find constants $A$ and $B$ such that $\dfrac{x}{(x-1)^2} \equiv \dfrac{A}{x-1} + \dfrac{B}{x-1}$.

**E5** (a) Can you find constants $A$ and $B$ such that

(i) $\dfrac{x}{(x-1)^2} \equiv \dfrac{A}{x-1} + \dfrac{B}{(x-1)^2}$  (ii) $\dfrac{3x+7}{(x+2)^2} \equiv \dfrac{A}{x+2} + \dfrac{B}{(x+2)^2}$

(b) (i) Show that $\dfrac{Ax+B}{(x+C)^2} \equiv \dfrac{A}{x+C} + \dfrac{B-AC}{(x+C)^2}$ where $A$, $B$ and $C$ are any constants.

(ii) Hence express $\dfrac{5x+16}{(x+3)^2}$ in the form $\dfrac{P}{x+3} + \dfrac{Q}{(x+3)^2}$.

**E6** Express $\dfrac{3}{2x-5} + \dfrac{2}{x+1} + \dfrac{1}{(x+1)^2}$ as a single fraction in its simplest form.

> **K** Any proper algebraic fraction with a denominator that is a product of linear factors, some of which are repeated twice, can be written as partial fractions where numerators are constant values and denominators are the linear factors and the squares of the repeated factors.

An example should help to clarify this.

Consider the algebraic fraction $\dfrac{x-8}{(x+1)(x-2)^2}$.

The denominator is $(x + 1)(x - 2)^2$, so the denominators of the partial fractions will be $(x + 1)$, $(x - 2)$ and $(x - 2)^2$.

So we have $\dfrac{x-8}{(x+1)(x-2)^2} \equiv \dfrac{A}{x+1} + \dfrac{B}{x-2} + \dfrac{C}{(x-2)^2}$, where $A$, $B$ and $C$ are constants to be found.

Hence $\dfrac{x-8}{(x+1)(x-2)^2} \equiv \dfrac{A(x-2)^2 + B(x+1)(x-2) + C(x+1)}{(x+1)(x-2)^2}$.

So $A(x-2)^2 + B(x + 1)(x - 2) + C(x + 1) \equiv x - 8$ for all values of $x$.

In particular, it must be true for $x = 2$ (chosen to eliminate $A$ and $B$), which gives

$$A(0) + B(0) + C(2 + 1) = 2 - 8$$

$$\Rightarrow \qquad\qquad\qquad 3C = -6$$

$$\Rightarrow \qquad\qquad\qquad C = -2$$

It must also be true for $x = -1$ (chosen to eliminate $B$ and $C$), which gives

$$A(-1 - 2)^2 + B(0) + C(0) = -1 - 8$$

$$\Rightarrow \qquad\qquad\qquad 9A = -9$$

$$\Rightarrow \qquad\qquad\qquad A = -1$$

We cannot choose a value for $x$ to eliminate $A$ and $C$ but we can choose a value to give an equation in $A$, $B$ and $C$ that we can solve to find the value of $B$.

A suitable value is $x = 3$, which gives $A(3-2)^2 + B(3+1)(3-2) + C(3+1) = 3-8$

$$\Rightarrow \qquad A + 4B + 4C = -5$$
$$\Rightarrow \qquad -1 + 4B - 8 = -5$$
$$\Rightarrow \qquad 4B = 4$$
$$\Rightarrow \qquad B = 1$$

Hence $\dfrac{x-8}{(x+1)(x-2)^2} \equiv -\dfrac{1}{x+1} + \dfrac{1}{x-2} - \dfrac{2}{(x-2)^2}$.

## Exercise E (answers p 148)

**1** Express each of these as partial fractions.

(a) $\dfrac{x+4}{(x+2)^2}$

(b) $\dfrac{8}{(x+3)(x+1)^2}$

(c) $\dfrac{x^2-3}{(x-2)(x-1)^2}$

(d) $\dfrac{3x+13}{(x-1)(x+3)^2}$

(e) $\dfrac{x^2+2}{(x-4)(x+2)^2}$

(f) $\dfrac{7x+4}{(x+4)(x-2)^2}$

(g) $\dfrac{x^2+2}{(x-5)(2-x)^2}$

(h) $\dfrac{13-2x^2}{(2x+1)(x+3)^2}$

(i) $\dfrac{7-x^2}{(2x-1)(x-5)^2}$

(j) $\dfrac{3-2x}{(x+2)(3x-1)^2}$

(k) $\dfrac{4x+3}{x(4x-1)^2}$

(l) $\dfrac{2x^2+5}{x^2(2x+5)}$

---

## Key points

- When a polynomial $p(x)$ is divided by $(bx-a)$, the remainder is $p\left(\dfrac{b}{a}\right)$. (p 18)

- An algebraic fraction is proper if the degree of the polynomial that is the numerator is less than the degree of the polynomial that is the denominator. (p 19)

- When a polynomial $p(x)$ is divided by $d(x)$, a polynomial that is not a factor of and is of a degree less than or equal to $p(x)$, then we can write
$\dfrac{p(x)}{d(x)} = q(x) + \dfrac{R(x)}{d(x)}$, where $\dfrac{R(x)}{d(x)}$ is a proper fraction. (pp 19–21)

- Any proper algebraic fraction with distinct or repeated linear factors in the denominator can be expressed as partial fractions where the numerators are constants. For example,

$\dfrac{5x+1}{(x-1)(2x+1)(x-5)}$ can be expressed in the form $\dfrac{A}{x-1} + \dfrac{B}{2x+1} + \dfrac{C}{x-5}$

and $\dfrac{5x+1}{(x-1)(2x+1)^2}$ can be expressed in the form $\dfrac{A}{x-1} + \dfrac{B}{2x+1} + \dfrac{C}{(2x+1)^2}$. (pp 24–30)

**30** | 2 Rational expressions 2

## Test yourself (answers p 148)

**1** The polynomials $p(x)$ and $q(x)$ are defined by

$$p(x) = 3x^2 + 11x - 4$$
$$q(x) = 3x^3 - x^2 + 3x - 1$$

(a) By evaluating $p\left(\frac{1}{3}\right)$ and $q\left(\frac{1}{3}\right)$, or otherwise, show that $p(x)$ and $q(x)$ have a common linear factor.

(b) Hence write $\dfrac{p(x)}{q(x)}$ as a simplified algebraic fraction.

**2** Find the values of the constants $A$, $B$ and $C$ so that

$$\frac{3x^2 + 14x + 1}{x + 5} \equiv Ax + B + \frac{C}{x + 5}$$

**3** The function f is defined by

$$f(x) = \frac{x^3 + 8}{x^2 - 4}, \quad x > 2$$

(a) Show that $f(x) \equiv x + \dfrac{4}{x - 2}$.

(b) Hence show that $f'(x) = 1 - \dfrac{4}{(x - 2)^2}$.

**4** Write $\dfrac{1}{4(x + 1)} + \dfrac{3}{4(x - 1)} + \dfrac{1}{2(x - 1)^2}$ as a single algebraic fraction in its simplest form.

**5** Express $\dfrac{7 - x}{(x + 3)(2x + 1)}$ in the form $\dfrac{A}{x + 3} + \dfrac{B}{2x + 1}$.

**6** Express $\dfrac{7x + 11}{(1 + 5x)(3 - x)}$ as partial fractions.

**7** Find the values of the constants $A$, $B$ and $C$ so that

$$\frac{4x^2 - 5x - 13}{(x + 1)(x - 3)} \equiv A + \frac{B}{x + 1} + \frac{C}{x - 3}$$

**8** Express $\dfrac{x - 1}{(2x + 3)^2}$ as partial fractions.

**9** Express $\dfrac{3x - 1}{(2 - 3x)(1 - x)^2}$ as partial fractions.

**10** Express $\dfrac{18}{(x + 2)(x - 1)(x - 4)}$ as partial fractions.

# 3 Parametric equations

In this chapter you will learn how to
- work with curves defined by two parametric equations, including the circle and ellipse
- convert between parametric and cartesian equations

## A Coordinates in terms of a third variable (answers p 149)

Computer animators make objects on the screen change their position over time. An object's position at any moment can be given using $(x, y)$ coordinates (also known as 'cartesian coordinates'). To instruct the computer to produce a required movement, the $x$-coordinate and $y$-coordinate can be separately defined in terms of time.

**A1** A computer animator uses these equations to define the movement of a dot on the screen ($x$ and $y$ are in centimetres; $t$ is in seconds).

$$x = 3t$$
$$y = 6t - t^2$$

(a) Copy this table and use the equations to complete it.

(b) On squared paper, using axes labelled $x$ and $y$, plot the motion of the dot.
What might the dot represent?

| $t$ | 0 | 1 | 2 | 3 | 4 | 5 | 6 |
|-----|---|---|---|---|---|---|---|
| $x$ |   | 3 |   |   |   |   |   |
| $y$ |   | 5 |   |   |   |   |   |

**A2** Here a dot has been made to move in a straight line.

(a) By reading off values of $x$ at $t = 1$, $t = 2$ and so on, state an equation for $x$ in terms of $t$.

(b) Similarly, express $y$ as a function of $t$.

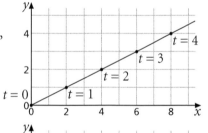

**A3** Here, too, a dot moves in a straight line.

(a) How does the motion differ from that in question A2?

(b) Give an equation for $x$ as a function of $t$.

(c) Give an equation for $y$ as a function of $t$.

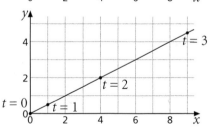

Two equations that separately define the $x$- and $y$-coordinates of a graph in terms of a third variable are called **parametric equations**.

The third variable is called the **parameter**.

If you have done Mechanics 1, you have already seen the $x$- and $y$-coordinates of a projectile's position separately defined as functions of time.

We have used $t$ for the parameter here, but the parameter does not have to represent time, and a different letter could be used.

Many graph plotting calculators and programs will let you define a graph parametrically. The manual (often available on-line) should tell you how. You may be restricted to using $t$ as the parameter.

You can also use a spreadsheet to plot a graph given by a pair of parametric equations, as here.

Column A contains values of $t$, increasing in steps of $0.2$.
Column B gives the $x$-coordinate, defined by the function $x = t^3$.
Column C gives the $y$-coordinate, defined by the function $y = t^2$.

Enter –2

Enter =A2+0.2 and copy down as far as 2.

Enter =A2^3 and copy down.

Enter =A2^2 and copy down.

| | A | B | C |
|---|---|---|---|
| | t | x | y |
| 1 | | | |
| 2 | –2 | –8 | 4 |
| 3 | –1.8 | –5.832 | 3.24 |
| 4 | –1.6 | –4.096 | 2.56 |
| 5 | –1.4 | –2.744 | 1.96 |
| 6 | –1.2 | –1.728 | 1.44 |
| 7 | –1 | –1 | 1 |
| 8 | –0.8 | –0.512 | 0.64 |
| 9 | | –0.216 | 0.36 |

To plot the graph, first select the whole of columns B and C.
On the chart toolbar, select the 'scatter chart' button.
(In some versions of Excel, you have to make a 'First column contains ...' selection; if so choose 'category ($x$)-axis labels' or '$x$-values for $xy$-chart'.)

This method plots unjoined points for the graph. You may be able to obtain a scatter diagram with lines drawn between the points, but using a joined-up line chart option does not work with parametric equations on some spreadsheet programs.

**A4** Obtain the graph given by $x = t^3$, $y = t^2$ $(-2 \le t \le 2)$ by plotting on squared paper or by using a graph plotter or spreadsheet. Call this graph G.

**A5** Each of the following graphs is obtained by applying a transformation to graph G. In each case, plot the graph and describe the transformation.

(a) $x = t^3$, $y = t^2 + 2$     (b) $x = t^3 - 1$, $y = t^2$     (c) $x = 3t^3$, $y = t^2$

(d) $x = t^3$, $y = \frac{1}{2}t^2$     (e) $x = t^3$, $y = -t^2$     (f) $x = t^3 + 4$, $y = t^2 - 1$

An advantage of defining a graph parametrically is that transformations are simple to apply.

To apply a translation $\begin{bmatrix} a \\ b \end{bmatrix}$ add $a$ to the function for $x$ and $b$ to the function for $y$.

To stretch in the $x$-direction, multiply the $x$-function by the required factor; similarly, to stretch in the $y$-direction, multiply the $y$-function.

To reflect in the $y$-axis multiply the $x$-function by $-1$; to reflect in the $x$-axis multiply the $y$-function by $-1$.

**A6** State a pair of parametric equations for each of these.

(a) The graph $x = t^2 + t$, $y = 1 - t$ translated by $\begin{bmatrix} 3 \\ -1 \end{bmatrix}$

(b) The graph $x = t^2 + t$, $y = 1 - t$ stretched by a factor of 2 in the $x$-direction

You can find where a parametrically defined graph meets an axis, or a line parallel to an axis, as follows.

---

### Example 1

Find the coordinates of the points where the curve $x = t^3 + 4$, $y = t^2 - t$ meets the line $y = 12$.

### Solution

*Substitute 12 for y in the y-equation.*

$$12 = t^2 - t$$
$$\Rightarrow \quad t^2 - t - 12 = 0$$

*Factorise.*

$$(t - 4)(t + 3) = 0$$
$$\Rightarrow \quad t = 4 \text{ or } -3$$

*Substitute these values of t into the x-equation.*

When $t = 4$, $x = 4^3 + 4 = 68$
When $t = -3$, $x = (-3)^3 + 4 = -23$

So the points are $(68, 12)$ and $(-23, 12)$.

---

### Exercise A (answers p 149)

**1** A curve is defined by $x = \dfrac{1}{t}$, $y = t^2$.

Find the coordinates of the points on the curve where $t = -3, -2, -1, 1, 2$ and $3$.

**2** A curve $K$ is defined by $x = t$, $y = t^2$.

Give the parametric equations of a curve obtained by

(a) stretching $K$ by factor 3 in the $y$-direction

(b) translating $K$ by the vector $\begin{bmatrix} 2 \\ 1 \end{bmatrix}$

**3** For each of the pairs of parametric equations below,

    (i) find the cartesian coordinates for $t = -2, -1, 0, 1, 2$, then plot these points and sketch the graph

    (ii) obtain the graph using a graph plotter or spreadsheet; if it differs from your sketch try to sort out why this has happened

(a) $x = t + 4$, $y = 1 - t^2$     (b) $x = 2 - t$, $y = t^3 - 2t$     (c) $x = t^3$, $y = t^2 - t$

**4** Use the fact that $x = 0$ for all points on the $y$-axis to find where the curve defined by $x = t^2 - 4$, $y = t^3 + t$ meets the $y$-axis.

**5** Find the coordinates of the point(s) where each of the following curves meets the $y$-axis.

(a) $x = t - 2$, $y = 2t + 1$            (b) $x = 3 - t$, $y = t^2 - t$

(c) $x = t^2 + t - 2$, $y = 3t - 6$      (d) $x = 8 - t^3$, $y = \dfrac{t - 1}{t + 1}$

**6** Find the coordinates of the points where the curves in question 5 meet the $x$-axis.

**7** Show that the curve $x = \sqrt{t+1}$, $y = \dfrac{t}{t^2 - 2}$ meets the line $y = 1$ at
$(0, 1)$ and $(\sqrt{3}, 1)$.

**8** The curve $x = t^2 + 1$, $y = t^3 - 1$ meets the line $x = 3$ at points $A$ and $B$.
Find the exact length of the line segment $AB$.

**\*9** On the graphs below, the value of the parameter $t$ is shown at each dot.
The parametric equations involve only low powers of $t$.
Write down possible parametric equations and test them on a graph plotter
or spreadsheet.

**(a)**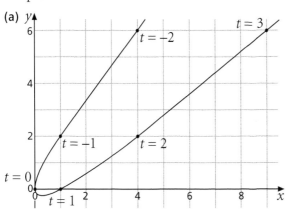

**(b)**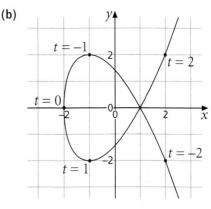

## B Converting between parametric and cartesian equations (answers p 150)

**B1** A graph is defined by these parametric equations.

$$x = 2t - 1$$
$$y = 4t$$

**(a)** Copy this table and complete it using the equations.

| $t$ | −2 | −1.5 | −1 | −0.5 | 0 | 0.5 | 1 | 1.5 | 2 |
|---|---|---|---|---|---|---|---|---|---|
| $x$ | | | | | | | | | |
| $y$ | | | | | | | | | |

**(b)** Make $t$ the subject of the second equation.

**(c)** Substitute this expression for $t$ into the first equation, and show that
this leads to

$$2x - y + 2 = 0$$

**(d)** Check that this equation is consistent with the last two lines of the table.

**(e)** What type of graph is this?

**B2** Use the method of parts (b) and (c) in the previous question to convert each
pair of parametric equations to an equation of the form $ax + by + c = 0$.

**(a)** $x = 3t + 4$, $y = 2t$  　　　　**(b)** $x = 5 - 2t$, $y = \frac{1}{3}t$

**B3** Here again are the parametric equations from question A1:

$$x = 3t, \ y = 6t - t^2$$

(a) Make $t$ the subject of the first equation.

(b) Show that substituting this expression for $t$ into the second equation gives

$$y = 2x - \frac{x^2}{9}$$

(c) Check that the last two lines in your table from question A1 are consistent with this formula.

The method of questions B1–B3 can often be used to convert a pair of parametric equations into the equation that connects $x$ and $y$ directly (the cartesian equation). It involves first choosing the simpler equation and making $t$ the subject of it.

**B4** Obtain a single cartesian equation for each pair of parametric equations. Your equation does not have to be of the form $y = \ldots$

(a) $x = 5t, \ y = 4t - 3$     (b) $x = t^2, \ y = 2t$     (c) $x = 2t, \ y = t^3$

---

### Example 2

Obtain a cartesian equation for the graph defined by $x = t^3, \ y = \sqrt{t} \ \ (t \geq 0)$.

#### Solution

| | |
|---|---|
| *The second equation is the simpler.* | $y = \sqrt{t}$ |
| *Square both sides.* | $y^2 = t$ |
| *Substitute for $t$ in the first equation.* | $x = (y^2)^3$ |
| | $\Rightarrow \ x = y^6$ |

---

### Example 3

Obtain a cartesian equation for the graph defined by $x = t + 5, \ y = t^3 - t$.

#### Solution

| | |
|---|---|
| *The first equation is the simpler.* | $x = t + 5$ |
| *Make $t$ the subject.* | $t = x - 5$ |
| *Substitute for $t$ in the second equation.* | $y = (x - 5)^3 - (x - 5)$ |
| *Expand the brackets.* | $y = x^3 - 15x^2 + 75x - 125 - x + 5$ |
| *Simplify.* | $y = x^3 - 15x^2 + 74x - 120$ |

---

**B5** Obtain a single cartesian equation for each pair of parametric equations.

(a) $x = \sqrt{t}, \ y = t^2$     (b) $x = t + 3, \ y = 3 - t^2$     (c) $x = t + 1, \ y = t^3 - 3t$

The examples opposite show a variety of ways of eliminating the parameter. In example 4, it is $t^2$, rather than $t$, that is first made the subject of one of the equations and eliminated. Example 5 again involves making $t$ the subject, though the working is harder. In example 6, the method is one that happens to work with the given equations.

## Example 4

Obtain a cartesian equation for the graph defined by $x = 3t^2 - 4$, $y = 8 - t^2$.

### Solution

*Take the y-equation and make $t^2$ the subject.*      $t^2 = 8 - y$

*Substitute $8 - y$ for $t^2$ in the x-equation.*      $x = 3(8 - y) - 4$

*Tidy the equation.*      $x = 20 - 3y$

## Example 5

Obtain a cartesian equation for the graph defined by $x = \dfrac{t}{t+1}$, $y = \dfrac{t}{t-3}$ $(t \neq -1, t \neq 3)$.

### Solution

*Multiply both sides of the x-equation by $t + 1$.*      $tx + x = t$

*Bring all the t-terms together.*      $tx - t = -x$

$$\Rightarrow \quad t(x - 1) = -x$$

$$\Rightarrow \quad t = \frac{-x}{x-1}$$

*You will also need an expression for $t - 3$.*

$$t - 3 = \frac{-x}{x-1} - 3$$

$$= \frac{-x}{x-1} - \frac{3(x-1)}{x-1}$$

$$= \frac{-x - 3(x-1)}{x-1}$$

$$= \frac{-4x + 3}{x-1}$$

*Substitute the expressions for t and t − 3 into the y-equation.*

$$y = \frac{-x}{x-1} \div \frac{-4x+3}{x-1} = \frac{-x}{x-1} \times \frac{x-1}{-4x+3} = \frac{-x}{-4x+3}$$

So the required cartesian equation is $y = \dfrac{-x}{-4x+3}$ .

## Example 6

Obtain a cartesian equation for the graph defined by $x = t + \dfrac{1}{t}$, $y = t - \dfrac{1}{t}$ $(t \neq 0)$.

### Solution

*Add the two parametric equations.*      $x + y = 2t$

*Subtract the second parametric equation from the first.*      $x - y = \dfrac{2}{t}$

*Multiply the 'sum' equation by the 'difference' equation.*      $(x + y)(x - y) = 4$, or $x^2 - y^2 = 4$

A statement like $t \neq -2$ or $t \geq 0$ after a pair of parametric equations is often warning you about a value or values of the parameter for which one or more of the equations is invalid (perhaps because division by zero or finding the square root of a negative number would be involved). You do not normally have to do anything about this.

**Exercise B** (answers p 150)

**1** Obtain a single cartesian equation for each pair of parametric equations.

(a) $x = \frac{1}{4}t$, $y = 5t - 1$

(b) $x = 4t$, $y = \frac{4}{t}$ $(t \neq 0)$

(c) $x = t^2 + 4t$, $y = \frac{1}{3}t$

(d) $x = \frac{1}{t}$, $y = \frac{1}{2}t$ $(t \neq 0)$

(e) $x = 2 - t$, $y = t^2 + 4$

(f) $x = 2t - 1$, $y = 3 - 4t$

(g) $x = \sqrt{t}$, $y = t^2 + t$ $(t \geq 0)$

(h) $x = \frac{1}{t}$, $y = 4 - t$ $(t \neq 0)$

(i) $x = t^3 - t$, $y = t + 2$

(j) $x = 1 + t$, $y = 2t^2 - t^3$

(k) $x = \frac{t-1}{2}$, $y = (t + 1)(t + 2)$

(l) $x = 4t^3 + 3$, $y = 6 - t^3$

(m) $x = \sqrt{t}$, $y = t(5 - t)$ $(t \geq 0)$

(n) $x = \frac{1}{t-3}$, $y = t^2$ $(t \neq 3)$

(o) $x = \frac{1}{t-2}$, $y = t^3$ $(t \neq 2)$

(p) $x = \frac{1}{t+2}$, $y = \frac{1}{t-1}$ $(t \neq -2, t \neq 1)$

(q) $x = 5 - \sqrt{t}$, $y = 4\sqrt{t} - 3$ $(t \geq 0)$ (r) $x = \frac{t}{2t-1}$, $y = \frac{t}{t-1}$ $(t \neq \frac{1}{2}, t \neq 1)$

**2** A curve is defined parametrically by $x = t^3 + \frac{3}{t}$, $y = t^3 - \frac{3}{t}$ $(t \neq 0)$.

By first expressing $x + y$ and $x - y$ in terms of $t$, show that $(x + y)(x - y)^3 = 432$.

**3** A curve is defined by $x = \frac{1}{t}$, $y = \frac{1}{t(t-1)}$. By first expressing $x + y$ and $\frac{y}{x}$ in terms of $t$, find the cartesian equation.

**\*4** Show that the graph defined by $x = \frac{1}{2t-1}$, $y = \frac{t}{2t-1}$ is a straight line.

---

**Useful curves**

Parametric equations can be used to study curves with interesting mathematical properties that have uses in optics and other branches of science and technology. Here are two. In each case $a$ is a scale factor. Try working out their cartesian equations.

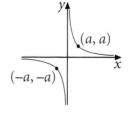

Standard parabola

Rectangular hyperbola

$x = at^2$, $y = 2at$

$x = at$, $y = \frac{a}{t}$

'Rectanglar' means the asymptotes are at right angles.

## C Circle and ellipse (answers p 151)

You know from your work on trigonometry that $\cos\theta$ and $\sin\theta$
are defined as the $x$- and $y$-coordinates of a point rotating
around a circle of radius 1 unit:

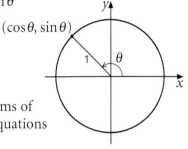

$$x = \cos\theta, \quad y = \sin\theta$$

You can also regard these equations as defining $x$ and $y$ in terms of
a third value $\theta$. Seen this way, they are a pair of parametric equations
for a circle, with $\theta$ as the parameter.

**C1** Put $x = \cos\theta$, $y = \sin\theta$ into a graph plotter and check that you get a circle
with its centre at the origin.

**C2** What do you expect these pairs of parametric equations to give?
Check with a graph plotter.

    **(a)** $x = 3\cos\theta$, $y = 3\sin\theta$          **(b)** $x = 0.5\cos\theta$, $y = 0.5\sin\theta$

In section A we applied a translation to a parametrically defined graph by
adding a constant to the $x$-equation or the $y$-equation (or both).

**C3** Write parametric equations for each of these, then check on a graph plotter.

    **(a)** A circle with unit radius, centre $(0, 2)$

    **(b)** A circle with unit radius, centre $(-3, 0)$

    **(c)** A circle with unit radius, centre $(1, -6)$

    **(d)** A circle with radius 2 units, centre $(5, 4)$

> **K** The curve $x = r\cos\theta$, $y = r\sin\theta$ is a circle with radius $r$, centre the origin.
>
> The curve $x = r\cos\theta + p$, $y = r\sin\theta + q$ is a circle with radius $r$, centre $(p, q)$.

**C4** Sketch these circles, indicating the radius and the position of the centre
in each case.

    **(a)** $x = \cos\theta - 3$, $y = \sin\theta + 2$      **(b)** $x = \cos\theta + 1$, $y = \sin\theta$

    **(c)** $x = 2\cos\theta - 5$, $y = 2\sin\theta + 5$    **(d)** $x = 0.6\cos\theta$, $y = 0.6\sin\theta - 3$

**C5** Put each of these pairs of equations into a graph plotter.
What transformation of the circle $x = \cos\theta$, $y = \sin\theta$ do you obtain
in each case?

    **(a)** $x = \cos\theta$, $y = 2\sin\theta$          **(b)** $x = 4\cos\theta$, $y = \sin\theta$

    **(c)** $x = \cos\theta$, $y = 0.6\sin\theta$       **(d)** $x = 0.5\cos\theta$, $y = 1.2\sin\theta$

When you stretch a circle with unit radius, centre the origin, by factors of $a$ in the $x$-direction and $b$ in the $y$-direction you get an **ellipse** that cuts the $x$-axis at $(-a, 0)$ and $(a, 0)$ and cuts the $y$-axis at $(0, b)$ and $(0, -b)$.

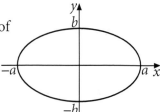

 The curve $x = a\cos\theta$, $y = b\sin\theta$ is an ellipse, centre the origin.
Its width is $2a$ units and its height is $2b$ units.

**C6** Write a pair of parametric equations for each of these ellipses.

(a) 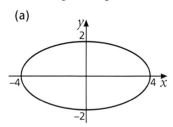   (b) 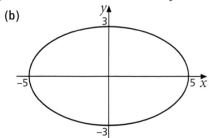   (c)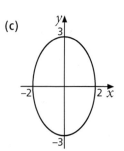

Like a circle, an ellipse can also be defined parametrically when its centre is not the origin.

**C7** Write a pair of parametric equations for each of these ellipses.

(a) 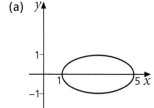   (b) 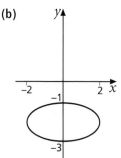   (c) 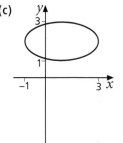   (d)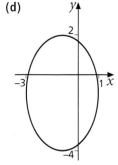

To convert a pair of parametric equations for an ellipse to a cartesian equation, first obtain expressions for $\cos\theta$ and $\sin\theta$ from the parametric equations, then use the identity $\cos^2\theta + \sin^2\theta = 1$, as in the next example.

---

### Example 7

An ellipse is defined by the parametric equations $x = 4\cos\theta$, $y = 5\sin\theta$.
Find its cartesian equation.

### Solution

From the $x$-equation, $\cos\theta = \dfrac{x}{4}$   From the $y$-equation, $\sin\theta = \dfrac{y}{5}$

Substituting these expressions in $\cos^2\theta + \sin^2\theta = 1$, $\left(\dfrac{x}{4}\right)^2 + \left(\dfrac{y}{5}\right)^2 = 1$

So the cartesian equation is $\dfrac{x^2}{16} + \dfrac{y^2}{25} = 1$.

---

**C8** Use the method of example 7 to show that the general ellipse, defined by $x = a\cos\theta$, $y = b\sin\theta$, has the cartesian equation $\dfrac{x^2}{a^2} + \dfrac{y^2}{b^2} = 1$.

**C9** An ellipse has the equation $9x^2 + 4y^2 = 36$. Rewrite this in the form $\dfrac{x^2}{a^2} + \dfrac{y^2}{b^2} = 1$ and hence write down a pair of parametric equations for this ellipse.

**C10** Find a pair of parametric equations for each of these ellipses.

(a) $4x^2 + y^2 = 36$  (b) $x^2 + 9y^2 = 9$  (c) $9x^2 + 0.25y^2 = 2.25$

The method of example 7 can be applied to a circle.

Consider a circle, radius 3 units and centre $(2, -1)$.
It can be defined parametrically as $x = 3\cos\theta + 2$, $y = 3\sin\theta - 1$.
Hence $\cos\theta = \dfrac{x-2}{3}$, $\sin\theta = \dfrac{y+1}{3}$

Substituting into $\cos^2\theta + \sin^2\theta = 1$, $\left(\dfrac{x-2}{3}\right)^2 + \left(\dfrac{y+1}{3}\right)^2 = 1$

Hence the cartesian equation of the circle is $(x-2)^2 + (y+1)^2 = 3^2$.
This corresponds to $(x-a)^2 + (y-b)^2 = r^2$, (from Core 1, a circle with centre $(a, b)$ and radius $r$) with $a = 2$, $b = -1$ and $r = 3$, as given above.

## Exercise C (answers p 151)

**1** A circle is defined by $x = 2\cos\theta$, $y = 2\sin\theta$, where $\theta$ is in radians.
Give the exact values of the cartesian coordinates of the point where $\theta = \dfrac{\pi}{3}$.

**2** Write a pair of parametric equations for each ellipse produced as follows.

(a) From a circle, centre the origin and of unit radius, that has been stretched by a factor of 4 in the $x$-direction

(b) From a circle, centre the origin and of unit radius, that has been 'stretched' by a factor of 0.7 in the $y$-direction

**3** An ellipse is defined by the parametric equations $x = 3\cos\theta$, $y = 4\sin\theta$.
Find the exact coordinates of the points where $\theta$ has values $0$, $\dfrac{\pi}{4}$, $\dfrac{\pi}{2}$, $\pi$ radians.

**4** Find the cartesian equation of the ellipse defined by $x = \tfrac{1}{2}\cos\theta$, $y = \tfrac{1}{3}\sin\theta$.

**5** The curves shown are ellipses. In each case, write

(i) a pair of parametric equations  (ii) the cartesian equation

(a) 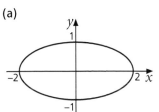 (b) 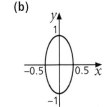 (c)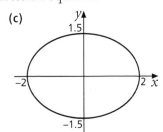

**6** A circle is defined by the cartesian equation $(x - 3)^2 + (y + 2)^2 = 25$.

   (a) State its centre.       (b) State its radius.       (c) Define it parametrically.

**\*7** A curve is given by $x = 2\cos\theta + 3,\ y = \sin\theta - 1$.

   (a) Draw a sketch of it.

   (b) Find the cartesian equation for it.

**\*8** Define the circle $x^2 + y^2 - 6x + 8y - 11 = 0$ parametrically.

**\*9** Obtain a cartesian equation for each of these pairs of parametric equations.

   (a) $x = \cot\theta,\ y = 2\operatorname{cosec}\theta$       (b) $x = 2\sec\theta,\ y = 3\tan\theta$

---

## Conic sections

Four curves highlighted in this chapter, the circle, ellipse, parabola and hyperbola, have the interesting property that they can all be obtained by slicing through the surface of a cone. (The hyperbola requires two identical cones, point to point.)

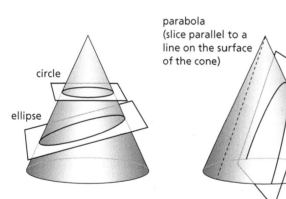

The path traced out by a body moving in space under the gravitational influence of a large body (such as our Sun) can be any of these conic sections.

Most planets in the solar system have an orbit that is nearly circular, but Mercury and Pluto have significantly elliptical orbits, while comets follow very stretched-out ellipses. (In elliptical motion of this kind, the large body is not at the centre of the ellipse and the parameter $\theta$ does not represent time.)

A body that does not orbit the Sun, but passes by and is deflected by the Sun's gravity, follows a hyperbolic path.

These curves are also used by architects and structural engineers, sometimes for aesthetic reasons but also often because their mathematical properties help with structural stability.

## Pattern parametrics

You can produce many interesting curves using parametric equations.
Most of those considered here go beyond what you will meet in the exam.
But it's interesting to feed them into a graph plotter and think about the result.

The one shown here uses only simple polynomials:

$$x = t^4 - 4t^2, \quad y = t^3 - 3t \quad (t = -3 \text{ to } 3)$$

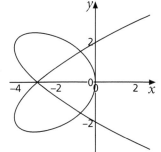

(It gets its swooping character because $x$ in terms of $t$ has three
stationary points within the stated limits of $t$, while $y$ in terms of $t$
has two stationary points. Bear this in mind if you want to want
to produce something similar of your own.)

Other curves besides a circle or ellipse – such as this one – can be
produced using sine and cosine. Try to work out what equations
have been used, then check with a graph plotter.

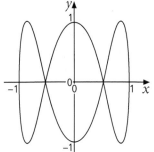

Plot some of these on a graph plotter, which must be set to degrees.
Some of them have established names, which are given. You can make up
your own names for the others.

Conjecture what effect a particular modification (such as changing a constant)
will have on the curve, then test and see if you were right.

**1** $x = \cos 5t, \ y = \sin 3t \ (t = 0 \text{ to } 400)$

**2** $x = \sin t - \cos 2t, \ y = \cos t - \sin 2t \ (t = 0 \text{ to } 360)$ (trefoil)

**3** $x = \dfrac{t^3}{50}, \ y = \sin 100t \ (t = -10 \text{ to } 10)$

**4** $x = 3 \cos 90t, \ y = 3 \sin 100t \ (t = 0 \text{ to } 40)$

**5** $x = \cos t + \cos^2 t, \ y = \sin t + \cos t \sin t \ (t = 0 \text{ to } 360)$ (cardioid)

**6** $x = 3(1 - 0.01t) \cos 99t, \ y = 3(1 - 0.01t) \sin 100t \ (t = 0 \text{ to } 95)$

**7** $x = 3 \sin t + \sin 12t, \ y = 3 \cos t + \cos 12t \ (t = 0 \text{ to } 360)$

**8** $x = 3 \sin t, \ y = \dfrac{3 \cos^2 t (2 + \cos t)}{3 + \sin^2 t} \ (t = 0 \text{ to } 360)$

**9** $x = at + \cos 100t$ (where $a = 0.2, 0.5, 1, 2$), $y = \sin 100t \ (t = -10 \text{ to } 10)$

**10** $x = 3 \sin t + \sin 10t, \ y = 3 \cos t + \cos 13t \ (t = 0 \text{ to } 360)$

### Test yourself (answers p 152)

1  A curve is defined by $x = \dfrac{1}{t^2}$, $y = 3t$ $(t \neq 0)$.

Find the coordinates of the points on the curve where $t = -3, -2, -1, 1, 2$ and $3$.

2  For each pair of parametric equations below, find the cartesian coordinates for $t = -2, -1, 0, 1, 2$, then plot these points and draw the graph.

   (a) $x = t + 1$, $y = 4 - t^2$  (b) $x = t^3 - 1$, $y = t^2 + 1$  (c) $x = 2 - t$, $y = t^3 + t^2 + t$

3  Find the coordinates of the point(s) where each of the following curves meets the *x*- and *y*-axes.

   (a) $x = t - 3$, $y = 3t + 1$  (b) $x = t^2 - 2t$, $y = 5 - t$

   (c) $x = 2t - 8$, $y = t^2 + t - 6$  (d) $x = \dfrac{t+1}{t-1}$, $y = t^3 + 27$ $(t \neq 1)$

4  Give the coordinates of the points where the curve defined by $x = t^2 - 5t$, $y = \dfrac{t+1}{t}$ meets the line $x = -6$.

5  Convert each of these pairs of parametric equations to an equation of the form $ax + by + c = 0$.

   (a) $x = 4t + 5$, $y = 3t$  (b) $x = 5 - 2t$, $y = \tfrac{1}{3}t$

**6** Obtain a single cartesian equation for each pair of parametric equations.

(a) $x = 3t$, $y = t^2$

(b) $x = t^3$, $y = \frac{1}{2}t$

(c) $x = \sqrt{t}$, $y = t^3$ $(t \geq 0)$

(d) $x = t - 1$, $y = 2 - t^2$

(e) $x = \dfrac{1}{t}$, $y = 3t$ $(t \neq 0)$

(f) $x = t^2 - t$, $y = \frac{1}{4}t$

(g) $x = t + 2$, $y = t^3 + 2t$

(h) $x = \dfrac{1}{2t}$, $y = 3 - t$ $(t \neq 0)$

(i) $x = 3t^3 + 2$, $y = 5 - t^3$

(j) $x = t(3 - t)$, $y = \sqrt{t}$ $(t \geq 0)$

(k) $x = t^2$, $y = \dfrac{1}{t - 2}$ $(t \neq 2)$

(l) $x = \dfrac{t}{t - 1}$, $y = \dfrac{t}{t + 1}$ $(t \neq -1, t \neq 1)$

(m) $x = 3\sqrt{t} - 2$, $y = 4 - \sqrt{t}$ $(t \geq 0)$ (n) $x = \dfrac{t}{2t - 3}$, $y = \dfrac{t}{t + 1}$ $(t \neq \frac{3}{2}, t \neq -1)$

**7** A curve is defined parametrically by $x = t^2 + \dfrac{2}{t}$, $y = t^2 - \dfrac{2}{t}$ $(t \neq 0)$.

By first expressing $x + y$ and $x - y$ in terms of $t$, find the cartesian equation.

**8** Describe the curve given by each of these pairs of parametric equations.

(a) $x = 4\cos\theta$, $y = 4\sin\theta$

(b) $x = \cos\theta$, $y = 3\sin\theta$

(c) $x = 0.6\cos\theta$, $y = 0.6\sin\theta$

(d) $x = 2\cos\theta$, $y = 3\sin\theta$

**9** Give a pair of parametric equations for each of these.

(a)      (b)      (c)

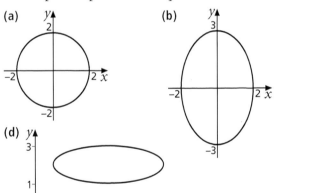
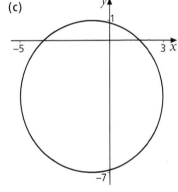

(d)

**10** An ellipse is defined by the parametric equations $x = 3\cos\theta$, $y = 4\sin\theta$.
Find its cartesian equation.

**11** Find a pair of parametric equations for each of these ellipses.

(a) $\dfrac{x^2}{4} + \dfrac{y^2}{16} = 1$

(b) $25x^2 + 4y^2 = 100$

**12** An ellipse is defined by the parametric equations $x = 6\cos\theta$, $y = 2\sin\theta$.
A chord of the ellipse has its ends at points on the ellipse where $\theta = \frac{1}{6}\pi$ and $\frac{5}{6}\pi$
respectively. Find the length of the chord, giving your answer as an exact value.

# 4 The binomial theorem

In this chapter you will learn how to use the binomial theorem for negative and fractional indices

## A Reviewing the binomial theorem for positive integers

In Core 2, you expanded expressions such as $(1 - 2x)^4$ using the binomial theorem. Using the theorem to expand $(1 + ax)^n$ gives

$$(1 + ax)^n = 1 + nax + \frac{n(n-1)}{2!}(ax)^2 + \frac{n(n-1)(n-2)}{3!}(ax)^3 + \dots + \frac{n(n-1)(n-2)\dots1}{n!}(ax)^n$$

So $(1 - 2x)^4 = (1 + (-2x))^4$

$$= 1 + 4\times(-2x) + \frac{4\times3}{2!}\times(-2x)^2 + \frac{4\times3\times2}{3!}\times(-2x)^3 + \frac{4\times3\times2\times1}{4!}\times(-2x)^4$$

$$= 1 - 8x + 24x^2 - 32x^3 + 16x^4$$

The expansion for $(1 + ax)^n$ can be used to expand an expression such as $(2 + 6x)^5$ as follows.

$$(2 + 6x)^5 = (2(1 + 3x))^5 = 2^5(1 + 3x)^5$$

Now $(1 + 3x)^5 = 1 + 5\times(3x) + \frac{5\times4}{2!}\times(3x)^2 + \frac{5\times4\times3}{3!}\times(3x)^3 +$

$$\frac{5\times4\times3\times2}{4!}\times(3x)^4 + \frac{5\times4\times3\times2\times1}{5!}\times(3x)^5$$

$$= 1 + 15x + 90x^2 + 270x^3 + 405x^4 + 243x^5$$

So $\quad (2 + 6x)^5 = 2^5(1 + 3x)^5$

$$= 2^5(1 + 15x + 90x^2 + 270x^3 + 405x^4 + 243x^5)$$

$$= 32 + 480x + 2880x^2 + 8640x^3 + 12\,960x^4 + 7776x^5$$

## Exercise A (answers p 153)

**1** Use the binomial theorem to expand $(1 + 5x)^6$ completely.

**2** Find the first five terms in the expansion of $(1 - 3x)^{12}$.

**3** Find the first three terms in the expansion of $(4 + 8x)^7$.

**4 (a)** Find the first four terms in the expansion of $\left(1 + \tfrac{1}{2}x\right)^8$.
   **(b)** Hence find the first four terms in the expansion of $(2 + x)^8$.

**5 (a)** Expand $(3 + x)^6$ fully.
   **(b)** Use the expansion to find the value of $3.01^6$ correct to two decimal places.

## B Extending the binomial theorem (answers p 153)

New ideas and techniques often arise when mathematicians consider extending the scope of a definition or formula.

We know that the binomial theorem helps us expand expressions of the form $(1 + ax)^n$ where $n$ is a positive integer.

Can we use the binomial theorem when $n$ is a negative integer?

For example, consider the expression $(1 + x)^{-2}$.

Using the formula for the binomial theorem gives

$$(1 + x)^{-2} = 1 + (-2)x + \frac{(-2)(-3)}{2!}x^2 + \frac{(-2)(-3)(-4)}{3!}x^3 + \frac{(-2)(-3)(-4)(-5)}{4!}x^4 + \dots$$

**D**

**B1** (a) Show that the expansion above simplifies to
$(1 + x)^{-2} = 1 - 2x + 3x^2 - 4x^3 + 5x^4 - \dots$

(b) Find and simplify the next three terms in this expansion.

(c) Why will the formula let us produce as many terms as we like when we apply it to $(1 + x)^{-2}$ but only produces a finite number of terms for, say, $(1 + x)^2$?

(d) What will be the 15th term in the expansion for $(1 + x)^{-2}$?

How is the expansion $1 - 2x + 3x^2 - 4x^3 + 5x^4 - \dots$ related to $(1 + x)^{-2}$?
We can try to answer this question by comparing $1 - 2x + 3x^2 - 4x^3 + 5x^4 - \dots$
with $(1 + x)^{-2}$ for different values of $x$.

**B2** (a) (i) Use your calculator to find the value of $(1 + x)^{-2}$ when $x = 0.2$, correct to 6 d.p.

(ii) Copy and complete the following table for the expansion
$1 - 2x + 3x^2 - 4x^3 + 5x^4 - \dots$ with $x = 0.2$.

| Number of terms | Expansion | Value when $x = 0.2$ |
|---|---|---|
| 1 | $1$ | 1 |
| 2 | $1 - 2x$ | 0.6 |
| 3 | $1 - 2x + 3x^2$ | |
| 4 | $1 - 2x + 3x^2 - 4x^3$ | |
| 5 | | |
| 6 | | |
| 7 | | |
| 8 | | |

(iii) What appears to be happening?

(b) (i) Work out the value of $(1 + x)^{-2}$ when $x = -2$.

(ii) In your table, complete a column for $x = -2$ and comment on your results.

(c) (i) Use your calculator to find the value of $(1 + x)^{-2}$ when $x = 0.9$, correct to 6 d.p.

(ii) In your table, complete a column for $x = 0.9$ and comment on your results.

With an infinite series such as $1 - 2x + 3x^2 - 4x^3 + 5x^4 - \ldots$ you may need to evaluate the sum of many terms before you can see whether or not the series is converging to a limit.

A spreadsheet is useful for this.

**B3** The spreadsheet below is set up to investigate further the value of the expansion $1 - 2x + 3x^2 - 4x^3 + 5x^4 - \ldots$ when $x = 0.9$.

The formula used here is
'=(-1)^(A2+1)*A2'
and it is filled down.

This is the value of $x$.

'1' is entered in cell C2.

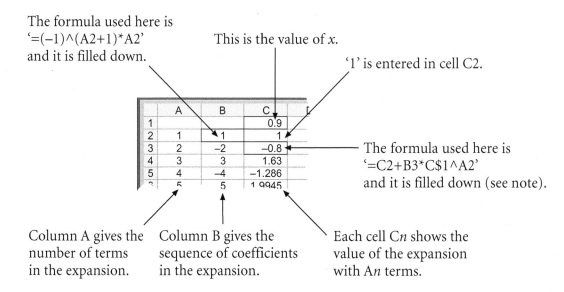

The formula used here is
'=C2+B3*C$1^A2'
and it is filled down (see note).

Column A gives the number of terms in the expansion.

Column B gives the sequence of coefficients in the expansion.

Each cell C$n$ shows the value of the expansion with A$n$ terms.

Note: 'C$1' ensures that cell C1 is always referred to (not 'the cell two rows above') when the formula is filled down.

(a) Set up a spreadsheet as above.
Do you think the expansion converges when $x = 0.9$?

(b) Try some different values of $x$, positive and negative, in cell C1.
Can you find a rule that tells you when $1 - 2x + 3x^2 - 4x^3 + 5x^4 - \ldots$ will converge?

**B4** Define functions f, g and h as

$$f(x) = (1 + x)^{-2}$$
$$g(x) = 1 - 2x + 3x^2 - 4x^3 + 5x^4 - 6x^5$$
$$h(x) = 1 - 2x + 3x^2 - 4x^3 + 5x^4 - 6x^5 + 7x^6 - 8x^7 + 9x^8 - 10x^9 + 11x^{10} - 12x^{11}$$

Use a graphic calculator or graph plotter to draw the graphs of $y = f(x)$, $y = g(x)$ and $y = h(x)$ for $-2 \leq x \leq 2$.

What do you notice about your graphs?

It can be proved (using methods outside the scope of this book) that the series expansion $1 - 2x + 3x^2 - 4x^3 + 5x^4 - \dots$ converges to $(1 + x)^{-2}$ for values of $x$ such that $-1 < x < 1$. This can be written as $|x| < 1$.

We say that the expansion $(1 + x)^{-2} = 1 - 2x + 3x^2 - 4x^3 + 5x^4 - \dots$ is **valid** for $|x| < 1$.

**B5** **(a)** Show that if the binomial theorem is used to find an expansion for $(1 - 2x)^{-1}$ then the first six terms are $1 + 2x + 4x^2 + 8x^3 + 16x^4 + 32x^5$.

**(b)** What will be the 12th term in this expansion for $(1 - 2x)^{-1}$?

**(c)** **(i)** Find the value of $(1 - 2x)^{-1}$ when $x = 0.7$.

**(ii)** Edit the spreadsheet used in B3 to investigate the value of the expansion $1 + 2x + 4x^2 + 8x^3 + 16x^4 + 32x^5 + \dots$ when $x = 0.7$.

**(d)** Try some different values of $x$, positive and negative. Can you find a rule that tells you when $1 + 2x + 4x^2 + 8x^3 + 16x^4 + 32x^5 + \dots$ will converge?

**K** The binomial theorem can produce an expansion for $(1 + ax)^n$ when $n$ is negative but it is only valid for certain values for $x$, namely the set of values for which $-1 < ax < 1$.

Will there be a similar result if $n$ is a fraction?

For example, applying the formula to $(1 + x)^{\frac{1}{2}}$ gives

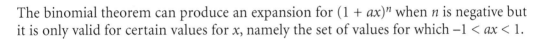

$$(1 + x)^{\frac{1}{2}} = 1 + \left(\tfrac{1}{2}\right)x + \frac{\left(\tfrac{1}{2}\right)\left(-\tfrac{1}{2}\right)}{2!}x^2 + \frac{\left(\tfrac{1}{2}\right)\left(-\tfrac{1}{2}\right)\left(-\tfrac{3}{2}\right)}{3!}x^3 + \dots$$

**B6** **(a)** Show that the expansion above simplifies to $(1 + x)^{\frac{1}{2}} = 1 + \tfrac{1}{2}x - \tfrac{1}{8}x^2 + \tfrac{1}{16}x^3 + \dots$

**(b)** Find and simplify the next two terms in the expansion.

**(c)** When $x = 0.8$, find the value of

**(i)** $(1 + x)^{\frac{1}{2}}$
    **(ii)** $1 + \tfrac{1}{2}x - \tfrac{1}{8}x^2 + \tfrac{1}{16}x^3$

**(d)** Use a graphic calculator or graph plotter to show that the graph of $y = 1 + \tfrac{1}{2}x - \tfrac{1}{8}x^2 + \tfrac{1}{16}x^3$ is very close to the graph of $y = (1 + x)^{\frac{1}{2}}$ when $|x| < 1$.

It was Isaac Newton who discovered the following.

**K** The **binomial expansion**
$$(1 + ax)^n = 1 + nax + \frac{n(n-1)}{2!}(ax)^2 + \frac{n(n-1)(n-2)}{3!}(ax)^3 + \dots$$
holds for **all** negative and fractional values of $n$ provided that $-1 < ax < 1$, that is $|ax| < 1$.

Newton's work on infinite series led directly to the development of calculus. The binomial expansion is still an important tool today in many areas of advanced mathematics.

To work out when a binomial expansion is valid you need to be able to solve inequalities that involve the modulus function.

**B7** Show that

**(a)** $|2x| < 1$ is equivalent to $|x| < \tfrac{1}{2}$
    **(b)** $|-4x| < 1$ is equivalent to $|x| < \tfrac{1}{4}$

**(c)** $|\tfrac{1}{3}x| < 1$ is equivalent to $|x| < 3$
    **(d)** $|\tfrac{3}{4}x| < 1$ is equivalent to $|x| < \tfrac{4}{3}$

**Example 1**

Find the binomial expansion of $\dfrac{1}{(1+3x)^2}$ in ascending powers of $x$ as far as the term in $x^3$ and state the set of values of $x$ for which the expansion is valid.

**Solution**

$$\frac{1}{(1+3x)^2} = (1+3x)^{-2} = 1 + (-2)(3x) + \frac{(-2)(-3)}{2!}(3x)^2 + \frac{(-2)(-3)(-4)}{3!}(3x)^3 + \dots$$

$$\approx 1 - 6x + 27x^2 - 108x^3$$

The expansion is valid when $-1 < 3x < 1$.

This simplifies to $-\frac{1}{3} < x < \frac{1}{3}$, or $|x| < \frac{1}{3}$.

---

**Example 2**

Expand $(1-2x)^{\frac{1}{2}}$ in ascending powers of $x$ as far as the term in $x^3$.
Show that you can use the expansion to find an approximate value for $\sqrt{0.94}$.
Hence find $\sqrt{0.94}$ correct to two decimal places.

**Solution**

$$(1-2x)^{\frac{1}{2}} = 1 + \left(\tfrac{1}{2}\right)(-2x) + \frac{\left(\tfrac{1}{2}\right)\left(-\tfrac{1}{2}\right)}{2!}(-2x)^2 + \frac{\left(\tfrac{1}{2}\right)\left(-\tfrac{1}{2}\right)\left(-\tfrac{3}{2}\right)}{3!}(-2x)^3 + \dots$$

$$\approx 1 - x - \tfrac{1}{2}x^2 - \tfrac{1}{2}x^3$$

The expansion is valid when $|-2x| < 1$, which gives $|x| < \frac{1}{2}$.

$\sqrt{0.94} = 0.94^{\frac{1}{2}} = (1 - 2 \times 0.03)^{\frac{1}{2}}$, which can be obtained by substituting $x = 0.03$ into $(1-2x)^{\frac{1}{2}}$.

As $|0.03| < \frac{1}{2}$, the expansion is valid for this value.

So $\sqrt{0.94} = (1 - 2 \times 0.03)^{\frac{1}{2}} \approx 1 - (0.03) - \tfrac{1}{2}(0.03)^2 - \tfrac{1}{2}(0.03)^3 = 1 - 0.03 - 0.000\,45 - 0.000\,013\,5$

$$= 0.969\,536\,5$$

Further terms in the expansion will not change the first three decimal places,
so we have $\sqrt{0.94} = 0.97$ correct to two decimal places.

---

**Example 3**

Find the series expansion of $(3+x)^{-1}$ as far as the term in $x^3$ and state the set of values of $x$ for which the expansion is valid.

**Solution**

$$(3+x)^{-1} = \left(3\left(1 + \tfrac{1}{3}x\right)\right)^{-1} = 3^{-1}\left(1 + \tfrac{1}{3}x\right)^{-1} = \tfrac{1}{3}\left(1 + \tfrac{1}{3}x\right)^{-1}$$

$$= \tfrac{1}{3}\left(1 + (-1)\left(\tfrac{1}{3}x\right) + \frac{(-1)(-2)}{2!}\left(\tfrac{1}{3}x\right)^2 + \frac{(-1)(-2)(-3)}{3!}\left(\tfrac{1}{3}x\right)^3 + \dots\right)$$

$$\approx \tfrac{1}{3} - \tfrac{1}{9}x + \tfrac{1}{27}x^2 - \tfrac{1}{81}x^3$$

The expansion is valid when $\left|\tfrac{1}{3}x\right| < 1$, which gives $|x| < 3$.

---

**Example 4**

Expand $(1 + x)^{\frac{2}{3}}$ in ascending powers of $x$ as far as the term in $x^2$.

Use the expansion to find an approximate value for $1.6^{\frac{2}{3}}$ and comment on its accuracy.

**Solution**

$(1 + x)^{\frac{2}{3}} = 1 + \left(\frac{2}{3}\right)x + \dfrac{\left(\frac{2}{3}\right)\left(-\frac{1}{3}\right)}{2!}x^2 + \dots \approx 1 + \frac{2}{3}x - \frac{1}{9}x^2$

So $1.6^{\frac{2}{3}} = (1 + 0.6)^{\frac{2}{3}} \approx 1 + \frac{2}{3}\times 0.6 - \frac{1}{9}\times(0.6)^2$   $\qquad |0.6| < 1$ *so we can use the expansion.*

$\qquad\qquad = 1 + 0.4 - 0.04$

$\qquad\qquad = 1.36$

Using a calculator gives $1.6^{\frac{2}{3}} = 1.367\,980\,757\dots$ which agrees with the approximate value when both values are rounded to two significant figures (to give 1.4). So the approximate value is accurate to two significant figures.

---

**Exercise B** (answers p 154)

**1** Expand each of these as a series of ascending powers of $x$ as far as the term in $x^3$.
For each expansion, give the range of values, in the form $|x| < k$, for which it is valid.

(a) $(1 + x)^{-1}$   (b) $(1 - x)^{-2}$   (c) $(1 + 2x)^{-4}$

(d) $\left(1 + \frac{1}{2}x\right)^{-2}$   (e) $\dfrac{1}{1 + 3x}$   (f) $\dfrac{1}{\left(1 - \frac{1}{3}x\right)^2}$

(g) $(1 - x)^{\frac{1}{2}}$   (h) $\sqrt{1 + \frac{1}{4}x}$   (i) $\dfrac{1}{\sqrt{1 + 2x}}$

**2 (a)** Show that the first four terms of the binomial expansion for $(1 + 3x)^{\frac{1}{3}}$ are
$$1 + x - x^2 + \tfrac{5}{3}x^3$$

**(b)** State the range of values for which the expansion is valid.

**3 (a)** Obtain the binomial expansion of $(1 + 4x)^{\frac{1}{2}}$ as far as the term in $x^6$.

**(b)** Show that this expansion can be used to find an approximation for $\sqrt{1.4}$ .
Hence find the value of $\sqrt{1.4}$ correct to two decimal places.

**4 (a)** Obtain the binomial expansion of $(1 + 2x)^{\frac{3}{2}}$ as far as the term in $x^2$.

**(b)** Use this expansion to find an approximate value for $1.8^{\frac{3}{2}}$.
Comment on its accuracy.

**5 (a)** Obtain the binomial expansion of $\left(1 + \frac{1}{2}x\right)^{\frac{1}{2}}$ as far as the term in $x^2$.

**(b) (i)** Hence find the series expansion of $(16 + 8x)^{\frac{1}{2}}$ as far as the term in $x^2$.

**(ii)** Find the range of values of $x$ for which this expansion is valid.

**6** Find the coefficient of $x^2$ in the series expansion of $\dfrac{1}{\sqrt{9 - x}}$.

**7** Expand each of these as a series of ascending powers of $x$ as far as the term in $x^2$. In each case give the range of values for which the expansion is valid.

(a) $(2 + x)^{-1}$

(b) $\dfrac{1}{(4 - x)^3}$

(c) $(6 + 3x)^{-2}$

(d) $(4 + x)^{\frac{1}{2}}$

(e) $(3 + 2x)^{-1}$

(f) $\sqrt[5]{32 - 64x}$

## C Multiplying to obtain expansions

Sometimes a series expansion can be obtained for a more complicated rational expression by finding expansions for simpler rational expressions and then multiplying.

---

### Example 5

Expand $\dfrac{1 + 3x}{(1 + x)^3}$, $|x| < 1$, in ascending powers of $x$ as far as the term in $x^3$.

### Solution

$\dfrac{1 + 3x}{(1 + x)^3} = (1 + 3x)(1 + x)^{-3}$

$= (1 + 3x)\left(1 + (-3)x + \dfrac{(-3)(-4)}{2!}x^2 + \dfrac{(-3)(-4)(-5)}{3!}x^3 + \dots \right)$   *You only need to go as far as the term in $x^3$.*

$= (1 + 3x)(1 - 3x + 6x^2 - 10x^3 + \dots)$

$= 1 - 3x + 6x^2 - 10x^3 + \dots \ + 3x - 9x^2 + 18x^3 - \dots$   *Multiply as far as terms in $x^3$.*

$\approx 1 - 3x^2 + 8x^3$

---

### Exercise C (answers p 155)

**1** For each of these, find an expansion in ascending powers of $x$ as far as the term in $x^3$.

(a) $\dfrac{5}{(1 - x)^2}$, $|x| < 1$

(b) $\dfrac{x}{1 + 3x}$, $|x| < \frac{1}{3}$

(c) $\dfrac{x + 1}{\sqrt{1 - 4x}}$, $|x| < \frac{1}{4}$

(d) $\dfrac{1 - 2x}{(1 - 3x)^3}$, $|x| < \frac{1}{3}$

**2 (a) (i)** Show that the first three terms of the expansion for $\dfrac{1}{1 - 3x}$ are $1 + 3x + 9x^2$.

**(ii)** State the range of values for which the expansion is valid.

**(b) (i)** Show that the first three terms of the expansion for $\dfrac{1}{(1 + x)^4}$ are $1 - 4x + 10x^2$.

**(ii)** State the range of values for which the expansion is valid.

**(c) (i)** By considering the product $(1 + 3x + 9x^2 + \dots)(1 - 4x + 10x^2 - \dots)$, find an expansion for $\dfrac{1}{(1 - 3x)(1 + x)^4}$ in ascending powers of $x$ as far as the term in $x^2$.

**(ii)** Explain why this expansion is only valid for $|x| < \frac{1}{3}$.

# D Adding (using partial fractions) to obtain expansions

An expansion for an expression such as $\dfrac{10-x}{(3-x)(1+2x)}$ can be obtained by finding expansions for simpler rational expressions and then multiplying, but the product is quite complicated. An alternative method is to use partial fractions and then **add** the resulting expansions.

---

### Example 6

The function f is given by $f(x) = \dfrac{10-x}{(3-x)(1+2x)}$.

Express $f(x)$ in partial fractions and hence obtain the expansion of $f(x)$ as far as the term in $x^2$. State the range of values for which the expansion is valid.

### Solution

Let
$$\frac{10-x}{(3-x)(1+2x)} \equiv \frac{A}{3-x} + \frac{B}{1+2x}$$

Then
$$\frac{10-x}{(3-x)(1+2x)} \equiv \frac{A(1+2x)+B(3-x)}{(3-x)(1+2x)}$$

giving
$$A(1+2x) + B(3-x) \equiv 10 - x$$

Substituting $x = 3$ in this identity gives    $7A = 7$, which gives $A = 1$.

Substituting $x = -\frac{1}{2}$ in this identity gives    $\frac{7}{2}B = \frac{21}{2}$, which gives $B = 3$.

Hence
$$f(x) \equiv \frac{1}{3-x} + \frac{3}{1+2x}$$

Now, $\dfrac{1}{3-x} = (3-x)^{-1} = 3^{-1}\left(1 - \tfrac{1}{3}x\right)^{-1} = \tfrac{1}{3}\left(1 - \tfrac{1}{3}x\right)^{-1}$

$$= \tfrac{1}{3}\left(1 + (-1)\left(-\tfrac{1}{3}x\right) + \frac{(-1)(-2)}{2!}\left(-\tfrac{1}{3}x\right)^2 + \ldots\right)$$

$$= \tfrac{1}{3}\left(1 + \tfrac{1}{3}x + \tfrac{1}{9}x^2 + \ldots\right)$$

$$= \tfrac{1}{3} + \tfrac{1}{9}x + \tfrac{1}{27}x^2 + \ldots$$

Also, $\dfrac{3}{1+2x} = 3(1+2x)^{-1} = 3\left(1 + (-1)(2x) + \frac{(-1)(-2)}{2!}(2x)^2 + \ldots\right)$

$$= 3(1 - 2x + 4x^2 - \ldots)$$

$$= 3 - 6x + 12x^2 - \ldots$$

So $f(x) = \tfrac{1}{3} + \tfrac{1}{9}x + \tfrac{1}{27}x^2 + \ldots + 3 - 6x + 12x^2 - \ldots$

$$\approx \tfrac{10}{3} - \tfrac{53}{9}x + \tfrac{325}{27}x^2$$

The expansion for $\left(1 - \tfrac{1}{3}x\right)^{-1}$ is valid for $\left|-\tfrac{1}{3}x\right| < 1$, which gives $|x| < 3$.

The expansion for $(1 + 2x)^{-1}$ is valid for $|2x| < 1$, which gives $|x| < \tfrac{1}{2}$.

The expansion for $f(x)$ is valid for the values that satisfy both inequalities, that is for $|x| < \tfrac{1}{2}$.

---

**Exercise D** (answers p 155)

**1** The function f is given by $f(x) = \dfrac{4+5x}{(1-x)(1+2x)}$.

    **(a)** Express $f(x)$ as partial fractions.

    **(b)** Hence obtain the expansion of $f(x)$ in ascending powers of $x$ as far as the term in $x^2$.

    **(c)** Show that the expansion is valid when $|x| < \frac{1}{2}$.

**2** The function g is given by $g(x) = \dfrac{8-x}{(2+x)(1-2x)}$.

    **(a)** Express $g(x)$ as partial fractions.

    **(b)** **(i)** Show that the first three terms in the expansion of $\dfrac{1}{2+x}$ in
            ascending powers of $x$ are $\frac{1}{2} - \frac{1}{4}x + \frac{1}{8}x^2$.

        **(ii)** Obtain a similar expansion for $\dfrac{1}{1-2x}$.

    **(c)** Hence obtain the first three terms in the expansion of $g(x)$ in ascending powers of $x$.

    **(d)** Find the range of values of $x$ for which this expansion of $g(x)$ is valid.

**3** Find the first four terms of the series expansion for each of these rational expressions. Find the range of values for which each expansion is valid.

    **(a)** $\dfrac{2+x}{(1+4x)(1-3x)}$
    **(b)** $\dfrac{7+x}{(3-x)(1+3x)}$
    **(c)** $\dfrac{9-x}{(1+x)(3-2x)}$

**4** Show that the first three terms in the expansion of $\dfrac{11x-3}{(4-3x)(1+x)}$ are $-\frac{3}{4} + \frac{47}{16}x - \frac{83}{64}x^2$.

---

**Key points**

- The binomial expansion

$$(1+ax)^n = 1 + nax + \frac{n(n-1)}{2!}(ax)^2 + \frac{n(n-1)(n-2)}{3!}(ax)^3 + \dots$$

  is valid for negative and fractional values of $n$ for $|ax| < 1$.       (p 49)

---

**Mixed questions** (answers p 156)

**1** **(a)** Expand $\dfrac{4}{(1+2x)^3}$ in ascending powers of $x$ as far as the term in $x^2$.

    **(b)** For what values of $x$ is this expansion valid?

**2** **(a)** Expand $(100 - 400x)^{\frac{1}{2}}$ in ascending powers of $x$ up to and including the term in $x^3$.

    **(b)** **(i)** What value of $x$ gives an approximate value for $\sqrt{60}$ when used in this expansion?

        **(ii)** Use the series expansion in part (a) to find an approximate value for $\sqrt{60}$.

        **(iii)** Comment on the accuracy of this approximate value.

**3** In the expansion of $(1 + ax)^n$ the coefficients of $x$ and $x^2$ are $-10$ and $75$ respectively. Find the value of $a$ and the value of $n$.

**4 (a)** Expand $(1 + x)^{-1}$ in ascending powers of $x$ as far as the term in $x^3$.

**(b)** By integrating $(1 + x)^{-1}$ and its expansion, find a series expansion for $\ln(1 + x)$ as far as the term in $x^4$.

**(c)** State, with a reason, whether your series expansion in part (b) could be used to find an approximation for $\ln 3$.

**5 (a)** Obtain the first four terms in the expansion of $(1 - 2x)^{-1}$ in ascending powers of $x$.

**(b)** Hence show that, for small $x$, $\dfrac{1-x}{1-2x} \approx 1 + x + 2x^2 + 4x^3$.

**(c)** Taking a suitable value for $x$, which should be stated, use the series expansion in part (b) to find an approximate value for $\frac{99}{98}$, giving your answer correct to 5 d.p.

**(d)** Hence write down an approximate value for $\frac{1}{98}$.

## Test yourself (answers p 157)

**1** The binomial expansion of $(1 - 2x)^{-3}$ in ascending powers of $x$ up to and including the term in $x^3$ is $1 + 6x + px^2 + qx^3$, $|x| < \frac{1}{2}$.

**(a)** Find the value of $p$ and the value of $q$.

**(b)** Hence obtain the first three terms of the expansion for $\dfrac{1 - 3x}{(1 - 2x)^3}$.

**2 (a)** Express $\dfrac{8 + 3x}{(1 + 3x)(2 - x)}$ in the form $\dfrac{A}{1 + 3x} + \dfrac{B}{2 - x}$.

**(b)** Obtain the first three terms in the expansion of $\dfrac{1}{1 + 3x}$ in ascending powers of $x$.

**(c)** Show that the first three terms in the expansion of $\dfrac{1}{2 - x}$ in ascending powers of $x$ are $\frac{1}{2} + \frac{x}{4} + \frac{x^2}{8}$.

**(d)** Hence, or otherwise, obtain the first three terms in the expansion of $\dfrac{8 + 3x}{(1 + 3x)(2 - x)}$ in ascending powers of $x$.

**(e)** State the range of values of $x$ for which the expansion in part (d) is valid.　　AQA 2004

**3 (a)** Obtain the binomial expansion of $(1 + x)^{\frac{1}{2}}$ as far as the term in $x^2$.

**(b) (i)** Hence, or otherwise, find the series expansion of $(4 + 2x)^{\frac{1}{2}}$ as far as the term in $x^2$.

**(ii)** Find the range of values of $x$ for which this expansion is valid.　　AQA 2003

**4 (a)** Expand $(1 - 10x)^{\frac{1}{5}}$, $|x| < \frac{1}{10}$, in ascending powers of $x$ as far as the term in $x^3$.

**(b)** By substituting $x = 0.001$ in your expansion, find $\sqrt[5]{99\,000}$ correct to 5 s.f.

**5** Find the coefficient of $x^2$ in the series expansion of $\dfrac{x + 8}{\sqrt{4 - x}}$.

# 5 Trigonometric formulae

In this chapter you will learn how to
- use the formulae for $\sin(A + B)$, $\cos(A + B)$, etc.
- use the formulae for $\sin 2A$, $\cos 2A$ and $\tan 2A$
- use equivalent expressions for $a\cos\theta + b\sin\theta$
- solve equations of the form $a\cos\theta + b\sin\theta = c$

## A Addition formulae (answers p 157)

The diagram shows a rectangle with diagonal 1 unit long, touching two parallel lines.

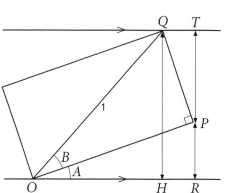

**A1** (a) Write down the length of $OP$ in terms of angle $B$.

    (b) Use your answer to (a) to write down an expression for the length of $RP$.

    (c) Show that angle $QPT$ = angle $A$, and use this to find an expression for the length of $PT$.

    (d) Hence write down an expression for $RP + PT$, the distance between the parallel lines.

    (e) Find $QH$ in terms of angle $(A + B)$, and thus show that
$\sin(A + B) = \sin A \cos B + \cos A \sin B$.

**A2** By using the fact that $OH = OR - HR$, show that $\cos(A + B) = \cos A \cos B - \sin A \sin B$.

The formulae you derived in questions A1 and A2 are called the **addition formulae**.

**A3** By replacing $B$ by $-B$ in the two addition formulae, and simplifying, establish formulae for $\sin(A - B)$ and $\cos(A - B)$.

> **K**
> $\sin(A + B) = \sin A \cos B + \cos A \sin B$
> $\sin(A - B) = \sin A \cos B - \cos A \sin B$
> $\cos(A + B) = \cos A \cos B - \sin A \sin B$
> $\cos(A - B) = \cos A \cos B + \sin A \sin B$

**A4** Put $B = A$ in the formula for $\sin(A + B)$. What result do you get for $\sin 2A$?

**A5** By putting $B = A$ in the formula for $\cos(A + B)$,

    (a) show that $\cos 2A = 2\cos^2 A - 1$

    (b) show also that $\cos 2A = 1 - 2\sin^2 A$

> **K**
> $\sin 2A = 2\sin A \cos A$
> $\cos 2A = \cos^2 A - \sin^2 A = 2\cos^2 A - 1 = 1 - 2\sin^2 A$

These are sometimes referred to as double angle formulae.

## Example 1

Use an addition formula to show that $\cos(x + 90)° = -\sin x°$.
Explain your result graphically.

### Solution

*In the addition formula for $\cos(A + B)$, substitute $x°$ for $A$ and $90°$ for $B$.*

$$\cos(x + 90)° = \cos x° \cos 90° - \sin x° \sin 90°$$
$$= \cos x° \times 0 - \sin x° \times 1$$
$$= -\sin x°$$

The graph of $\cos(x + 90)°$ is the graph of $\cos x°$ translated by $\begin{bmatrix} -90° \\ 0 \end{bmatrix}$.

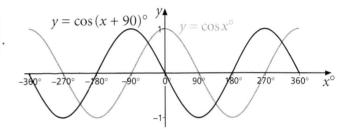

The graph of $-\sin x°$ is the graph of $\sin x°$ reflected in the $x$-axis.

The two graphs are clearly identical, illustrating that $\cos(x + 90)° = -\sin x°$.

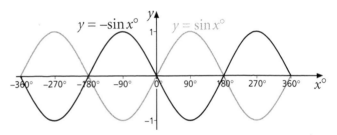

## Example 2

By writing $\cos 15°$ as $\cos(60° - 45°)$, show that $\cos 15° = \dfrac{1 + \sqrt{3}}{2\sqrt{2}}$.

### Solution

$$\cos 15° = \cos(60° - 45°)$$
$$= \cos 60° \cos 45° + \sin 60° \sin 45°$$
$$= \tfrac{1}{2} \times \frac{1}{\sqrt{2}} + \frac{\sqrt{3}}{2} \times \frac{1}{\sqrt{2}}$$
$$= \frac{1 + \sqrt{3}}{2\sqrt{2}}$$

## Example 3

Given that $\sin A = \tfrac{1}{4}$, find    (a) $\cos 2A$    (b) $\sin 2A$

### Solution

(a) $\cos 2A = 1 - 2\sin^2 A = 1 - 2 \times \tfrac{1}{16} = 1 - \tfrac{1}{8} = \tfrac{7}{8}$

(b) Since $\sin^2 2A + \cos^2 2A = 1$, $\sin 2A = \pm\sqrt{1 - \cos^2 2A}$

so $\sin 2A = \pm\sqrt{1 - \dfrac{49}{64}} = \pm\sqrt{\dfrac{15}{64}} = \pm\dfrac{\sqrt{15}}{8}$

**D** **A6** In example 3, there is only one value for $\cos 2A$, but two values for $\sin 2A$. Explain why this is so.

There are addition formulae for the tangent function as well as sine and cosine.

**A7** (a) Rewrite $\tan (A + B)$ in terms of $\sin (A + B)$ and $\cos (A + B)$.

   (b) Use the addition formulae to expand $\sin (A + B)$ and $\cos (A + B)$ in the expression you wrote in part (a).

   (c) Divide top and bottom of the fraction by $\cos A \cos B$, to obtain an expression solely in terms of $\tan A$ and $\tan B$.

**A8** (a) Replace $B$ by $-B$ to obtain an expression for $\tan (A - B)$ in terms of $\tan A$ and $\tan B$.

   (b) In the expression for $\tan (A + B)$, put $B = A$ and thus obtain an expression for $\tan 2A$ in terms of $\tan A$.

**K**

$$\tan (A + B) = \frac{\tan A + \tan B}{1 - \tan A \tan B}$$

$$\tan (A - B) = \frac{\tan A - \tan B}{1 + \tan A \tan B}$$

$$\tan 2A = \frac{2 \tan A}{1 - \tan^2 A} \qquad \text{(This is another double angle formula.)}$$

---

### Example 4

Given that $\tan 2A = 2$, find in surd form the two possible values of $\tan A$.

### Solution

$$\tan 2A = \frac{2 \tan A}{1 - \tan^2 A} = 2$$

$\Rightarrow \qquad 2 \tan A = 2(1 - \tan^2 A)$

$\Rightarrow \qquad \tan A = 1 - \tan^2 A$

$\Rightarrow \qquad \tan^2 A + \tan A - 1 = 0$

*Use the quadratic formula.* $\qquad \tan A = \dfrac{-1 \pm \sqrt{1^2 - 4 \times 1 \times -1}}{2 \times 1}$

$\Rightarrow \qquad \tan A = \dfrac{-1 \pm \sqrt{5}}{2}$

$\Rightarrow \qquad \tan A = -\frac{1}{2} + \dfrac{\sqrt{5}}{2} \ \text{ or } \ -\frac{1}{2} - \dfrac{\sqrt{5}}{2}$

---

## Example 5

Find a formula for $\tan 3A$ in terms of $\tan A$.

### Solution

Use the addition formula.
$$\tan 3A = \tan(A + 2A) = \frac{\tan A + \tan 2A}{1 - \tan A \tan 2A}$$

Use the double angle formula.
$$= \frac{t + \dfrac{2t}{1 - t^2}}{1 - t\dfrac{2t}{1 - t^2}} \quad \text{where } t = \tan A$$

Multiply top and bottom by $(1 - t^2)$.
$$= \frac{t(1 - t^2) + 2t}{(1 - t^2) - t \times 2t}$$

$$= \frac{3t - t^3}{1 - 3t^2} = \frac{3 \tan A - \tan^3 A}{1 - 3 \tan^2 A}$$

## Example 6

Solve $3 \sin 2x = \cos x$, giving answers between 0 and $2\pi$ in radians to two decimal places.

### Solution

$$3 \sin 2x = \cos x$$
$$\Rightarrow \quad 3 \times 2 \sin x \cos x = \cos x$$
$$\Rightarrow \quad 6 \sin x \cos x - \cos x = 0$$
$$\Rightarrow \quad \cos x (6 \sin x - 1) = 0$$

So $\cos x = 0$, or $6 \sin x - 1 = 0$ giving $\sin x = \frac{1}{6}$

$\cos x = 0$ gives $x = \frac{\pi}{2}$ or $\frac{3\pi}{2}$, i.e. $x = 1.57$ or $4.71$ (to 2 d.p.)

$\sin x = \frac{1}{6}$ gives $x = \arcsin \frac{1}{6} = 0.167\ldots$, or $\pi - 0.167\ldots$ which is $2.974\ldots$

So $x = 0.17, 1.57, 2.97$ or $4.71$ (to 2 d.p.)

## Example 7

Prove that $\dfrac{1 - \cos 2A}{\sin 2A} = \tan A$ $(A \neq n\pi, n \in \mathbb{Z})$

### Solution

$$\frac{1 - \cos 2A}{\sin 2A} = \frac{1 - (1 - 2 \sin^2 A)}{2 \sin A \cos A} = \frac{2 \sin^2 A}{2 \sin A \cos A} = \frac{\sin A}{\cos A} = \tan A$$

$n \in \mathbb{Z}$ means '$n$ is a member of the integers' $(\ldots, -2, -1, 0, 1, 2, \ldots)$
So $(A \neq n\pi, n \in \mathbb{Z})$ means that $A$ cannot be $\ldots, -2\pi, -\pi, 0, \pi, 2\pi, \ldots$

These are the values of $A$ where $\sin 2A = 0$ and where $\tan A$ is not defined.
You are not expected to prove that the equality does not hold for these values;
the question is simply telling you that it does not hold.

**Example 8**

Show that $\cos x - \sin x - 1 = -2 \sin \frac{x}{2}\left(\sin \frac{x}{2} + \cos \frac{x}{2}\right).$

**Solution**

$\cos 2A = 1 - 2\sin^2 A$. Replacing $A$ by $\frac{x}{2}$, we have $\cos x = 1 - 2\sin^2 \frac{x}{2}$.

Similarly $\sin 2A = 2\sin A \cos A$. Replacing $A$ by $\frac{x}{2}$, we have $\sin x = 2\sin \frac{x}{2}\cos \frac{x}{2}$.

Hence
$$\cos x - \sin x - 1 = \left(1 - 2\sin^2 \frac{x}{2}\right) - 2\sin \frac{x}{2}\cos \frac{x}{2} - 1$$
$$= -2\sin^2 \frac{x}{2} - 2\sin \frac{x}{2}\cos \frac{x}{2}$$
$$= -2\sin \frac{x}{2}\left(\sin \frac{x}{2} + \cos \frac{x}{2}\right)$$

---

**Exercise A** (answers p 158)

**1** Use an addition formula to simplify $\sin(x + 180)°$.
Explain your result graphically.

**2 (a)** By writing $\sin 75°$ as $\sin(45° + 30°)$, show that $\sin 75° = \dfrac{\sqrt{3}+1}{2\sqrt{2}}$.

**(b)** Use a similar method to express $\sin 15°$ using surds.

**3** Given that $\cos A = \frac{4}{5}$, where $A$ is acute, find the exact value of

**(a)** $\sin A$        **(b)** $\sin 2A$        **(c)** $\cos 2A$        **(d)** $\operatorname{cosec} 2A$

**4 (a)** If $\tan A = \frac{1}{2}$ and $\tan B = \frac{1}{3}$, find $\tan(A + B)$.

**(b)** If $\tan 2C = \frac{3}{4}$, find the two possible values of $\tan C$.

**5 (a)** Show that $\cos(A + B) + \cos(A - B) = 2\cos A \cos B$.

**(b)** Simplify $\cos(A - B) - \cos(A + B)$.

**6** Simplify

**(a)** $\cos 2A \cos A - \sin 2A \sin A$        **(b)** $\cos(A + B)\cos A + \sin(A + B)\sin A$

**(c)** $2\sin 3C \cos 3C$        **(d)** $\sin 3D \cos 2D + \cos 3D \sin 2D$

**7** Show that

**(a)** $(\cos A + \sin A)(\cos B + \sin B) = \cos(A - B) + \sin(A + B)$

**(b)** $(\cos A + \sin A)^2 = 1 + \sin 2A$

**(c)** $\sin 3A = 3\sin A - 4\sin^3 A$

**(d)** $(\sin A + \cos B)^2 + (\cos A - \sin B)^2 = 2(1 + \sin(A - B))$

**8** Show that $\cot 2x + \operatorname{cosec} 2x = \cot x$.

**9** Show that $\dfrac{\cos\theta}{1-\sqrt{2}\sin\theta} - \dfrac{\cos\theta}{1+\sqrt{2}\sin\theta} = \sqrt{2}\tan 2\theta \ \left(\theta \neq n\pi \pm \dfrac{\pi}{4}, n\in\mathbb{Z}\right)$.

**10** Prove that $\dfrac{\tan a}{\sec a - 1} = \cot\tfrac{1}{2}a \ (a \neq n\pi, n\in\mathbb{Z})$.

**11** If $t = \tan\tfrac{1}{2}\theta$, show that

(a) $\dfrac{2t}{1+t^2} = \sin\theta$ (b) $\dfrac{1-t^2}{1+t^2} = \cos\theta$

**12** Solve these equations for $0° \leq x° \leq 360°$.

(a) $\sin 2x° = \cos x°$ (b) $\sin x° + \cos 2x° = 0$ (c) $\cos 2x° = 7\cos x° + 3$

(d) $\cos 2x° = 1 + \sin x°$ (e) $\sin 2x° = \tan x°$

**13** Show that

(a) $\sin(\theta + \phi) + \sin(\theta - \phi) = 2\sin\theta\cos\phi$

(b) $\sin(\theta + \phi) - \sin(\theta - \phi) = 2\cos\theta\sin\phi$

**14** (a) Show that $\dfrac{\cot^2\theta}{1+\cot^2\theta} \equiv \cos^2\theta$.

(b) Hence solve $\dfrac{\cot^2\theta}{1+\cot^2\theta} = 2\sin 2\theta$ for $0° \leq \theta \leq 360°$. AQA 2002

## B Equivalent expressions (answers p 160)

You already know how to solve several types of trigonometric equations.

**B1** Solve each of these equations to the nearest degree. Give all solutions between 0° and 360°.
Check that each of your answers is reasonable by using a graph plotter.

(a) $2\sin(x + 30)° = 1$ (b) $3\cos(x - 50)° = 2$ (c) $3\cos x° + 4\sin x° = 0$

**D** **B2** Can you solve $3\sin x° + 4\cos x° = 1$ using any of the methods you used in B1? Explain your answer.

In order to solve $3\sin x° + 4\cos x° = 1$, it will be useful to look at the trigonometric function $y = 3\sin x° + 4\cos x°$.

**B3** (a) On a graph plotter, draw the graph of $y = 3\sin x° + 4\cos x°$, for values of $x°$ roughly between −360° and 360°.

(b) The graph of $y = 3\sin x° + 4\cos x°$ appears to be a sine curve.

(i) What is the period of $y = 3\sin x° + 4\cos x°$?

(ii) What is the amplitude of $y = 3\sin x° + 4\cos x°$?

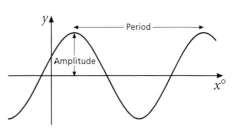

**B4** Using a graph plotter, find the period and amplitude of each of these.

    **(a)** $y = 5\sin x° + 12\cos x°$    **(b)** $y = 7\sin x° + 24\cos x°$    **(c)** $y = \sin x° + \cos x°$

**B5** Look at your results in questions B3 and B4.

    **(a)** What do you think the period of $y = 2\sin x° + 3\cos x°$ would be?

    **(b)** What do you think the amplitude of $y = 2\sin x° + 3\cos x°$ would be?

    **(c)** Check your conjectures by plotting the graph of $y = 2\sin x° + 3\cos x°$.

    **(d)** What do you think the period and amplitude of $y = a\sin x° + b\cos x°$ would be?

**B6** **(a)** Draw again the graph of $y = \sin x° + \cos x°$ on your plotter.
        Draw also the graph of $y = \sin x°$.

    **(b)** It looks as though you can transform the graph of $y = \sin x°$ on to
        that of $y = \sin x° + \cos x°$ using two transformations:
        an enlargement in the $y$-direction scale factor $\sqrt{2}$, followed by a translation of $\begin{bmatrix} -45° \\ 0 \end{bmatrix}$.
        What does the equation of $y = \sin x°$ become after these two transformations?

    **(c)** Use the fact that $\sin(x + \alpha)° = \sin x° \cos \alpha° + \cos x° \sin \alpha°$ to show that the
        equation of the graph you obtained in part (b) is identical to $y = \sin x° + \cos x°$.

**K**

$$r\sin(x + \alpha) = r(\sin x \cos \alpha + \cos x \sin \alpha)$$
$$= (r\cos \alpha)\sin x + (r\sin \alpha)\cos x$$

If we have an expression such as $2\sin x + 3\cos x$, we can change it into the form
$r\sin(x + \alpha)$ provided we can find values of $r$ and $\alpha$, such that

$$r\cos \alpha = 2 \text{ and } r\sin \alpha = 3$$

An example will show how this can be useful.

---

## Example 9

Find the maximum value of the expression $2\sin x° + 3\cos x°$,
and the value of $x°$ $(0° \leq x° \leq 360°)$ at which the maximum occurs.

### Solution

*First express $2\sin x° + 3\cos x°$ in the form $r\sin(x + \alpha)°$.*

If $2\sin x° + 3\cos x° = r\sin x° \cos \alpha° + r\cos x° \sin \alpha°$ then,
equating coefficients, $r\cos \alpha° = 2$ and $r\sin \alpha° = 3$.

*Eliminate $\alpha°$ from these two equations by squaring and adding.*

$$r^2 \cos^2 \alpha° + r^2 \sin^2 \alpha° = 4 + 9 = 13$$

$\Rightarrow\quad\quad r^2(\cos^2 \alpha° + \sin^2 \alpha°) = 13$

$\Rightarrow\quad\quad\quad\quad\quad r^2 = 13\quad\quad$ *since* $\cos^2 \alpha° + \sin^2 \alpha° = 1.$

$\Rightarrow\quad\quad\quad\quad\quad r = \sqrt{13}\quad\quad$ *Take the positive value.*

*You could use this value of $r$ to find the value of $\alpha°$ using $r\cos \alpha° = 2$ or $r\sin \alpha° = 3$.*
*But you can easily find $\alpha°$ by eliminating $r$ directly from $r\cos \alpha° = 2$ and $r\sin \alpha° = 3$.*

$r\cos\alpha° = 2$ and $r\sin\alpha° = 3$

$\Rightarrow \dfrac{r\sin\alpha°}{r\cos\alpha°} = \dfrac{3}{2} \Rightarrow \tan\alpha° = 1.5 \Rightarrow \alpha° = 56°$ (to the nearest degree)

Hence $2\sin x° + 3\cos x° = \sqrt{13}\,\sin(x + 56)°$

This expression has a maximum value of $\sqrt{13}$, when $\sin(x + 56)° = 1$.
$\sin(x + 56)° = 1$ when $(x + 56)° = 90°$

Hence $x° = 34°$      *There is only one solution for x between $0°$ and $360°$.*

---

**B7** In the example above, $r^2 = 13$. Hence $r$ could be $-\sqrt{13}$.
In this case, $\cos\alpha°$ and $\sin\alpha°$ will both be negative, so $180° \le \alpha° \le 270°$.
Using $r = -\sqrt{13}$ and an appropriate value of $\alpha°$, check that this
leads to the same solution as above.

An expression such as $4\sin x° - 3\cos x°$ can be put in the form $r\sin(x - \alpha)°$.

**B8** (a) Expand the expression $r\sin(x - \alpha)°$ using the addition formula.

(b) Given that $4\sin x° - 3\cos x° = r\sin(x - \alpha)°$, by equating coefficients
and squaring, find the value of $r$, where $r > 0$.

(c) Similarly, show that $\tan\alpha° = 0.75$ and hence find $\alpha°$ to the nearest degree.

(d) Hence express $4\sin x° - 3\cos x°$ in the form $r\sin(x - \alpha)°$.

(e) (i) What is the minimum value of $4\sin x° - 3\cos x°$?

(ii) At what value of $x°$, between $0°$ and $360°$, does the minimum occur?

(f) Check that your answer is correct by plotting $y = 4\sin x° - 3\cos x°$
and your answer to (d) using a graph plotter.

You can also use the expressions $r\cos(x + \alpha)$ and $r\cos(x - \alpha)$ in the same way.

---

## Example 10

(a) Express $4\cos x + 3\sin x$ in the form $R\cos(x - \alpha)$, where $R > 0$ and $0 < \alpha < \dfrac{\pi}{2}$.

(b) Hence solve $4\cos x + 3\sin x = 2$ for $0 < x < \pi$, giving answers to two decimal places.

## Solution

(a) $R\cos(x - \alpha) = R\cos x\cos\alpha + R\sin x\sin\alpha$

If $4\cos x + 3\sin x = R\cos(x - \alpha)$, we require $R\cos\alpha = 4$ and $R\sin\alpha = 3$.

Hence $\tan\alpha = \dfrac{3}{4}$, $\alpha = \tan^{-1}0.75 = 0.64$ radians (to 2 d.p.) and $R^2 = 4^2 + 3^2 = 25$, so $R = 5$.

So $4\cos x + 3\sin x = 5\cos(x - 0.64)$.

(b) $4\cos x + 3\sin x = 2 \quad\Rightarrow\quad 5\cos(x - 0.64) = 2$

$\Rightarrow \quad \cos(x - 0.64) = 0.4$

One solution is given by $\qquad\quad x - 0.64 = \cos^{-1}0.4 = 1.159...$

$\Rightarrow \qquad\qquad\qquad x = 1.799... = 1.80$ (to 2 d.p.)

This is the only solution between $0$ and $\pi$.

---

## Example 11

(a) Express $\cos\theta - \sin\theta$ in the form $r\cos(\theta + \alpha)$.

(b) Hence solve the equation $\cos\theta - \sin\theta = 0.5$ for $0 \le \theta \le \dfrac{\pi}{2}$.

### Solution

(a) Let $\cos\theta - \sin\theta = r\cos(\theta + \alpha)$

$$= r(\cos\theta\cos\alpha - \sin\theta\sin\alpha)$$
$$= (r\cos\alpha)\cos\theta - (r\sin\alpha)\sin\theta$$

Then, equating coefficients, we have $r\cos\alpha = 1$ and $r\sin\alpha = 1$.

Hence $r^2 = 1^2 + 1^2 = 2$, so $r = \sqrt{2}$.

$\dfrac{r\sin\alpha}{r\cos\alpha} = \dfrac{1}{1} \Rightarrow \tan\alpha = 1$, so $\alpha = \dfrac{\pi}{4}$

Hence $\cos\theta - \sin\theta = \sqrt{2}\cos\left(\theta + \dfrac{\pi}{4}\right)$

(b) Thus $\cos\theta - \sin\theta = 0.5 \Rightarrow \sqrt{2}\cos\left(\theta + \dfrac{\pi}{4}\right) = 0.5 \Rightarrow \cos\left(\theta + \dfrac{\pi}{4}\right) = \dfrac{0.5}{\sqrt{2}} = 0.3536...$

$\Rightarrow \left(\theta + \dfrac{\pi}{4}\right) = 1.209...$        *Remember you are working in radians.*

$\Rightarrow \qquad \theta = 1.209... - \dfrac{\pi}{4} = 0.42$ (to 2 d.p.)    *This is the only solution between 0 and $\dfrac{\pi}{2}$.*

---

## Example 12

Solve the equation $9\sin\theta° - 6\cos\theta° = 7$ for $0° \le \theta° \le 360°$.

### Solution

*$9\sin\theta° - 6\cos\theta°$ could be expressed in the form $r\sin(\theta - \alpha)°$ or $-r\cos(\theta + \alpha)°$; either would be suitable. Here $r\sin(\theta - \alpha)°$ is used.*

Let $9\sin\theta° - 6\cos\theta° = r\sin(\theta - \alpha)° = r\sin\theta°\cos\alpha° - r\cos\theta°\sin\alpha°$.

Hence $r\cos\alpha° = 9$ and $r\sin\alpha° = 6$

$\Rightarrow r^2 = 9^2 + 6^2 = 117$, so $r = 10.82...$

Also $\dfrac{r\sin\alpha°}{r\cos\alpha°} = \dfrac{6}{9} \Rightarrow \tan\alpha° = 0.666...$, from which $\alpha° = 33.69...°$

So $9\sin\theta° - 6\cos\theta° = 10.82... \times \sin(\theta - 33.69)° = 7$

$\Rightarrow \sin(\theta - 33.69)° = 7 \div 10.82... = 0.6472...$

$\theta°$ is between $0°$ and $360°$, so $(\theta - 33.69)°$ is between $-33.69°$ and $326.31°$.

$\sin(\theta - 33.69)° = 0.6472...$ gives $(\theta - 33.69)° = 40.33°$ (to the nearest 0.01°)

$$\text{and } (\theta - 33.69)° = 180° - 40.33° = 139.67°$$

*We also have $(\theta - 33.69)° = 40.33° + 360°$ etc., but these give values of $\theta°$ outside the required range.*

The two values above are within the range $-33.69°$ to $326.31°$, and they lead to

$(\theta - 33.69)° = 40.33°$     $\Rightarrow$     $\theta = 74.0°$

and $(\theta - 33.69)° = 139.67°$     $\Rightarrow$     $\theta = 173.4°$ (answers correct to 0.1°)

## Exercise B (answers p 161)

1 The graph shown may be regarded either as a sine graph or a cosine graph, translated left or right.
Express the equation of the graph in the following forms, where $r > 0$ and $0° < \alpha° < 360°$.

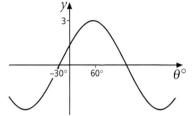

(a) $r\sin(\theta + \alpha)°$     (b) $r\cos(\theta - \alpha)°$

(c) $r\sin(\theta - \alpha)°$     (d) $r\cos(\theta + \alpha)°$

2 (a) Express $5\sin\theta° + 2\cos\theta°$ in the form $r\sin(\theta + \alpha)°$, where $r > 0$ and $0° < \alpha° < 90°$.

  (b) Hence find the maximum value of $5\sin\theta° + 2\cos\theta°$, and the value of $\theta°$ $(0° < \theta° < 90°)$ at which it occurs.

3 (a) Express $\sin\theta° + 2\cos\theta°$ in the form $r\sin(\theta + \alpha)°$, where $r > 0$ and $0° < \alpha° < 90°$.

  (b) Express $\sin\theta° + 2\cos\theta°$ in the form $r\cos(\theta - \alpha)°$, where $r > 0$ and $0° < \alpha° < 90°$.

  (c) Show that your answers in parts (a) and (b) are equivalent.

4 (a) Express $2\sin\theta° - 3\cos\theta°$ in the form $r\sin(\theta - \alpha)°$, where $r > 0$ and $0° < \alpha° < 90°$.

  (b) By writing $2\sin\theta° - 3\cos\theta°$ as $-(3\cos\theta° - 2\sin\theta°)$, write $2\sin\theta° - 3\cos\theta°$ in the form $-r\cos(\theta + \alpha)°$, where $r > 0$ and $0° < \alpha° < 90°$.

  (c) Using your answer to (a) or to (b), solve the equation $2\sin\theta° - 3\cos\theta° = 1$ for $0° < \theta° < 90°$.

5 Solve each of these equations for $0° < x° < 360°$.

  (a) $7\sin x° + 10\cos x° = 8$    (b) $3\sin x° - 4\cos x° = 2$    (c) $9\cos x° - 5\sin x° = 4$

6 Prove that if $\cos(x + 45)° = 2\cos(x - 45)°$, then $\tan x° = -\frac{1}{3}$.

7 (a) Express $\sqrt{3}\sin\theta - \cos\theta$ in the form in the form $r\sin(\theta - \alpha)$ $\left(r > 0 \text{ and } 0 < \alpha < \frac{\pi}{2}\right)$.

  (b) Hence solve $\sqrt{3}\sin\theta - \cos\theta = 1$, giving exact solutions between $0$ and $2\pi$.

8 (a) Show that $\tan(\theta - 45)° = \dfrac{\tan\theta° - 1}{1 + \tan\theta°}$.

  (b) Hence find the exact value of $\tan 15°$, giving your answer in the form $p + q\sqrt{3}$.

9 (a) Given that $\cos A = \frac{5}{13}$ $\left(0 < A < \frac{\pi}{2}\right)$, find the exact value of $\sin A$.

  (b) Given that $\sin B = \frac{3}{5}$ $\left(0 < B < \frac{\pi}{2}\right)$, find the exact value of $\cos(A + B)$.

10 (a) Given that $\tan x \neq 1$, show that $\dfrac{\cos 2x}{\cos x - \sin x} \equiv \cos x + \sin x$.

  (b) By expressing $\cos x + \sin x$ in the form $R\sin(x + a)$, solve, for $0° \leq x \leq 360°$,
$$\dfrac{\cos 2x}{\cos x - \sin x} = \frac{1}{2}.$$

AQA 2001

## Key points

- $\sin (A + B) = \sin A \cos B + \cos A \sin B$
  $\sin (A - B) = \sin A \cos B - \cos A \sin B$
  $\cos (A + B) = \cos A \cos B - \sin A \sin B$
  $\cos (A - B) = \cos A \cos B + \sin A \sin B$       (p 56)

- $\tan (A + B) = \dfrac{\tan A + \tan B}{1 - \tan A \tan B}$      $\tan (A - B) = \dfrac{\tan A - \tan B}{1 + \tan A \tan B}$     (p 58)

- $\sin 2A = 2 \sin A \cos A$
  $\cos 2A = \cos^2 A - \sin^2 A = 2\cos^2 A - 1 = 1 - 2\sin^2 A$     (p 56)

- $\tan 2A = \dfrac{2 \tan A}{1 - \tan^2 A}$     (p 58)

- $a \sin x + b \cos x$ can be written in the form
  $r \sin (x + \alpha)$, where $a = r \cos \alpha$ and $b = r \sin \alpha$
  $r \cos (x - \alpha)$, where $a = r \sin \alpha$ and $b = r \cos \alpha$     (pp 62–63)

- $a \sin x - b \cos x$ can be written in the form
  $r \sin (x - \alpha)$, where $a = r \cos \alpha$ and $b = r \sin \alpha$
  $r \cos (x + \alpha)$, where $a = -r \sin \alpha$ and $b = -r \cos \alpha$     (p 63)

## Test yourself (answers p 162)

1 Use an addition formula to simplify $\sin (x + 90)°$, and explain your result with the aid of a sketch graph.

2 Express the equation of the graph shown in the following forms, where $r > 0$ and $0° < \alpha° < 360°$.

(a) $r \sin (\theta + \alpha)°$      (b) $r \cos (\theta - \alpha)°$

(c) $r \sin (\theta - \alpha)°$      (d) $r \cos (\theta + \alpha)°$

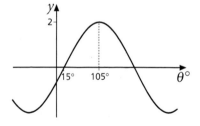

3 (a) By writing $\cos 105°$ as $\cos (60 + 45)°$, show that $\cos 105° = \dfrac{1 - \sqrt{3}}{2\sqrt{2}}$.

(b) Use a similar method to express $\sin 105°$ using surds.

4 Given that $\sin x = \frac{3}{5}$, where $0 < x < \dfrac{\pi}{2}$, find exactly

(a) $\cos x$      (b) $\cos 2x$      (c) $\sin 2x$      (d) $\tan 2x$

**5** Given that $\sin\theta = \frac{12}{13}$, where $\frac{\pi}{2} < \theta < \pi$, find the exact value of

    **(a)** $\cos\theta$               **(b)** $\cos 2\theta$              **(c)** $\operatorname{cosec} 2\theta$           **(d)** $\cot 2\theta$

**6** Given that $\tan 2\theta = 3$, find the two possible values of $\tan\theta$ in surd form.

**7** Solve $\cos^2\theta° = \sin 2\theta°$ for $0° < \theta° < 360°$.

**8** Solve these equations, giving your solutions in radians between 0 and $2\pi$ in terms of $\pi$ or (where that is not possible) to two decimal places.

    **(a)** $2\cos x = \sin 2x$        **(b)** $\cos 2x = 1 + \sin 2x$       **(c)** $\cos 2x = 3\cos x + 2$

**9** Prove that $\cot\dfrac{\theta}{2} - \tan\dfrac{\theta}{2} = 2\cot\theta$.

**10** Show that $\tan(A+B) + \tan(A-B) = 2\cot A\,\dfrac{\sec^2 B}{\cot^2 A - \tan^2 B}$.

**11 (a)** Use the identity $\cos(A+B) = \cos A\cos B - \sin A\sin B$ to show that

    the equation $\cos\left(x + \dfrac{5\pi}{6}\right) = \sin x$ can be written as $\cos x + \sqrt{3}\sin x = 0$.

  **(b)** Hence solve the equation $\cos\left(x + \dfrac{5\pi}{6}\right) = \sin x$ giving all solutions,

    in terms of $\pi$, in the interval $0 < x < 2\pi$.                           AQA 2004

**12 (a)** Find the value of $\tan^{-1} 2.4$, giving your answer in radians to three decimal places.

  **(b)** Express $10\sin\theta + 24\cos\theta$ in the form $R\sin(\theta + \alpha)$, where $R > 0$ and $0 < \alpha < \dfrac{\pi}{2}$.

  **(c)** Hence

     **(i)** write down the maximum value of $10\sin\theta + 24\cos\theta$

     **(ii)** find a value of $\theta$ at which this maximum occurs             AQA 2004

**13 (a)** Express $3\sin x° + 4\cos x°$ in the form $r\sin(x + \alpha)°$,

    where $r > 0$ and $0° < \alpha° < 90°$.

  **(b)** Hence find the maximum and minimum values of the expression

    $\dfrac{4}{3\sin x° + 4\cos x° + 11}$ and the values of $x°$ at which they occur $(0° < x° < 360°)$.

**14 (a) (i)** Express $5\sin\theta° - 4\cos\theta°$ in the form $r\sin(\theta - \alpha)°$ $(r > 0,\ 0° < \alpha° < 90°)$.

     **(ii)** Hence solve the equation $5\sin\theta° - 4\cos\theta° = 3$, giving solutions

       to the nearest degree in the range $0°$ to $360°$.

  **(b) (i)** Express $4\cos\theta° - 5\sin\theta°$ in the form $r\cos(\theta + \alpha)°$ $(r > 0$ and $0° < \alpha° < 90°)$.

     **(ii)** Hence solve the equation $4\cos\theta° - 5\sin\theta° = -3$, giving solutions

       to the nearest degree in the range $0°$ to $360°$.

  **(c)** Compare your answers to parts (a) and (b) and comment.

**15** Solve the following equations for $0 < x < 2\pi$, giving solutions to two decimal places.

    **(a)** $\sin x + 4\cos x = 3$        **(b)** $\sin x - 4\cos x = 3$       **(c)** $3\cos x - \sin x = 0.2$

    **(d)** $\sin x + \sqrt{3}\cos x = 1$      **(e)** $\sqrt{2}\cos x + \sin x = 1$     **(f)** $2\sqrt{2}\cos x - \sin x = 2$

# 6 Differential equations

In this chapter you will learn how to
- form a first-order differential equation
- solve a first-order differential equation by separating the variables
- solve problems involving exponential growth or decay

---

**Key points from Core 3**

- The derivative of $e^{ax}$ is $ae^{ax}$.

- $\int e^{ax}\,dx = \dfrac{1}{a}e^{ax} + c$

- $\int \dfrac{1}{ax+b}\,dx = \dfrac{1}{a}\ln|ax+b| + c$

- $\int \dfrac{f'(x)}{f(x)}\,dx = \ln|f(x)| + c$

- $\int \dfrac{1}{a^2 + x^2}\,dx = \dfrac{1}{a}\tan^{-1}\left(\dfrac{x}{a}\right) + c$

- $\int \dfrac{1}{\sqrt{a^2 - x^2}}\,dx = \sin^{-1}\left(\dfrac{x}{a}\right) + c$

---

## A Integration revisited

The integrals listed above are all expressed in terms of the variable $x$.
For the work in this chapter you will often need to use other letters.

Of course it makes no essential difference which letter is used, but the use of letters other than $x$ may make it harder to see what to do.

For example, you should be familiar with the fact that $\int x\,dx = \frac{1}{2}x^2 + c$.

This statement remains true when $x$ is replaced by, for example, $t$ or $P$ or $y$:

$$\int t\,dt = \tfrac{1}{2}t^2 + c \qquad \int P\,dP = \tfrac{1}{2}P^2 + c \qquad \int y\,dy = \tfrac{1}{2}y^2 + c$$

Similarly, the second statement in the key points above could be written $\int e^{at}\,dt = \dfrac{1}{a}e^{at} + c$.

### Exercise A (answers p 163)

**1** Find each of these indefinite integrals.

(a) $\int t^2\,dt$  (b) $\int y^3\,dy$  (c) $\int e^{4s}\,ds$  (d) $\int \cos 2\theta\,d\theta$

**2** Find each of these indefinite integrals.

(a) $\int \sqrt{u}\,du$  (b) $\int \dfrac{1}{2P-1}\,dP$  (c) $\int \dfrac{1}{\sqrt{q+1}}\,dq$  (d) $\int \dfrac{v}{v^2-1}\,dv$

## B Forming a differential equation (answers p 163)

Imagine a population of organisms (say bacteria) in which individual organisms reproduce. The more organisms there are in the population, the faster the population will grow. Suppose that the rate of growth is proportional to the size of the population.

Let the population at time $t$ hours be $P$.

The rate of growth of the population, in organisms per hour, is given by $\dfrac{dP}{dt}$.

The fact that the rate of growth is proportional to the size of the population can be written as

$$\frac{dP}{dt} \propto P \text{ or } \frac{dP}{dt} = kP, \text{ where } k \text{ is a constant.}$$

Suppose that the value of $k$ for a particular population is known to be $0.1$.

Then

$$\frac{dP}{dt} = 0.1P$$

An equation that involves a derivative (or more than one derivative) is called a **differential equation**. Differential equations are used to model situations involving rates of change.

The differential equation above is a **first-order** differential equation as it involves a first-order derivative $\dfrac{dP}{dt}$ but no derivatives of higher order, such as $\dfrac{d^2P}{dt^2}$.

**B1** The rate of growth of a population $P$ at time $t$ is given by $0.05P^2$.
Write this information as a differential equation.

**B2** The temperature of an oven at time $t$ minutes is $T$ °C. The rate at which the temperature is increasing is given by $(2t + 0.01t^2)$ degrees per minute.
Write this information as a differential equation.

**B3** The population $P$ of a region at time $t$ years is **decreasing** at a rate given by $0.1Pt$.
Explain why it is incorrect to write this information as $\dfrac{dP}{dt} = 0.1Pt$, and write the differential equation correctly.

**B4** An object moves along a straight track. Its distance at time $t$ seconds is $s$ metres.
The distance decreases at a rate given by $0.02s$ metres per second.
Write this information as a differential equation.

**B5** A researcher is modelling the sales of a music CD. She suggests that if the total number sold $t$ weeks from launching the CD is $N$, then the rate at which the total grows is proportional to $N(20\,000 - N)$.

(a) Write the suggested model as a differential equation, including a constant $k$.

(b) Explain why the model predicts that the total number sold will not exceed $20\,000$.

# C Solving by separating variables (answers p 163)

Here again is the differential equation for the population of organisms described at the beginning of the previous section:

$$\frac{dP}{dt} = 0.1P$$

Solving this differential equation means finding the equation connecting $P$ and $t$. The process of solving will involve integration.

It is possible to rewrite this differential equation so that the left-hand side of the equation involves only $P$ and the right-hand side only $t$. This is called **separating the variables**.

The first step is to separate the numerator and denominator of $\frac{dP}{dt}$.

(You have met this idea when doing integration by substitution.)

$$dP = 0.1P\,dt$$

Now divide both sides by $P$ (or multiply by $\frac{1}{P}$), so that the variables are completely separated.

$$\frac{1}{P}\,dP = 0.1\,dt$$

With the equation in this form, both sides can be integrated.

$$\int \frac{1}{P}\,dP = \int 0.1\,dt$$

$$\ln|P| = 0.1t + c$$

By 'exponentiating' both sides (that is, $e^{\text{left side}} = e^{\text{right side}}$), we get

$$e^{\ln|P|} = e^{0.1t + c}$$
$$= e^{0.1t}\,e^{c}$$

$c$ is just a constant whose value at this stage is unknown. So is $e^c$. We can let $A$ stand for $e^c$, so that $A$ is now the unknown constant.

$$= Ae^{0.1t}$$

Because $e^{\ln|P|} = |P|$ it follows that

$$|P| = Ae^{0.1t}$$

In this case we know that $P > 0$, so we can write

$$P = Ae^{0.1t}$$

This equation is called the **general solution** of the differential equation.
It contains an unknown constant $A$.
To fix the value of $A$ we need some more information.
Suppose we know that when $t = 0$, the value of $P$ is 200. Then

$$200 = Ae^{0}, \text{ so } A = 200$$

The resulting equation is called a **particular solution**.

$$P = 200e^{0.1t}$$

> **K** The method of solving a differential equation by separating the variables can be summarised as follows.
>
> - Rearrange the equation so that the left-hand side involves only one variable and the right-hand side only the other.
>
> - Integrate each side to get the general solution of the differential equation. This will include an unknown constant.
>
> - Use information about known values of the variables to fix the value of the constant. (This information is sometimes called the 'boundary conditions'.) The resulting solution is the particular solution which fits the given information.

**C1** By differentiating, show that if $P = Ae^{0.1t}$ then $\frac{dP}{dt} = 0.1P$.

(This verifies that $P = Ae^{0.1t}$ is the general solution of the differential equation.)

**C2 (a)** Given that $\dfrac{dP}{dt} = \dfrac{5}{P}$, $P > 0$

  **(i)** complete this rearrangement of the differential equation: $P\,dP = \ldots$

  **(ii)** by integrating each side, show that $P^2 = 10t + A$, where $A$ is a constant.

 **(b)** Verify by differentiation that if $P = \sqrt{10t + A}$ then $\dfrac{dP}{dt} = \dfrac{5}{P}$.

 **(c)** Given that $P = 6$ when $t = 0$, show that $A = 36$.

 **(d)** Find the value of $P$ when $t = 10.8$.

**C3 (a)** Given that $\dfrac{dP}{dt} = 0.01P^2$

  **(i)** complete this rearrangement of the differential equation: $\dfrac{1}{P^2}\,dP = \ldots$

  **(ii)** by integrating each side, show that $P = -\dfrac{1}{0.01t + c}$

 **(b)** Given that $P = 10$ when $t = 0$, show that $c = -0.1$ and hence that $P = \dfrac{100}{10 - t}$.

 **(c)** What happens to $P$ as $t$ gets closer and closer to 10?

**D** **C4** A student was given this differential equation: $\dfrac{dy}{dx} = 3y^2$.

 **(a)** Explain what is wrong with this working:
$$dy = 3y^2\,dx$$
$$\int dy = \int 3y^2\,dx$$
$$\int 1\,dy = \int 3y^2\,dx$$
$$y = y^3 + c$$

 **(b)** Show that the correct general solution of the equation is $y = -\dfrac{1}{3x + c}$.

---

## Example 1

Show that the general solution of the differential equation $\dfrac{dy}{dx} = 2x(y + 4)$, $y > 0$,
is $y = Ae^{x^2} - 4$.

## Solution

*First separate the variables.*    $\dfrac{dy}{y + 4} = 2x\,dx$   $\left(\dfrac{dy}{y + 4} \text{ is the same as } \dfrac{1}{y + 4}\,dy.\right)$

*Integrate both sides.*    $\displaystyle\int \dfrac{1}{y + 4}\,dy = \int 2x\,dx$

$\Rightarrow \quad \ln(y + 4) = x^2 + c$    *Since $y > 0$, $|y + 4|$ is unnecessary.*

*Exponentiate both sides.*    $y + 4 = e^{x^2 + c} = e^{x^2}e^c = Ae^{x^2}$ *(where $A = e^c$)*

$\Rightarrow \qquad y = Ae^{x^2} - 4$

---

## Example 2

A water tank is filled in such a way that the rate at which the depth of the water increases is proportional to the square root of the depth.

Initially the depth is 4 m. After a time $t$ hours the depth is $h$ m.

(a) Write down a differential equation for $h$.

(b) Show that $\sqrt{h} = \frac{1}{2}kt + 2$, where $k$ is a constant.

(c) Given that $h = 16$ when $t = 6$, find the value of $k$.

(d) Find the time taken to fill the tank to a depth of 36 m.

### Solution

(a) The rate of increase of $h$ is $\dfrac{dh}{dt}$, and this is proportional to $\sqrt{h}$. So $\dfrac{dh}{dt} = k\sqrt{h}$.

(b) *Separate the variables and integrate.* $\qquad \dfrac{dh}{\sqrt{h}} = k\,dt$

$$\int h^{-\frac{1}{2}}\,dh = \int k\,dt$$

$$\Rightarrow \qquad 2h^{\frac{1}{2}} = kt + c$$

$$\Rightarrow \qquad \sqrt{h} = \tfrac{1}{2}(kt + c)$$

When $t = 0, h = 4,$ so $\qquad \sqrt{4} = \tfrac{1}{2}(k \times 0 + c)$

$$\Rightarrow \qquad 2 = \tfrac{1}{2}c \ \text{ so } \ c = 4$$

so $\qquad \sqrt{h} = \tfrac{1}{2}(kt + 4) = \tfrac{1}{2}kt + 2$

(c) $4 = 3k + 2$, so $k = \frac{2}{3}$.

(d) The equation for $\sqrt{h}$ is $\sqrt{h} = \frac{1}{3}t + 2$. When $h = 36$, $6 = \frac{1}{3}t + 2$, so $t = 12$.

---

## Exercise C (answers p 164)

**1** (a) Show that the general solution of the differential equation $\dfrac{dy}{dx} = \dfrac{x^3}{y}$ can be written in the form $y^2 = \frac{1}{2}x^4 + A$, where $A$ is a constant.

   (b) Find the particular solution for which $y = 4$ when $x = 0$.

**2** (a) Show that the general solution of the differential equation $\dfrac{dy}{dx} = \dfrac{1+x}{y}$ can be written in the form $y^2 = x^2 + 2x + A$, where $A$ is a constant.

   (b) Find the value of $A$ given that $y = 3$ when $x = 1$.

**3** (a) Show that the general solution of the differential equation $\dfrac{dy}{dx} = xy$ can be written in the form $y = Ae^{\frac{1}{2}x^2}$, where $A$ is a constant.

   (b) Find the value of $A$ given that $y = 6$ when $x = 0$.

**4** Solve the differential equation $\dfrac{dy}{dx} = 1 + y \ (y > 0)$ given that $y = 5$ when $x = 0$.

**5 (a)** Show that the general solution of the differential equation $\dfrac{dy}{dx} = 2x\sqrt{y}$

can be written in the form $\sqrt{y} = \frac{1}{2}x^2 + A$, where $A$ is a constant.

**(b)** Given that $y = 4$ when $x = 0$, find the value of $A$.

**(c)** Find, to three significant figures, the value of $x$ for which $y = 20$.

**6** As a result of a disease, the population of a colony of animals is decreasing at a rate proportional to the size of the population. Initially the population is 20 000; after time $t$ days the population is $P$.

**(a)** Write down a differential equation for $P$, including a constant of proportionality $k$.

**(b)** Show that the general solution of the differential equation can be written in the form $P = Ae^{-kt}$, where $A$ is a constant.

**(c)** Use the fact that initially $P = 20\,000$ to find the value of $A$.

**(d)** Given that $P = 10\,000$ when $t = 10$, find the value of $k$ to three significant figures.

**(e)** Find, to three significant figures, the value of $t$ for which $P = 1000$.

**7 (a)** Find the general solution of the differential equation $\dfrac{dy}{dx} = \dfrac{y}{x^2}$ $(x > 0, y > 0)$, giving $y$ in terms of $x$.

**(b)** Find the particular solution for which $y = e$ when $x = 1$.

**8** Solve the differential equation $\dfrac{dy}{dx} = xy^2$ given that $y = 1$ when $x = 0$.

**9** Solve the differential equation $\dfrac{dy}{dx} = \dfrac{y^2}{x}$ $(x > 0, y > 0)$ given that $y = \frac{1}{2}$ when $x = 1$.

**10 (a)** Find $\displaystyle\int \dfrac{x}{x^2 + 1}\,dx$.

**(b) (i)** Show that the general solution of the differential equation $\dfrac{dy}{dx} = \dfrac{xy}{x^2 + 1}$,

where $x \geq 0$ and $y > 0$, can be expressed in the form $y = A\sqrt{x^2 + 1}$, where $A$ is a constant.

**(ii)** Given that $y = 10$ when $x = 1$, find the exact value of $A$.

**(c) (i)** Find the general solution of the differential equation $\dfrac{dy}{dx} = \dfrac{xy^2}{x^2 + 1}$ $(x \geq 0, y > 0)$.

**(ii)** Given that $y = 1$ when $x = 0$, show that $y = \dfrac{1}{1 - \frac{1}{2}\ln(x^2 + 1)}$.

**11** Newton's law of cooling states that the rate at which an object's temperature decreases is proportional to the difference between the object's temperature and the temperature of its surroundings.

**(a)** Write this as a differential equation using $T\,°C$ for the object's temperature and $A\,°C$ for the surrounding temperature.

**(b)** Show that the general solution can be written as $T = A + Be^{-kt}$, where $k$ and $B$ are constants.

## D Exponential growth and decay (answers p 165)

This is the differential equation for the population of organisms described at the beginning of section B:

$$\frac{dP}{dt} = 0.1P$$

The rate of growth of the population is proportional to the size of the population. The constant of proportionality is $0.1$.

In section C it was shown that the general solution of the equation is     $P = Ae^{0.1t}$

For the case where $P = 200$ at $t = 0$, the particular solution is     $P = 200e^{0.1t}$

The graph of $P$ against $t$ is shown here. (Both negative and positive values of $t$ are shown.)

This is an example of **exponential growth**.

The general form of an exponential growth function of $t$ is $Ae^{bt}$, where $A$ and $b$ are both positive.

If $P = Ae^{bt}$, then $\frac{dP}{dt} = Abe^{bt} = bP$, which shows that the rate of growth is proportional to the value of $P$.

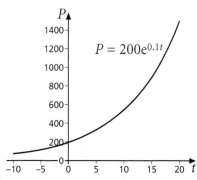

**D1** Given that $P = 200e^{0.1t}$, find, to three significant figures, the value of $t$ for which $P$ is

(a) 300          (b) 400          (c) 150

If $A$ is positive but $b$ is negative in the equation $P = Ae^{bt}$, then we have **exponential decay**.

For example, here is the graph of $P = 50e^{-0.5t}$.

**D2 (a)** Given that $P = 50e^{-0.5t}$, find, to three significant figures, the value of $t$ for which $P$ is

(i) 30          (ii) 20          (iii) 60

**(b)** What happens to $P$ as $t$ gets larger and larger?

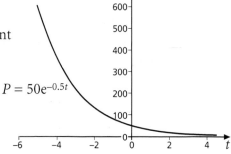

Exponential decay functions are often used to model processes where a quantity gets closer and closer to a given limiting value as time goes on.

The phrase '$t$ gets larger and larger' is usually expressed in symbols as '$t \to \infty$' (read as '$t$ tends to infinity').

As $t \to \infty$, the value of $Ae^{-bt}$, where $b > 0$, gets closer and closer to 0, so the value of $C + Ae^{-bt}$ gets closer and closer to $C$ from above.

The value of $C - Ae^{-bt}$ gets closer and closer to $C$ from below.

This is illustrated in the graphs on the right.

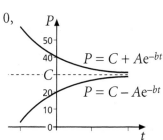

**D3** Given that $y = 40 + 10e^{-2t}$,

    (a) find the value of $y$ when $t = 0$

    (b) find the limiting value of $y$ as $t \to \infty$

    (c) sketch the graph of $y$ against $t$

**D4** A sample of liquid is heated to a temperature of $80\,°C$ and then allowed to cool down. The temperature gradually falls towards that of the surrounding atmosphere, which is $20\,°C$. The equation $T = c + ae^{-bt}$ $(b > 0)$ is used to model the cooling process, where $T\,°C$ is the temperature of the liquid and $t$ is the time in minutes since cooling started.

    (a) By considering what happens as $t \to \infty$, find the value of $c$.

    (b) By considering the situation at $t = 0$, find the value of $a$.

    (c) Given that it takes 10 minutes for the temperature to fall to $35\,°C$, show that $e^{-10b} = 0.25$ and hence find the value of $b$ to three significant figures.

    (d) Find the rate of cooling, in degrees per minute, when the temperature of the liquid is $35\,°C$.

**K** An equation of the form $y = ae^{bt}$ $(a > 0, b > 0)$ represents exponential growth.

An equation of the form $y = ae^{-bt}$ $(a > 0, b > 0)$ represents exponential decay.

The equation $y = c \pm ae^{-bt}$ $(a > 0, b > 0)$ represents a process in which the value of $y$ gets closer and closer to $c$ as $t \to \infty$.

---

### Example 3

A population $P$ is modelled by the equation $P = r - se^{-0.5t}$, where $r$ and $s$ are constants and $t$ is the time in years.

(a) Given that $P = 200$ when $t = 0$ and $P = 360$ when $t = 4$, find the values of $r$ and $s$ to three significant figures.

(b) What happens to the population as $t$ gets larger and larger?

(c) At what rate is the population growing when $t = 6$?

### Solution

(a) *Substitute the given values into the equation.*     $200 = r - s$

                                                    $360 = r - se^{-2}$

    *Subtract the first equation from the second.*     $160 = s(1 - e^{-2})$

$$\Rightarrow \quad s = \frac{160}{1 - e^{-2}} = 185 \text{ to 3 s.f.}$$

    *Use the first equation to find the value of $r$.*     $r = 200 + 185 = 385$ to 3 s.f.

(b) The equation for $P$ is $P = 385 - 185e^{-0.5t}$.
    As $t \to \infty$, $P$ gets closer and closer to 385.

(c) When $t = 6$, $\dfrac{dP}{dt} = -185 \times (-0.5e^{-0.5t}) = 92.5e^{-3} = 4.61$ per year (to 3 s.f.)

---

## Exercise D (answers p 165)

**1** The growth of a population $P$ is modelled by the equation $P = 5000e^{0.04t}$, where $t$ is the time in years from the first count.

(a) What was the size of the population when it was first counted?

(b) What is the population at time $t = 20$?

(c) Find the rate of increase at time $t = 20$, to the nearest whole number.

**2** Given that $y = 50 - 10e^{-\frac{1}{2}t}$, find

(a) the value of $y$ when $t = 0$          (b) the limiting value of $y$ as $t \to \infty$

**3** The size of a population is modelled by the equation $P = ae^{-kt}$.

(a) Given that $P = 800$ when $t = 0$, write down the value of $a$.

(b) Given that $P = 500$ when $t = 5$, show that $k = 0.0940$ to 3 s.f.

(c) Find, to three significant figures,

    (i) the value of $P$ when $t = 4$      (ii) the value of $t$ for which $P = 400$

**4** The temperature, $T\,°C$, at the centre of a bonfire is modelled by the equation $T = 200 - qe^{-kt}$, where $t$ is the time in minutes since the fire was lit and $k > 0$.

(a) The temperature at the centre when the fire was lit was $15\,°C$. Find the value of $q$.

(b) What happens to the temperature as $t \to \infty$?

(c) It takes 10 minutes for the centre to reach a temperature of $100\,°C$. Find the value of $k$, to three significant figures.

**5** When a radioactive isotope decays, the number of atoms that remain radioactive after $t$ years is given by $N = N_0e^{-kt}$, where $N_0$ is the initial number of radioactive atoms and $k$ is a constant. In a particular case $k = 0.04$. Show that the time taken for half the atoms to lose their radioactivity is about 17.3 years. (This called the 'half-life' of the substance.)

## E Further exponential functions (answers p 165)

Exponential functions are normally expressed in terms of e, because the derivative of $e^x$ or $e^t$ is simple to find and because logarithms to base e are readily available on calculators and as a spreadsheet function.

However, for any positive value of $a$, the functions $a^x$ and $a^{-x}$ are exponential functions and could be used to model exponential growth or decay.

There is a straightforward way of converting an exponential function of the form $a^x$ into the normal exponential form using e.

**E1** (a) Use the fact that $5 = e^{\ln 5}$ to write $5^x$ in the form $e^{kx}$, giving $k$ to 3 s.f.

(b) Use the fact that $8 = e^{\ln 8}$ to write $8^x$ in the form $e^{kx}$.

(c) Write $2^x$ in the form $e^{kx}$.

(d) Write $a^x$ in the form $e^{kx}$.

**K** The expression $a^x$ is equivalent to $e^{(\ln a)x}$.

**E2** Show that the derivative of $a^x$ is $(\ln a)a^x$.

**K** The derivative of $a^x$ is $(\ln a)a^x$.

**E3** The value $£V$ of a car $t$ years after initial purchase is modelled by the equation $V = 20\,000 \times 0.85^t$.

    (a) What was the initial value of the car?

    (b) What is its value after 5 years?

    (c) The value of $t$ for which $V = 8000$ is given by $20\,000 \times 0.85^t = 8000$,

        from which $0.85^t = \frac{8000}{20\,000} = 0.4$.

        Use logarithms to find the value of $t$, to three significant figures.

    (d) Find the value of $\dfrac{dV}{dt}$ when $t = 5$.

**E4** The population of an animal colony increases by 20% each year.

    (a) By what number is the population multiplied each year?

    (b) Given that the initial population is 8000, write down an expression for the population after $t$ years.

**E5** Redo question E4 for the case where the population decreases by 20% each year.

---

## Example 4

The population $P$ of an animal colony is modelled by the equation $P = A \times (1.08)^t$, where $A$ is a constant and $t$ is the time in years since the population was first counted.

(a) Given that the population 3 years after the first count is 5400, find the population at the first count, to three significant figures.

(b) How many years after the first count will the population reach 10 000?

(c) Find the rate at which the population is increasing 3 years after the first count.

## Solution

(a) The population at the first count is the value of $A$.

    Since $5400 = A \times (1.08)^3$, it follows that $A = \dfrac{5400}{(1.08)^3} = 4290$ to 3 s.f.

(b)     $10\,000 = 4290 \times 1.08^t$           (c)         $P = 4290 \times 1.08^t$

    $\Rightarrow$   $1.08^t = \frac{10\,000}{4290}$               So $\dfrac{dP}{dt} = 4290 \times \ln 1.08 \times 1.08^t$

    $\Rightarrow t \ln 1.08 = \ln\left(\frac{10\,000}{4290}\right)$      When $t = 3$, $\dfrac{dP}{dt} = 4290 \times \ln 1.08 \times 1.08^3$

    $\Rightarrow$   $t = \dfrac{\ln\left(\frac{10\,000}{4290}\right)}{\ln 1.08} = 11.0$ to 3 s.f.              $= 416$ individuals per year to 3 s.f.

---

**1** The population $P$ of a city region is modelled by the equation $P = P_0 \times (1.04)^t$, where $P_0$ is the population now and $t$ is the time in years measured from now. Given that $P_0 = 240\,000$, find

    **(a)** the time taken from now for the population to reach $300\,000$

    **(b)** the rate of increase of the population 4 years from now

**2** The value $£V$ of a vehicle is modelled by the equation $V = 16\,000 \times (0.8)^t$, where $t$ is the time in years since the vehicle was purchased. Find

    **(a)** the time taken from the time of purchase for the vehicle to halve in value

    **(b)** the rate at which the value is decreasing 1 year after purchase

**3** Given that $y = p + qa^x$, where $p$, $q$ and $a$ are constants, show that $\dfrac{dy}{dx} = (\ln a)(y - p)$.

---

## Key points

- To solve a differential equation by separating variables, rewrite the equation so that each variable appears on only one side, integrate each side to find the general solution and use any additional information (boundary conditions) to find the particular solution.     (p 70)

- An equation of the form $y = ae^{bt}$ $(a > 0, b > 0)$ represents exponential growth. An equation of the form $y = ae^{-bt}$ $(a > 0, b > 0)$ represents exponential decay. The equation $y = c \pm ae^{-bt}$ $(a > 0, b > 0)$ represents a process in which the value of $y$ gets closer and closer to $c$ as $t \to \infty$.     (p 75)

- The expression $a^x$ is equivalent to $e^{(\ln a)x}$. The derivative of $a^x$ is $(\ln a)a^x$.     (p 77)

---

## Mixed questions (answers p 165)

**1 (a)** Write down $\displaystyle\int \frac{1}{1 + y^2}\,dy$.

    **(b)** Solve the differential equation $\dfrac{dy}{dx} = 1 + y^2$, given that $y = 1$ when $x = 0$.

**2** Liquid is poured into a reservoir whose shape is an upturned pyramid. At time $t$ minutes the depth of the water is $h$ m. The rate at which $h$ increases is inversely proportional to $h^2$.

    **(a)** Write down a differential equation for $h$, including a constant of proportionality.

    **(b)** Show that the general solution of the differential equation can be written in the form $h^3 = At + B$, where $A$ and $B$ are constants.

    **(c)** Given that $h = 4$ when $t = 0$ and $h = 5$ when $t = 1$, find the values of $A$ and $B$.

**3** The rotational speed, $r$ revolutions per second, of a flywheel satisfies the differential equation $\dfrac{\mathrm{d}r}{\mathrm{d}t} = \dfrac{50-r}{2}$.

(a) Find the general solution of this equation and show that it can be written in the form $r = 50 - Ae^{-\frac{1}{2}t}$.

(b) What happens to $r$ as $t \to \infty$?

(c) Given that $r = 20$ when $t = 0$, find the value of $A$.

(d) Find, to three significant figures, the value of $t$ for which $r = 40$.

## Test yourself (answers p 166)

**1** (a) Solve the differential equation $\dfrac{\mathrm{d}y}{\mathrm{d}x} = \dfrac{1}{y^2}$, giving the general solution for $y$ in terms of $x$.

(b) Find the particular solution of this differential equation for which $y = -1$ when $x = 1$. AQA 2002

**2** A microbiologist is studying the growth of populations of simple organisms. For one such organism, the model proposed is $P = 100 - 50e^{-\frac{1}{4}t}$, where $P$ is the population after $t$ minutes.

(a) Write down

   (i) the initial value of the population

   (ii) the value which the population approaches as $t$ becomes large

(b) Find the time at which the population will have a value of 75, giving your answer to two significant figures. AQA 2004

**3** The speed $v\,\mathrm{m\,s^{-1}}$ of a pebble falling through still water after $t$ seconds can be modelled by the differential equation $\dfrac{\mathrm{d}v}{\mathrm{d}t} = 10 - 5v$.

A pebble is placed carefully on the surface of the water at time $t = 0$ and begins to sink.

(a) Show that $t = \frac{1}{5}\ln\left(\dfrac{2}{2-v}\right)$.

(b) Use the model to find the speed of the pebble after 0.5 seconds, giving your answer to two significant figures. AQA 2004

**4** (a) Solve the differential equation $\dfrac{\mathrm{d}y}{\mathrm{d}x} = \dfrac{y-3}{2}$, giving the general solution for $y$ in terms of $x$.

(b) Find the particular solution of this differential equation for which $y = 2$ when $x = 0$.

**5** Show that the general solution of the differential equation $\dfrac{\mathrm{d}y}{\mathrm{d}x} = x(y+1)$ $(y > 0)$ can be written in the form $y = Ae^{\frac{1}{2}x^2} - 1$.

# 7 Differentiation

In this chapter you will learn how to
- differentiate a function defined parametrically
- differentiate a function defined implicitly
- find the equation of the tangent and the normal to a curve defined parametrically or implicitly

## Key points from previous books

- The line through the point $(x_1, y_1)$ with gradient $m$ has the equation $y - y_1 = m(x - x_1)$.

- A line perpendicular to a line with gradient $m$ has gradient $-\dfrac{1}{m}$.

- The derivative of $e^x$ is $e^x$.

- The derivative of $\ln x$ is $\dfrac{1}{x}$.

- $\dfrac{dy}{dx} = \dfrac{1}{\frac{dx}{dy}}$

- If $y = uv$, then $\dfrac{dy}{dx} = u\dfrac{dv}{dx} + v\dfrac{du}{dx}$ (product rule)

- If $y = \dfrac{u}{v}$, then $\dfrac{dy}{dx} = \dfrac{v\dfrac{du}{dx} - u\dfrac{dv}{dx}}{v^2}$ (quotient rule)

- The derivative of $\sin x$ is $\cos x$.
  The derivative of $\cos x$ is $-\sin x$.
  The derivative of $\tan x$ is $\sec^2 x$.

- $\dfrac{dy}{dx} = \dfrac{dy}{du} \times \dfrac{du}{dx}$ (chain rule)

- The derivative of $f(ax)$ is $af'(ax)$.
  The derivative of $f(ax + b)$ is $af'(ax + b)$.

## A Functions defined parametrically (answers p 166)

In each of the equations below, $y$ is defined **explicitly** in terms of $x$.

$$y = 3x^2 - 1 \qquad y = \sqrt{x+2} \ (x \geq -2) \qquad y = \ln x \ (x > 0) \qquad y = x^2 e^x$$

If $x$ and $y$ are each defined in terms of a third variable $t$, the third variable is called a **parameter**. The function that links $y$ to $x$ is said to be defined **parametrically**.

For example, the equations $x = 3t$ and $y = t^2 + 1$ together define a function connecting $x$ and $y$, as the table of values shows.

| $t$ | -3 | -2 | -1 | 0 | 1 | 2 | 3 |
|---|---|---|---|---|---|---|---|
| $x = 3t$ | -9 | -6 | -3 | 0 | 3 | 6 | 9 |
| $y = t^2 + 1$ | 10 | 5 | 2 | 1 | 2 | 5 | 10 |

The graph of $y$ against $x$ is shown here.
Points on the graph are labelled by the value of $t$.

The gradient at any point on this graph is the value
of $\frac{dy}{dx}$ at the point.

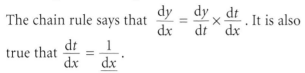

We can find an expression for $\frac{dy}{dx}$ **in terms of $t$** from
the two parametric equations.

The chain rule says that $\frac{dy}{dx} = \frac{dy}{dt} \times \frac{dt}{dx}$ . It is also

true that $\frac{dt}{dx} = \dfrac{1}{\frac{dx}{dt}}$ .

It follows that

$$\frac{dy}{dx} = \dfrac{\frac{dy}{dt}}{\frac{dx}{dt}}$$

For the example above, $\frac{dy}{dt} = 2t$ and $\frac{dx}{dt} = 3$, so $\frac{dy}{dx} = \frac{2t}{3}$.

**A1** Given that $x = t^2$ and $y = t^3$, find $\frac{dy}{dx}$ in terms of $t$.

**A2** Find $\frac{dy}{dx}$ in terms of $t$ given that

(a) $x = 2t$, $y = t^2 + t$   (b) $x = 3t$, $y = \frac{1}{t}$ $(t \neq 0)$   (c) $x = \cos t$, $y = \sin t$

The diagram shows again the graph whose parametric
equations are

$$x = 3t, \ y = t^2 + 1$$

$P$ is the point on this graph where $t = 2$.
The coordinates of $P$ are $(6, 5)$.

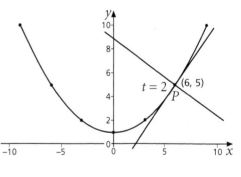

The gradient of the tangent, that is $\frac{dy}{dx}$, is $\frac{2t}{3}$ (as shown

above). So at $P$ the gradient of the tangent is $\frac{2 \times 2}{3} = \frac{4}{3}$.

To find the equation of the tangent at $P$, we use the fact that the equation of
the line through $(x_1, y_1)$ with gradient $m$ is $y - y_1 = m(x - x_1)$.

**A3** Show that the equation of the tangent at $P$ is
$$y = \tfrac{4}{3}x - 3$$

The normal at $P$ is perpendicular to the tangent, so its gradient is $-\dfrac{1}{\frac{4}{3}} = -\frac{3}{4}$.

**A4** Show that the equation of the normal is
$$y = -\tfrac{3}{4}x + \tfrac{19}{2}$$

**A5** A curve is given by the parametric equations $x = 2t$, $y = \dfrac{1}{t}$ $(t \neq 0)$.

(a) Find $\dfrac{dy}{dx}$ in terms of $t$.

(b) What are the coordinates of the point on the curve where $t = 4$?

(c) Show that the equation of the tangent at the point where $t = 4$ is
$$y = -\tfrac{1}{32}x + \tfrac{1}{2}$$

(d) Rewrite this equation in the form $ax + by = c$, where $a$, $b$ and $c$ are integers.

**A6** A curve is given by the parametric equations $x = t^3$, $y = t^2$.

(a) Find $\dfrac{dy}{dx}$ in terms of $t$.

(b) Find the equation of the normal to the curve at the point where $t = 2$.

---

### Example 1

A curve is given by the parametric equations $x = t + \dfrac{1}{t}$, $y = t - \dfrac{1}{t}$ $(t > 0)$.

(a) Find the equation of the tangent to the curve at the point where $t = 2$, in the form $ax + by = c$, where $a$, $b$ and $c$ are integers.

(b) Find the equation of the normal to the curve at the point where $t = 2$, in the form $ax + by = c$, where $a$, $b$ and $c$ are integers.

### Solution

$$x = t + \frac{1}{t} = t + t^{-1} \qquad y = t - \frac{1}{t} = t - t^{-1}$$

$$\frac{dx}{dt} = 1 - \frac{1}{t^2} \quad \frac{dy}{dt} = 1 + \frac{1}{t^2} \quad \frac{dy}{dx} = \frac{\dfrac{dy}{dt}}{\dfrac{dx}{dt}} = \frac{1 + \dfrac{1}{t^2}}{1 - \dfrac{1}{t^2}} \quad \text{When } t = 2, \; \frac{dy}{dx} = \frac{1 + \dfrac{1}{4}}{1 - \dfrac{1}{4}} = \frac{\frac{5}{4}}{\frac{3}{4}} = \frac{5}{3}$$

The coordinates of the point where $t = 2$ are $\left(2 + \tfrac{1}{2}, 2 - \tfrac{1}{2}\right)$, or $\left(\tfrac{5}{2}, \tfrac{3}{2}\right)$.

(a) The gradient of the tangent is $\tfrac{5}{3}$, so the equation is $\quad y - \tfrac{3}{2} = \tfrac{5}{3}\left(x - \tfrac{5}{2}\right)$

*Expand the brackets.* $\qquad\qquad\qquad\qquad\qquad\qquad\qquad y - \tfrac{3}{2} = \tfrac{5}{3}x - \tfrac{25}{6}$

*Multiply through by 6.* $\qquad\qquad\qquad\qquad\qquad\qquad 6y - 9 = 10x - 25$

*Rearrange.* $\qquad\qquad\qquad\qquad\qquad\qquad\qquad\qquad 10x - 6y = 16$

$$\Rightarrow 5x - 3y = 8$$

(b) The gradient of the normal is $-\tfrac{3}{5}$, so the equation is $\quad y - \tfrac{3}{2} = -\tfrac{3}{5}\left(x - \tfrac{5}{2}\right)$

*Expand the brackets.* $\qquad\qquad\qquad\qquad\qquad\qquad\qquad y - \tfrac{3}{2} = -\tfrac{3}{5}x + \tfrac{3}{2}$

*Multiply through by 10.* $\qquad\qquad\qquad\qquad\qquad 10y - 15 = -6x + 15$

*Rearrange.* $\qquad\qquad\qquad\qquad\qquad\qquad\qquad\qquad 6x + 10y = 30$

$$\Rightarrow 3x + 5y = 15$$

---

**Exercise A** (answers p 166)

**1** A curve is defined by the parametric equations $x = t^2$, $y = t^3$.

   (a) Show that $\dfrac{dy}{dx} = \dfrac{3}{2}t$.

   (b) $A$ is the point on the curve where $t = 4$. Find

      (i)  the coordinates of $A$

      (ii) the equation of the tangent at $A$

      (iii) the equation of the normal at $A$

**2** A curve is defined by the parametric equations $x = 2t$, $y = \sqrt{t} + 1$ $(t \geq 0)$.

   (a) Find $\dfrac{dy}{dx}$ in terms of $t$.

   (b) Show that the equation of the tangent at the point where $t = 1$ is $y = \frac{1}{4}x + \frac{3}{2}$.

   (c) Find the equation of the normal at the point where $t = 1$, in the form $y = ax + b$.

**3** A curve is defined by the parametric equations $x = 2t + 1$, $y = \dfrac{2}{t} + 1$ $(t > 0)$.

   (a) Find $\dfrac{dy}{dx}$ in terms of $t$.

   (b) Show that the equation of the tangent at the point where $t = 2$ is $x + 4y = 13$.

   (c) Find the equation of the normal to the curve at the point where $t = 2$, in the form $ax + by = c$, where $a, b$ and $c$ are integers.

**4** A curve is defined by the parametric equations $x = \cos\theta$, $y = 2\sin\theta$ $(0 \leq \theta \leq 2\pi)$.

   (a) Show that $\dfrac{dy}{dx} = -\dfrac{2}{\tan\theta}$.

   (b) $A$ is the point on the curve for which $\theta = \dfrac{\pi}{4}$. State the exact values of the coordinates of $A$.

   (c) Show that the equation of the tangent at $A$ is $2x + y = 2\sqrt{2}$.

**5** A curve is defined by the parametric equations $x = t + \dfrac{1}{t^2}$, $y = t - \dfrac{1}{t^2}$ $(t > 0)$.

   Find, in the form $ax + by + c = 0$, where $a, b$ and $c$ are integers, the equation of

   (a) the tangent to the curve at the point where $t = 1$

   (b) the normal to the curve at the point where $t = 1$

**6** A curve is defined by the parametric equations $x = t - \dfrac{1}{t}$, $y = t^2$ $(t > 0)$.

   (a) Find $\dfrac{dy}{dx}$ in terms of $t$.

   (b) $A$ is the point on the curve for which $t = \frac{1}{2}$.
      Find, in the form $ax + by + c = 0$, where $a, b$ and $c$ are integers, the equation of

      (i)  the tangent to the curve at $A$

      (ii) the normal to the curve at $A$

## B Functions defined implicitly (answers p 167)

The equation $xy + y = 9$ is not written in the explicit form $y = $ a function of $x$.

However, for a given value of $x$ it is possible to find a corresponding value of $y$. For example, if $x = 2$, the equation becomes $2y + y = 9$, from which $3y = 9$ and so $y = 3$.

We say that in the equation $xy + y = 9$, $y$ is defined **implicitly** as a function of $x$.

By finding $y$ for different values of $x$ we can plot the graph of the equation $xy + y = 9$.

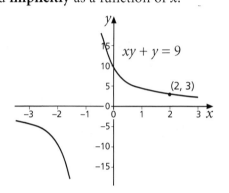

Other examples of implicit equations are

$$xy + x + y = 20$$
$$x + y + y^2 = 20$$
$$x^2 - y^2 = 1$$
$$x^2y + xy^2 = 16$$

In order to find the gradient function for a graph defined like this we need to be able to differentiate, with respect to $x$, expressions containing both $x$ and $y$, such as $x + y + y^2$. Before we do this, some notation is needed.

In the symbol $\dfrac{dy}{dx}$, the part $\dfrac{d}{dx}$ taken separately represents the operator 'differentiate with respect to $x$'. This operator can be used in statements such as

$$\frac{d}{dx}(x^2) = 2x \quad \text{('The derivative with respect to } x \text{ of } x^2 \text{ is } 2x.\text{')}$$

or $\dfrac{d}{dx}(e^{3x}) = 3e^{3x}$

It can also be used to state, for example, the product rule: $\dfrac{d}{dx}(uv) = u\dfrac{dv}{dx} + v\dfrac{du}{dx}$

**B1** Write each of these statements using the operator $\dfrac{d}{dx}$.

(a) The derivative with respect to $x$ of $\ln x$ is $\dfrac{1}{x}$.

(b) The derivative with respect to $x$ of $(x + \sin 3x)$ is $1 + 3\cos 3x$.

Return now to the equation $xy + y = 9$, whose graph is shown above.

The gradient function can be found by differentiating both sides of the equation with respect to $x$.

The first term $xy$ is a product, so you need to use the product rule for this:

$$\frac{d}{dx}(xy) = x\frac{dy}{dx} + y\frac{dx}{dx} = x\frac{dy}{dx} + y$$

Differentiating the whole equation term by term with respect to $x$ gives $xy + y = 9$.

$$x\frac{dy}{dx} + y + \frac{dy}{dx} = 0$$

This equation can be used to find the value of the gradient $\frac{dy}{dx}$ at a given point on the curve, by substituting the known values of $x$ and $y$.

**B2** The point $(2, 3)$ lies on the curve $xy + y = 9$.

  (a) By substituting $x = 2$, $y = 3$ into the derived equation $x\frac{dy}{dx} + y + \frac{dy}{dx} = 0$, find the value of $\frac{dy}{dx}$ at the point $(2, 3)$.

  (b) Show that for all values of $x$ and $y$, $\frac{dy}{dx} = -\frac{y}{x+1}$.

The result in B2(b) can be confirmed by using a different method, as follows.

The equation $xy + y = 9$ can be rearranged as $y = \frac{9}{x+1}$, with $y$ as an explicit function of $x$.

From this it follows that $\frac{dy}{dx} = -\frac{9}{(x+1)^2} = -\frac{9}{(x+1)(x+1)} = -\frac{y}{x+1}$.

However, it is not always possible to rewrite an implicit equation in explicit form. Even when it is possible, the result may be complicated. So you need to learn how to differentiate a function expressed implicitly.

This involves differentiating with respect to $x$ expressions containing both $x$ and $y$.

For example, $\frac{d}{dx}(x^2 + y) = \frac{d}{dx}(x^2) + \frac{d}{dx}(y) = 2x + \frac{dy}{dx}$

$\qquad$ or $\frac{d}{dx}(x^2 y) = x^2 \frac{d}{dx}(y) + y\frac{d}{dx}(x^2)$ $\qquad$ (using the product rule)

$\qquad\qquad = x^2 \frac{dy}{dx} + y(2x) = x^2 \frac{dy}{dx} + 2xy$

**B3** Write each of these in terms of $x$ and $\frac{dy}{dx}$.

  (a) $\frac{d}{dx}(x^3 + y)$ $\qquad$ (b) $\frac{d}{dx}(x^4 - y)$ $\qquad$ (c) $\frac{d}{dx}\left(\frac{1}{x} + 2y\right)$

**B4** Write each of these in terms of $x$, $y$ and $\frac{dy}{dx}$.

  (a) $\frac{d}{dx}(x^3 y)$ $\qquad$ (b) $\frac{d}{dx}(x^4 y)$ $\qquad$ (c) $\frac{d}{dx}(e^x y)$

**B5** The equation of a curve is $x^2 y + x + y = 9$.

  (a) Show that $(x^2 + 1)\frac{dy}{dx} + 2xy + 1 = 0$.

  (b) Verify that the point $(1, 4)$ lies on the curve and find the gradient at this point.

The phrase 'differentiate $y^2$' is incomplete and therefore unclear.

It could mean 'differentiate $y^2$ *with respect to* $y$' or 'differentiate $y^2$ *with respect to* $x$'.

These are different. In symbols, the first is $\dfrac{d}{dy}(y^2)$ and the second is $\dfrac{d}{dx}(y^2)$.

The two operators $\dfrac{d}{dx}$ and $\dfrac{d}{dy}$ are connected by the chain rule:

**K**
$$\frac{d}{dx}(\ ) = \frac{d}{dy}(\ )\frac{dy}{dx}$$

So, for example, $\dfrac{d}{dx}(y^2) = \dfrac{d}{dy}(y^2)\dfrac{dy}{dx} = 2y\dfrac{dy}{dx}$  'To differentiate $y^2$ with respect to $x$, differentiate it with respect to $y$ and then multiply by $\dfrac{dy}{dx}$.'

**B6** Write each of these in terms of $y$ and $\dfrac{dy}{dx}$.

(a) $\dfrac{d}{dx}(y^3)$     (b) $\dfrac{d}{dx}(y^4)$     (c) $\dfrac{d}{dx}(y-2)^3$     (d) $\dfrac{d}{dx}(2y+1)^2$     (e) $\dfrac{d}{dx}(y^{-2})$

Now we are in a position to differentiate with respect to $x$ a product such as $xy^2$.

$$\frac{d}{dx}(xy^2) = x\frac{d}{dx}(y^2) + y^2\frac{d}{dx}(x) \quad \text{(using the product rule)}$$

$$= x\frac{d}{dy}(y^2)\frac{dy}{dx} + y^2(1) \quad \text{(using the chain rule for the first part)}$$

$$= x(2y)\frac{dy}{dx} + y^2$$

$$= 2xy\frac{dy}{dx} + y^2$$

**B7** Write each of these in terms of $x$, $y$ and $\dfrac{dy}{dx}$.

(a) $\dfrac{d}{dx}(xy^3)$     (b) $\dfrac{d}{dx}(x^2y^2)$     (c) $\dfrac{d}{dx}(x^3y^4)$     (d) $\dfrac{d}{dx}(x(y-1)^2)$

**B8** A curve has the equation $y^2 + x + y = 7$.
(a) By differentiating both sides of this equation with respect to $x$, show that
$$(2y+1)\frac{dy}{dx} + 1 = 0$$
(b) Verify that the point $(1, 2)$ lies on the curve and find the value of $\dfrac{dy}{dx}$ at this point.

**B9** A curve has the equation $xy^2 + y = 6$.
(a) By differentiating both sides of this equation with respect to $x$, show that
$$(2xy + 1)\frac{dy}{dx} + y^2 = 0$$
(b) Verify that the point $(1, 2)$ lies on the curve and find the value of $\dfrac{dy}{dx}$ at this point.

## Example 2

A curve is defined by the equation $2x^2 + xy + y^2 = 28$.
Find the equations of the tangent and the normal to the curve at the point $(3, 2)$
in the form $ax + by + c = 0$, where $a$, $b$ and $c$ are integers.

### Solution

$$2x^2 + xy + y^2 = 28$$

*Differentiate both sides of the equation with respect to x.*

$$\frac{d}{dx}\left(2x^2 + xy + y^2\right) = 0$$

*Use the product rule for the term xy and the chain rule for the term $y^2$.*

$$4x + \left(x\frac{dy}{dx} + y\right) + 2y\frac{dy}{dx} = 0$$

Substitututing $x = 3$ and $y = 2$,

$$12 + 3\frac{dy}{dx} + 2 + 4\frac{dy}{dx} = 0$$

$$\Rightarrow \qquad 14 + 7\frac{dy}{dx} = 0 \quad \text{so} \quad \frac{dy}{dx} = -2$$

The gradient of the tangent at $(3, 2)$ is $-2$.

So the equation of the tangent is $y - 2 = -2(x - 3)$, or $2x + y - 8 = 0$.

The gradient of the normal at $(3, 2)$ is $\frac{1}{2}$.

The equation of the normal is $y - 2 = \frac{1}{2}(x - 3)$, or $x - 2y + 1 = 0$.

---

### Exercise B (answers p 167)

**1** A curve is defined by the equation $x^2 + xy + y = 7$.
Find the equations of the tangent and the normal to the curve at the point $(2, 1)$
in the form $ax + by + c = 0$, where $a$, $b$ and $c$ are integers.

**2** Find, in the form $ax + by + c = 0$, the equation of **(i)** the tangent **(ii)** the normal
to each of the curves defined below, at the given point.

(a) $2x^2 - y^2 = 1$, at $(1, 1)$        (b) $x^3 + xy + y = 11$, at $(2, 1)$

(c) $xy + x - y^2 = 9$, at $(5, 4)$      (d) $x^2y + xy^2 = 12$, at $(3, 1)$

(e) $x^3 + y^2 = 9$, at $(2, 1)$        (f) $(x - 2)^2 + 3(y - 1)^2 = 16$, at $(4, 3)$

**3** The curve whose equation is $x^2 + xy + (y - 4)^2 = 7$ crosses the line $x = 1$ at two points.

(a) Find the coordinates of the two points.

(b) Find the gradient of the curve at each of the two points.

**4** The curve whose equation is $x^2 + xy + y^2 = 13$ crosses the line $y = 1$ at two points.

(a) Find the coordinates of the two points.

(b) Find the gradient of the curve at each of the two points.

(c) Find the equation of the tangent at each of the two points.

## Key points

- If $x$ and $y$ are defined in terms of a parameter $t$, then $\dfrac{dy}{dx} = \dfrac{\frac{dy}{dt}}{\frac{dx}{dt}}$. (p 81)

- In equations such as $xy + x + y^2 = 5$, $x^2 + 3y + xy = 6$, and so on, $y$ is defined implicitly in terms of $x$. (p 84)

- The symbol $\dfrac{d}{dx}$ denotes the operator 'differentiate with respect to $x$'. (p 84)

- The chain rule is used when differentiating a function of $y$ with respect to $x$:

$$\frac{d}{dx}(\ \ ) = \frac{d}{dy}(\ \ )\frac{dy}{dx}$$

For example, $\dfrac{d}{dx}(y^2) = \dfrac{d}{dy}(y^2)\dfrac{dy}{dx} = 2y\dfrac{dy}{dx}$ (p 86)

- By differentiating both sides of the equation that defines a function implicitly, an equation for $\dfrac{dy}{dx}$ is obtained. (pp 86–87)

## Mixed questions (answers p 168)

**1** A curve is defined parametrically by the equations $x = 1 + 2t$, $y = 1 + \dfrac{1}{t}$ $(t > 0)$.

(a) (i) Find $\dfrac{dy}{dx}$ in terms of $t$.

    (ii) Find the value of $\dfrac{dy}{dx}$ when $t = 2$.

(b) $A$ is the point on the curve for which $t = 2$. Find the coordinates of $A$.

(c) (i) Show that the relationship between $x$ and $y$ can be written in the form $xy - x - y = 1$.

    (ii) By differentiating both sides of this equation with respect to $x$, find the value of $\dfrac{dy}{dx}$ at the point $A$.

(d) Check that the answers obtained in (a) (ii) and (c) (ii) agree.

**2** A curve $C$ is defined parametrically by the equations $x = \cos\theta$, $y = \cos 2\theta$.

(a) Plot the points obtained by letting $\theta$ be $0$, $\dfrac{\pi}{4}$, $\dfrac{\pi}{2}$, $\dfrac{3\pi}{4}$, ... up to $2\pi$.

(b) What happens when $\theta$ takes values greater than $2\pi$?

(c) Explain why the curve $C$ consists of a part, but not the whole, of the graph of $y = 2x^2 - 1$.

(d) Find $\dfrac{dy}{dx}$ in terms of $\theta$.

(e) Find the equation of the tangent to $C$ at the point where $\theta = \dfrac{\pi}{4}$.

(f) Find the equation of the normal to $C$ at the point where $\theta = \dfrac{\pi}{4}$.

**3** A curve is defined by the equation $xy + x^2 - y^2 = 11$.
The line $x = 3$ intersects the curve at two points $A$ and $B$.

(a) Find the coordinates of $A$ and $B$.

(b) Find, in the form $ax + by = c$, where $a$, $b$ and $c$ are integers, the equation of

(i) the tangent to the curve at each of the points $A$ and $B$

(ii) the normal to the curve at each of the points $A$ and $B$

**4** The equation of the circle with centre $(2, 3)$ and radius 5 can be written as
$$(x - 2)^2 + (y - 3)^2 = 25$$

(a) Find the coordinates of the two points where this circle intersects the line $x = 5$.

(b) Find the gradient of the circle at each of these points.

(c) Find the equation of the normal to the circle at each of these points.

(d) Verify that each of the two normals passes through the centre of the circle.

**5** A curve is defined by $\sqrt{x} + \sqrt{y} = 5$ $(x \geq 0, \ y \geq 0)$.

(a) Show that $\dfrac{dy}{dx} = -\sqrt{\dfrac{y}{x}}$.

(b) Hence find the equation of the tangent to the curve at the point where $x = 9$.

**6** A curve is defined by the equation $(x^2 - 1)y = x^2 + 1$.

(a) Show that $(x^2 - 1)\dfrac{dy}{dx} = 2x(1 - y)$.

(b) Hence find the gradient of the curve at the point where $x = 2$.

## Test yourself (answers p 168)

**1** A curve is given by the parametric equations $x = 3t - 1$, $y = \dfrac{1}{t}$.

(a) Find $\dfrac{dy}{dx}$ in terms of $t$.

(b) Hence find the equation of the normal to the curve at the point where $t = 1$.  AQA 2003

**2** A curve is defined by the parametric equations $x = 3\sin t$ and $y = \cos t$.

(a) Show that, at the point $P$ where $t = \dfrac{\pi}{4}$, the gradient of the curve is $-\frac{1}{3}$.

(b) Find the equation of the tangent to the curve at the point $P$, giving your answer in the form $y = mx + c$.  AQA 2003

**3** A curve is defined by the equation $x^2 + 3xy + 2y^2 = 12$.
Find the equations of the tangent and the normal to the curve at the point $(2, 1)$ in the form $ax + by + c = 0$, where $a$, $b$ and $c$ are integers.

**4** A curve is given by the equation $3(x + 1)^2 - 9(y - 1)^2 = 32$.

(a) Find the coordinates of the two points on the curve at which $x = 3$.

(b) Find the gradient of the curve at each of these two points.  AQA 2002

# 8 Integration

In this chapter you will learn how to
- integrate a rational function using partial fractions
- use trigonometric identities to integrate functions such as $\sin^2 x$

## A Using partial fractions (answers p 169)

The process of expressing a rational expression in a form involving partial fractions was introduced in chapter 2. There are two cases to consider:

(1) degree of numerator < degree of denominator (a 'proper' algebraic fraction)

(2) degree of numerator ≥ degree of denominator (an 'improper' algebraic fraction)

Example 1 below illustrates case (1).

---

### Example 1

Express $\dfrac{6x^2 + x + 1}{(x-1)(x+1)^2}$ as partial fractions.

### Solution

The degree of the numerator is 2. This is less than that of the denominator, which is 3.

There will be three partial fractions, with denominators $(x - 1)$, $(x + 1)$ and $(x + 1)^2$.

Let $\dfrac{6x^2 + x + 1}{(x-1)(x+1)^2} \equiv \dfrac{A}{x-1} + \dfrac{B}{x+1} + \dfrac{C}{(x+1)^2}$.

So $\dfrac{6x^2 + x + 1}{(x-1)(x+1)^2} \equiv \dfrac{A(x+1)^2 + B(x+1)(x-1) + C(x-1)}{(x-1)(x+1)^2}$.

So $A(x + 1)^2 + B(x - 1)(x + 1) + C(x - 1) \equiv 6x^2 + x + 1$.

In this identity, let $x = -1$ (so that $A$ and $B$ are eliminated): $\quad -2C = 6 - 1 + 1$, so $C = -3$.

Now let $x = 1$ (so that $B$ and $C$ are eliminated): $\quad 4A = 6 + 1 + 1$, so $A = 2$.

*With A and C now known, you can let x be any other value in order to find B.*

*Alternatively, you can look at the coefficient of $x^2$ on each side of the identity.*

On the left the coefficient of $x^2$ is $A + B$; on the right it is 6. So $A + B = 6$, from which $B = 4$.

So $\dfrac{6x^2 + x + 1}{(x-1)(x+1)^2} \equiv \dfrac{2}{x-1} + \dfrac{4}{x+1} - \dfrac{3}{(x+1)^2}$.

---

**A1** Express each of these as partial fractions.

(a) $\dfrac{5x - 4}{(x-2)(x+1)}$

(b) $\dfrac{2x + 11}{(x-2)(2x+1)}$

(c) $\dfrac{5x + 13}{(x-3)(x+1)^2}$

In case (2), where the degree of the numerator is greater than or equal to that of the denominator, there will be a **quotient** as well as partial fractions. The degree of the quotient is equal to the difference between the degrees of the numerator and denominator.

degree 2

$$\frac{2x^2 + x + 5}{x - 3} \equiv Ax + B + \frac{C}{x - 3}$$

degree 1     2 − 1 = 1,
             so quotient is **linear**

degree 2

$$\frac{x^2 + 4}{(x - 2)(x + 5)} \equiv A + \frac{B}{x - 2} + \frac{C}{x + 5}$$

degree 2     2 − 2 = 0,
             so quotient is a **constant**

---

### Example 2

Express $\dfrac{x^2 + 5}{(x - 1)(x + 2)}$ in a form involving partial fractions.

### Solution

The degree of the numerator is 2; that of the denominator is also 2. So there will be a quotient (a constant).

There are two possible methods.

**Method 1**

Let $\dfrac{x^2 + 5}{(x - 1)(x + 2)} \equiv A + \dfrac{B}{x - 1} + \dfrac{C}{x + 2}$ .

So $A(x - 1)(x + 2) + B(x + 2) + C(x - 1) \equiv x^2 + 5$.

Let $x = 1$. Then $3B = 6$, so $B = 2$.

Let $x = -2$. Then $-3C = 9$, so $C = -3$.

To find the value of $A$, choose another value for $x$, or equate coefficients of $x^2$, giving $A = 1$.

So $\dfrac{x^2 + 5}{(x - 1)(x + 2)} \equiv 1 + \dfrac{2}{x - 1} - \dfrac{3}{x + 2}$.

**Method 2**

$$\frac{x^2 + 5}{(x - 1)(x + 2)} \equiv \frac{x^2 + 5}{x^2 + x - 2}$$

$$\equiv \frac{(x^2 + x - 2) + 7 - x}{x^2 + x - 2}$$

$$\equiv 1 + \frac{7 - x}{x^2 + x - 2}$$

$$\equiv 1 + \frac{7 - x}{(x - 1)(x + 2)}$$

Let $\dfrac{7 - x}{(x - 1)(x + 2)} \equiv \dfrac{A}{x - 1} + \dfrac{B}{x + 2}$ .

Then $A(x + 2) + B(x - 1) \equiv 7 - x$

Let $x = -2$. Then $-3B = 9$, so $B = -3$.

Let $x = 1$. Then $3A = 6$, so $A = 2$.

So $\dfrac{x^2 + 5}{(x - 1)(x + 2)} \equiv 1 + \dfrac{2}{x - 1} - \dfrac{3}{x + 2}$.

---

**A2** Express each of these in a form involving partial fractions.

(a) $\dfrac{x^2 + 3}{(x + 1)(x + 2)}$  (b) $\dfrac{x^2}{(x - 2)(x + 3)}$  (c) $\dfrac{2x^2 - 3}{(2 - x)(x + 1)}$

Partial fractions can be used to help integrate a function.

For example, the function $\dfrac{x+9}{(x-3)(x+1)}$ is equivalent to $\dfrac{3}{x-3} - \dfrac{2}{x+1}$.

It follows that $\displaystyle\int \dfrac{x+9}{(x-3)(x+1)}\,dx = 3\int \dfrac{1}{x-3}\,dx - 2\int \dfrac{1}{x+1}\,dx$ .

The integrals on the right side above are of a type you have met before: $\displaystyle\int \dfrac{1}{x+b}\,dx = \ln|x+b| + c$ .

So $\displaystyle\int \dfrac{x+9}{(x-3)(x+1)}\,dx = 3\ln|x-3| - 2\ln|x+1| + c$ .

**A3** Use your answer to A1 (a) to find $\displaystyle\int \dfrac{5x-4}{(x-2)(x+1)}\,dx$ .

A more general type of integral that you have met before is $\displaystyle\int \dfrac{1}{ax+b}\,dx = \dfrac{1}{a}\ln|ax+b| + c$ .

**A4** Use your answer to A1 (b) to find $\displaystyle\int \dfrac{2x+11}{(x-2)(2x+1)}\,dx$ .

**A5** (a) Express $\dfrac{x-6}{x(x+2)}$ as partial fractions.

(b) Find $\displaystyle\int \dfrac{x-6}{x(x+2)}\,dx$ .

**A6** Use your answers to question A2 to find

(a) $\displaystyle\int \dfrac{x^2+3}{(x+1)(x+2)}\,dx$    (b) $\displaystyle\int \dfrac{x^2}{(x-2)(x+3)}\,dx$    (c) $\displaystyle\int \dfrac{2x^2-3}{(2-x)(x+1)}\,dx$

In example 1 it was shown that $\dfrac{6x^2+x+1}{(x-1)(x+1)^2} \equiv \dfrac{2}{x-1} + \dfrac{4}{x+1} - \dfrac{3}{(x+1)^2}$ .

It follows that $\displaystyle\int \dfrac{6x^2+x+1}{(x-1)(x+1)^2}\,dx = 2\int \dfrac{1}{x-1}\,dx + 4\int \dfrac{1}{x+1}\,dx - 3\int \dfrac{1}{(x+1)^2}\,dx$ .

The first two integrals on the right are of the same type as before, but the third is different.

$\displaystyle\int \dfrac{1}{(x+1)^2}\,dx$ is the same as $\displaystyle\int (x+1)^{-2}\,dx$, which is $\dfrac{(x+1)^{-1}}{-1} + c = -\dfrac{1}{x+1} + c$ .

**A7** Complete the working above to find $\displaystyle\int \dfrac{6x^2+x+1}{(x-1)(x+1)^2}\,dx$ .

**A8** Use your answer to A1 (c) to find $\displaystyle\int \dfrac{5x+13}{(x-3)(x+1)^2}\,dx$ .

## Example 3

(a) Express $\dfrac{x+5}{(2x+1)(x-1)^2}$ as partial fractions. (b) Hence find $\displaystyle\int \dfrac{x+5}{(2x+1)(x-1)^2}\,dx$.

### Solution

(a) Let $\dfrac{x+5}{(2x+1)(x-1)^2} \equiv \dfrac{A}{2x+1} + \dfrac{B}{x-1} + \dfrac{C}{(x-1)^2} \equiv \dfrac{A(x-1)^2 + B(2x+1)(x-1) + C(2x+1)}{(2x+1)(x-1)^2}$.

So $A(x-1)^2 + B(2x+1)(x-1) + C(2x+1) \equiv x+5$.

Let $x = 1$. Then $3C = 6$, so $C = 2$.

Let $x = -\frac{1}{2}$. Then $\frac{9}{4}A = 4\frac{1}{2} = \frac{9}{2}$, so $A = 2$.

Equate coefficients of $x^2$: $A + 2B = 0$, so $B = -\frac{1}{2}A = -1$.

So $\dfrac{x+5}{(2x+1)(x-1)^2} \equiv \dfrac{2}{2x+1} - \dfrac{1}{x-1} + \dfrac{2}{(x-1)^2}$.

(b) $\displaystyle\int \dfrac{x+5}{(2x+1)(x-1)^2}\,dx = 2\int \dfrac{1}{2x+1}\,dx - \int \dfrac{1}{x-1}\,dx + 2\int \dfrac{1}{(x-1)^2}\,dx$

$$= 2 \times \tfrac{1}{2}\ln|2x+1| - \ln|x-1| - \dfrac{2}{x-1} + c$$

$$= \ln|2x+1| - \ln|x-1| - \dfrac{2}{x-1} + c$$

## Example 4

Find $\displaystyle\int \dfrac{x^2}{(x-2)(x+1)}\,dx$.

### Solution

*The function here is an improper fraction. The degrees of numerator and denominator are both 2, so there is a constant quotient + partial fractions.*

Let $\dfrac{x^2}{(x-2)(x+1)} \equiv A + \dfrac{B}{x-2} + \dfrac{C}{x+1}$.

So $A(x-2)(x+1) + B(x+1) + C(x-2) \equiv x^2$.

Let $x = 2$. Then $3B = 4$, so $B = \frac{4}{3}$.

Let $x = -1$. Then $-3C = 1$, so $C = -\frac{1}{3}$.

By equating coefficients of $x^2$, $A = 1$.

So $\displaystyle\int \dfrac{x^2}{(x-2)(x+1)}\,dx = \int 1\,dx + \tfrac{4}{3}\int \dfrac{1}{x-2}\,dx - \tfrac{1}{3}\int \dfrac{1}{x+1}\,dx$

$$= x + \tfrac{4}{3}\ln|x-2| - \tfrac{1}{3}\ln|x+1| + c$$

## Exercise A (answers p 169)

**1** Find each of these indefinite integrals.

(a) $\int \dfrac{1}{x(x-1)}\,dx$

(b) $\int \dfrac{3}{(x-1)(x+2)}\,dx$

(c) $\int \dfrac{x}{(x-1)(x+3)}\,dx$

(d) $\int \dfrac{x+5}{(x-1)(x+4)}\,dx$

(e) $\int \dfrac{x+7}{(2x-1)(x+2)}\,dx$

(f) $\int \dfrac{5x+1}{(1-x)(2x+1)}\,dx$

**2** Find each of these indefinite integrals.

(a) $\int \dfrac{x^2}{(x+1)(x+2)}\,dx$

(b) $\int \dfrac{x^2+3}{x(x-3)}\,dx$

(c) $\int \dfrac{x^2-3}{(x+2)(x-1)}\,dx$

**3** Find each of these indefinite integrals.

(a) $\int \dfrac{x}{(x-2)(x+1)^2}\,dx$

(b) $\int \dfrac{x+3}{(x+1)(x-1)^2}\,dx$

(c) $\int \dfrac{x}{(2x-1)(x-1)^2}\,dx$

(d) $\int \dfrac{x-1}{x^2(x+1)}\,dx$

(e) $\int \dfrac{x+1}{(x+2)^2(2x+3)}\,dx$

(f) $\int \dfrac{x-1}{x(x-4)^2}\,dx$

## B Definite integrals

As with all integrals involving expressions such as $\dfrac{1}{x}$, $\dfrac{1}{x-2}$, $\dfrac{1}{2x+3}$, $\dfrac{1}{(x-2)^2}$, $\ldots$

you need to make sure that the range of a definite integral does not include any discontinuity.

For example, the definite integral $\displaystyle\int_1^4 \dfrac{1}{x-2}\,dx$

cannot be evaluated because between $x=1$ and $x=4$ there is a discontinuity at $x=2$.

In all the examples and questions that follow, this problem will not arise.

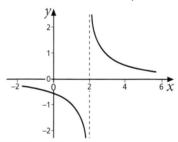

---

### Example 5

Find $\displaystyle\int_2^3 \dfrac{x+5}{(2x+1)(x-1)^2}\,dx$.

Give your answer in the form $a + \ln b$.

### Solution

The indefinite integral has been found already, in example 3.

$$\int_2^3 \dfrac{x+5}{(2x+1)(x-1)^2}\,dx = \left[\ln|2x+1| - \ln|x-1| - \dfrac{2}{x-1}\right]_2^3$$

$$= (\ln 7 - \ln 2 - 1) - (\ln 5 - \ln 1 - 2)$$

$$= 1 + \ln 7 - \ln 2 - \ln 5$$

$$= 1 + \ln\left(\dfrac{7}{2\times 5}\right) \quad \textit{from the laws of logarithms}$$

$$= 1 + \ln\tfrac{7}{10}$$

---

**Exercise B** (answers p 169)

**1** Find the exact value of each of these.

(a) $\displaystyle\int_1^2 \frac{1}{x(x+1)}\,dx$

(b) $\displaystyle\int_0^3 \frac{1}{(x+1)(x+4)}\,dx$

(c) $\displaystyle\int_1^4 \frac{x+1}{x(x-5)}\,dx$

(d) $\displaystyle\int_0^1 \frac{x+2}{(x+1)(x+5)}\,dx$

(e) $\displaystyle\int_3^4 \frac{x+3}{(x-2)(2x-1)}\,dx$

(f) $\displaystyle\int_0^1 \frac{x+6}{(x+1)(2x-3)}\,dx$

**2** Find the exact value of each of these.

(a) $\displaystyle\int_1^2 \frac{x^2+3}{x(x+1)}\,dx$

(b) $\displaystyle\int_2^5 \frac{x^2}{(x-1)(x+2)}\,dx$

(c) $\displaystyle\int_0^2 \frac{x^2-1}{(x+2)(x+4)}\,dx$

(d) $\displaystyle\int_0^2 \frac{x^2}{(x+5)(x-3)}\,dx$

(e) $\displaystyle\int_{-1}^1 \frac{x^2+2}{(2-x)(x+4)}\,dx$

(f) $\displaystyle\int_0^1 \frac{x^2}{x^2-4}\,dx$

**3** Find the exact value of each of these.

(a) $\displaystyle\int_0^2 \frac{x}{(x+1)(x-3)^2}\,dx$

(b) $\displaystyle\int_2^5 \frac{x+1}{(x-1)(x+2)^2}\,dx$

(c) $\displaystyle\int_1^3 \frac{x+4}{x^2(x+2)}\,dx$

(d) $\displaystyle\int_0^1 \frac{x}{(x+1)^2(x+2)}\,dx$

(e) $\displaystyle\int_0^2 \frac{x+2}{(2x+1)(x+1)^2}\,dx$

(f) $\displaystyle\int_0^2 \frac{x+2}{(x+3)^2(2x+5)}\,dx$

# C Using trigonometrical identities (answers p 169)

The integrals $\int \cos 2x\,dx$ and $\int \sin 2x\,dx$ should be familiar:

$$\int \cos 2x\,dx = \tfrac{1}{2}\sin 2x + c \qquad\qquad \int \sin 2x\,dx = -\tfrac{1}{2}\cos 2x + c$$

In chapter 5 you met formulae for $\sin 2x$ and $\cos 2x$ in terms of $\sin x$ and $\cos x$:

$$\sin 2x = 2\sin x \cos x \quad (1) \qquad\qquad \cos 2x = \cos^2 x - \sin^2 x \quad (2)$$
$$= 2\cos^2 x - 1 \qquad (3)$$
$$= 1 - 2\sin^2 x \qquad (4)$$

These formulae enable us to express $\sin^2 x$, $\cos^2 x$ and $\sin x \cos x$ in terms of $\sin 2x$ or $\cos 2x$, thus making it possible to integrate them.

**C1** (a) Use formula (1) above to express $\sin x \cos x$ in terms of $\sin 2x$.

    (b) Hence find $\int \sin x \cos x\,dx$.

**C2** (a) Use formula (3) above to express $\cos^2 x$ in terms of $\cos 2x$.

    (b) Hence find $\int \cos^2 x\,dx$.

**C3** By expressing $\sin^2 x$ in terms of $\cos 2x$, find $\int \sin^2 x\,dx$.

**C4** (a) By replacing $x$ by $\tfrac{1}{2}x$ in formula (4) above, show that $\sin^2 \tfrac{1}{2}x = \tfrac{1}{2}(1 - \cos x)$.

    (b) Hence find

      (i) $\displaystyle\int \sin^2 \tfrac{1}{2}x\,dx$

      (ii) $\displaystyle\int_0^{\frac{\pi}{2}} \sin^2 \tfrac{1}{2}x\,dx$

Here are the 'addition formulae' from chapter 5:

$$\cos(A + B) = \cos A \cos B - \sin A \sin B \qquad \sin(A + B) = \sin A \cos B + \cos A \sin B$$

These can be used to find formulae for $\cos 3x$, $\sin 3x$, $\cos 4x$, $\sin 4x$ and so on in terms of powers of $\cos x$ and $\sin x$. By rearranging the resulting formulae, we can express powers of $\cos x$ and $\sin x$ in terms of $\cos 3x$, $\sin 3x$, and so on, and thus integrate them.

**C5** (a) Use the formula for $\cos(A + B)$ with $A = 2x$ and $B = x$ to find an expression for $\cos 3x$ in terms of $\cos 2x$, $\cos x$, $\sin 2x$ and $\sin x$.

(b) By using formulae (1) and (3) above, together with the equation $\cos^2 x + \sin^2 x = 1$, show that $\cos 3x = 4\cos^3 x - 3\cos x$.

(c) Rearrange this last formula to express $\cos^3 x$ in terms of $\cos 3x$ and $\cos x$.

(d) Hence find $\int \cos^3 x \, dx$.

---

**Example 6**

Find $\displaystyle\int_0^{\frac{\pi}{8}} \cos^2 2x \, dx$.

**Solution**

Use the 'double angle' formula $\cos 2A = 2\cos^2 A - 1$, with $A = 2x$.

$$\cos 4x = 2\cos^2 2x - 1$$

Rearranging, we get $\cos^2 2x = \tfrac{1}{2}(\cos 4x + 1)$.

So $\displaystyle\int_0^{\frac{\pi}{8}} \cos^2 2x \, dx = \int_0^{\frac{\pi}{8}} \tfrac{1}{2}(\cos 4x + 1)\,dx$

$$= \tfrac{1}{2}\left[\tfrac{1}{4}\sin 4x + x\right]_0^{\frac{\pi}{8}}$$

$$= \tfrac{1}{2}\left(\tfrac{1}{4}\sin\tfrac{\pi}{2} + \tfrac{\pi}{8}\right) - 0 = \tfrac{1}{8} + \tfrac{\pi}{16}$$

---

**Exercise C** (answers p 170)

**1** Find
  (a) $\displaystyle\int_0^{\pi} \sin^2 x \, dx$
  (b) $\displaystyle\int_0^{\frac{\pi}{6}} \cos^2 x \, dx$
  (c) $\displaystyle\int_0^{\frac{\pi}{3}} \cos^2 \tfrac{1}{2}x \, dx$

**2** The region enclosed by the curve $y = \cos x$ and the $x$-axis between $x = 0$ and $x = \dfrac{\pi}{2}$ is rotated through $2\pi$ radians about the $x$-axis.

Show that the volume of the solid of revolution formed is $\dfrac{\pi^2}{4}$.

(Reminder: Volume of solid of revolution about $x$-axis $= \int \pi y^2 \, dx$.)

**3** (a) Show that $(1 + \cos x)^2 = \tfrac{3}{2} + 2\cos x + \tfrac{1}{2}\cos 2x$.

(b) Hence find $\displaystyle\int (1 + \cos x)^2 \, dx$.

(c) Find $\displaystyle\int (1 + \sin x)^2 \, dx$.

**4** (a) Show that $\displaystyle\int (\cos\theta + \sin\theta)^2 \, d\theta = \theta - \tfrac{1}{2}\cos 2\theta + c$.

(b) Find $\displaystyle\int_0^{\frac{\pi}{2}} (\cos\theta - \sin\theta)^2 \, d\theta$.

## Key points

- Functions such as $\dfrac{x^2}{(x-2)(x+3)}$, $\dfrac{x+5}{(2x+1)(x-1)^2}$ and so on can be integrated by using partial fractions.

  If degree of numerator $\geq$ degree of denominator, then there will be a quotient + partial fractions. (pp 90–91)

- Functions such as $\cos^2 x$, $\sin x \cos x$, $\sin^2 2x$ and so on can be integrated by using the double angle formulae $\cos 2x = 2\cos^2 x - 1 = 1 - 2\sin^2 x$ and $\sin 2x = 2\sin x \cos x$. (p 95)

## Mixed questions (answers p 170)

**1** The function f is given by $f(x) = \dfrac{9}{(1+2x)(4-x)}$.

(a) Express $f(x)$ as partial fractions.

(b) (i) Show that the first three terms in the expansion of $\dfrac{1}{4-x}$ in ascending powers of $x$ are $\dfrac{1}{4} + \dfrac{x}{16} + \dfrac{x^2}{64}$.

(ii) Obtain a similar expansion for $\dfrac{1}{1+2x}$.

(iii) Hence, or otherwise, obtain the first three terms in the expansion of $f(x)$ in ascending powers of $x$.

(iv) Find the range of values of $x$ for which the expansion of $f(x)$ in ascending powers of $x$ is valid.

(c) (i) Find $\int f(x)\,dx$.

(ii) Hence find, to two significant figures, the error in using the expansion of $f(x)$ up to the term in $x^2$ to evaluate $\displaystyle\int_0^{0.25} f(x)\,dx$. AQA 2001

**2 (a)** Show that $(\cos x + 2\sin x)^2 = \dfrac{5}{2} - \dfrac{3}{2}\cos 2x + 2\sin 2x$.

**(b)** Find $\displaystyle\int_0^{\frac{\pi}{2}} (\cos x + 2\sin x)^2\,dx$.

## Test yourself (answers p 171)

**1** Find

(a) $\displaystyle\int \dfrac{x+1}{x(3x+2)}\,dx$

(b) $\displaystyle\int \dfrac{x^2+1}{x(3x+2)}\,dx$

(c) $\displaystyle\int \dfrac{x+1}{x^2(3x+2)}\,dx$

(d) $\displaystyle\int_1^2 \dfrac{x}{(3x-1)(x+1)}\,dx$

(e) $\displaystyle\int_1^2 \dfrac{x^2}{(3x-1)(x+1)}\,dx$

(f) $\displaystyle\int_1^2 \dfrac{x-1}{(3x-1)(x+1)^2}\,dx$

**2** Find

(a) $\displaystyle\int_0^{\frac{\pi}{4}} \sin^2 x\,dx$

(b) $\displaystyle\int_0^{\frac{\pi}{2}} (1-\sin x)^2\,dx$

(c) $\displaystyle\int_0^{\pi} \cos^2 \tfrac{1}{2}x\,dx$

# 9 Vectors

In this chapter you will work in two and three dimensions.
You will learn how to
- find the magnitude of a vector
- add and subtract vectors and their scalar multiples
- use column vectors and **i, j, k** notation
- work with position vectors
- find and use the vector equation of a straight line
- find the scalar product of two vectors
- use the scalar product to find the angle between two straight lines

## A Vectors in two dimensions (answers p 171)

For those who have studied Mechanics 1 this section is mainly revision.

**A1** Towns $A$ and $B$ are 40 km apart and towns $B$ and $C$ are 30 km apart.
Is this enough information to find the distance between towns $A$ and $C$?

This sketch shows the relative positions of towns $A$, $B$ and $C$.

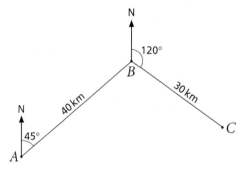

**A2 (a)** Find the size of angle $ABC$.

**(b)** Calculate the distance between towns $A$ and $C$.

The **distances** $AB$ and $BC$ do not add to give the distance $AC$.

The **displacement** from $A$ to $B$ (written as $\overrightarrow{AB}$) has a magnitude (which is the distance of 40 km) and a direction (NE).

The displacement from $A$ to $B$ followed by the displacement from $B$ to $C$ is equivalent to the displacement from $A$ to $C$; we can write this as
$$\overrightarrow{AB} + \overrightarrow{BC} = \overrightarrow{AC}$$

A quantity which behaves in this way is called a **vector** quantity.
A vector quantity has both **magnitude** and **direction**.

A quantity such as temperature or mass that has magnitude but no direction is called a **scalar** quantity.

We can represent a vector by a straight line segment where the length of the line represents the magnitude of the vector and the direction of the line (indicated by an arrow) represents the direction of the vector.

For example, using a scale of 1 cm to 10 km, we can represent the vector $\overrightarrow{AB}$ by this line.

The magnitude of a vector is sometimes called the **modulus**. The modulus of the vector $\overrightarrow{AB}$ is written as $|\overrightarrow{AB}|$.

Here we have $|\overrightarrow{AB}| = 40$.

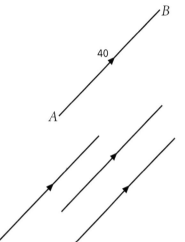

Two vectors are **equal** if they have the same magnitude and the same direction.

So any of these lines may represent the vector $\overrightarrow{AB}$.

An alternative way to label a vector is to use a lower-case letter which

• is in bold type in printed material

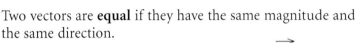

• has a wavy or straight line underneath when handwritten

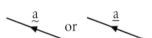 or

All vectors are added in the same way as the displacements on the previous page. This is sometimes called the 'triangle law'.

To add these two vectors …       … put them 'head to tail' …

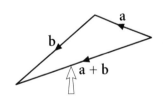

… and this vector represents the vector sum or **resultant**.

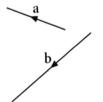

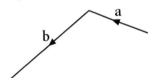 If two vectors **p** and **q** have the same magnitude but opposite directions then we say that **q** = −**p**.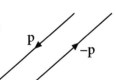

The resultant vector **a** − **b** is equivalent to **a** + −**b**.

| To find **a** − **b** … | … add **a** and −**b** … | … to obtain the resultant **a** + −**b**. |

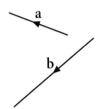

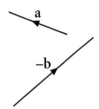

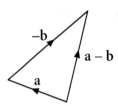

A vector can be multiplied by a number.

For example

- 2**x** is a vector with a magnitude that is twice the magnitude of **x** and in the same direction

- $-\frac{1}{3}$**x** is a vector with a magnitude a third of the magnitude of **x** and in the opposite direction

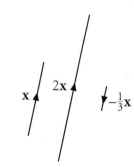

Clearly the vectors **x**, 2**x** and $-\frac{1}{3}$**x** are parallel.
Parallel vectors are sometimes called **scalar multiples** of each other.

**K**    In general, where $k$ is a number, vectors **a** and $k$**a** are parallel.

**A3** Vectors **a**, **b** and **c** are shown below on square centimetre dotty paper.

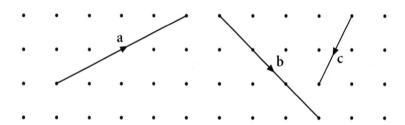

Draw diagrams to show the following vectors.

| (a) 2**c** | (b) $\frac{1}{2}$**a** | (c) $-\frac{1}{3}$**b** | (d) **a** + **b** |
| (e) **a** − **b** | (f) **b** − **a** | (g) $\frac{1}{2}$**a** + 3**b** | (h) **a** + **b** + **c** |

**D**   **A4** For any two vectors **x** and **y**, show that **x** + **y** = **y** + **x**.

**A5** Write each of these in its simplest form.

    (a) **a** + **b** + 4**b**                 (b) 2**a** + **b** + 3**a** − 5**b**

**A6** Show that for any two vectors **p** and **q**, the vector **p** + 2**q** is parallel to 2**p** + 4**q**.

**A7** Which of the vectors below are parallel to 2**x** − **y**?

    A 2**x** − 3**y**      B 6**x** − 3**y**      C 4**x** + 2**y**      D **y** − 2**x**      E **x** − $\frac{1}{2}$**y**

## Example 1

PQRS is a parallelogram.
$X$ is a point on $SR$ such that $SX = \frac{1}{3}SR$.

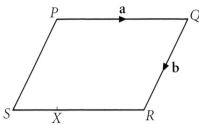

Given that $\overrightarrow{PQ} = \mathbf{a}$ and $\overrightarrow{QR} = \mathbf{b}$, find each of these in terms of $\mathbf{a}$ and $\mathbf{b}$.

(a) $\overrightarrow{SR}$      (b) $\overrightarrow{SX}$      (c) $\overrightarrow{PR}$      (d) $\overrightarrow{QS}$      (e) $\overrightarrow{PX}$      (f) $\overrightarrow{QX}$

### Solution

(a) $\overrightarrow{SR} = \overrightarrow{PQ} = \mathbf{a}$
(b) $\overrightarrow{SX} = \frac{1}{3}\overrightarrow{SR} = \frac{1}{3}\mathbf{a}$
(c) $\overrightarrow{PR} = \overrightarrow{PQ} + \overrightarrow{QR} = \mathbf{a} + \mathbf{b}$
(d) $\overrightarrow{QS} = \overrightarrow{QR} + \overrightarrow{RS} = \mathbf{b} + -\mathbf{a} = \mathbf{b} - \mathbf{a}$
(e) $\overrightarrow{PX} = \overrightarrow{PS} + \overrightarrow{SX} = \mathbf{b} + \frac{1}{3}\mathbf{a}$
(f) $\overrightarrow{QX} = \overrightarrow{QR} + \overrightarrow{RX} = \overrightarrow{QR} + \frac{2}{3}\overrightarrow{RS} = \mathbf{b} + \frac{2}{3}(-\mathbf{a}) = \mathbf{b} - \frac{2}{3}\mathbf{a}$

## Exercise A (answers p 172)

**1** Write each of these in its simplest form.

(a) $\mathbf{x} + \mathbf{y} + 2\mathbf{x}$      (b) $\mathbf{x} + \mathbf{y} - 2\mathbf{x} + 3\mathbf{y}$      (c) $\mathbf{x} - \frac{1}{2}\mathbf{y} + \mathbf{y} - \mathbf{x}$

**2** Which of the vectors below are parallel to $\mathbf{p} - 3\mathbf{q}$?

A $2\mathbf{p} - 6\mathbf{q}$      B $4\mathbf{p} - 8\mathbf{q}$      C $\mathbf{q} - \mathbf{p}$      D $\mathbf{q} - \frac{1}{3}\mathbf{p}$      E $4\mathbf{p} + 12\mathbf{q}$

**3** PQRST is a pentagon.
$\overrightarrow{PQ} = \mathbf{a}$, $\overrightarrow{QR} = \mathbf{b}$, $\overrightarrow{RS} = \mathbf{c}$ and $\overrightarrow{TS} = 3\mathbf{b}$.

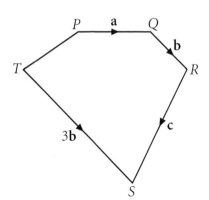

Find each of these in terms of $\mathbf{a}$, $\mathbf{b}$ and $\mathbf{c}$.

(a) $\overrightarrow{PR}$      (b) $\overrightarrow{PS}$      (c) $\overrightarrow{SR}$      (d) $\overrightarrow{TR}$      (e) $\overrightarrow{PT}$

**4** *ABCD* is a trapezium.
*AB* is parallel to *DC* and *DC* = 2*AB*.
*M* is the mid-point of *DC*.
$\overrightarrow{AB}$ = **p** and $\overrightarrow{BC}$ = **q**.

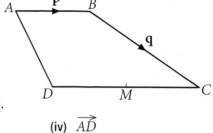

(a) Write down these vectors in terms of **p** and **q**.

   (i) $\overrightarrow{DC}$         (ii) $\overrightarrow{MC}$         (iii) $\overrightarrow{BM}$         (iv) $\overrightarrow{AD}$

(b) Show that *ABMD* is a parallelogram.

**5** *PQRS* is a quadrilateral.
*W*, *X*, *Y* and *Z* are the mid-points
respectively of *PQ*, *QR*, *RS* and *PS*.
$\overrightarrow{PQ}$ = **a**, $\overrightarrow{QR}$ = **b**, $\overrightarrow{RS}$ = **c** and $\overrightarrow{SP}$ = **d**.

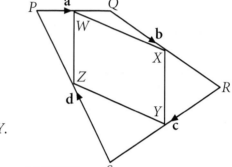

(a) (i) Show that *WX* is parallel to *PR*.

    (ii) Show that *ZY* is parallel to *PR*.

    (iii) Hence, show that *WX* is parallel to *ZY*.

(b) Show that *XY* is parallel to *WZ*.

(c) What have you proved about the quadrilateral *WXYZ*?

## B Components in two dimensions (answers p 172)

For those who have studied Mechanics 1 this section is mainly revision.

A vector can be written in column vector form.
For example, the vector on the right goes
4 units 'across to the right' and 1 unit 'down'
and, in column vector form, it is written as $\mathbf{a} = \begin{bmatrix} 4 \\ -1 \end{bmatrix}$

This is the **x-component**.

This is the **y-component**.

Vectors parallel to **a** are scalar multiples of **a**.

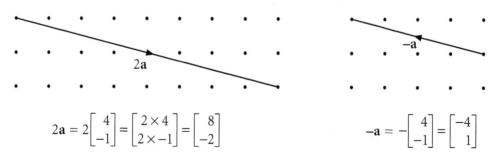

$$2\mathbf{a} = 2\begin{bmatrix} 4 \\ -1 \end{bmatrix} = \begin{bmatrix} 2 \times 4 \\ 2 \times -1 \end{bmatrix} = \begin{bmatrix} 8 \\ -2 \end{bmatrix}$$

$$-\mathbf{a} = -\begin{bmatrix} 4 \\ -1 \end{bmatrix} = \begin{bmatrix} -4 \\ 1 \end{bmatrix}$$

**B1** Which of these vectors are parallel to $\begin{bmatrix} 4 \\ -2 \end{bmatrix}$?

A $\begin{bmatrix} 12 \\ -3 \end{bmatrix}$         B $\begin{bmatrix} 8 \\ -4 \end{bmatrix}$         C $\begin{bmatrix} 2 \\ -1 \end{bmatrix}$         D $\begin{bmatrix} -16 \\ 8 \end{bmatrix}$         E $\begin{bmatrix} 20 \\ 10 \end{bmatrix}$

The notation can be used to find resultant vectors when adding or subtracting. For example, we can see from the diagram that

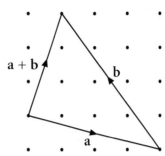

$$\mathbf{a} = \begin{bmatrix} 4 \\ -1 \end{bmatrix}, \quad \mathbf{b} = \begin{bmatrix} -3 \\ 4 \end{bmatrix} \text{ and } \mathbf{a} + \mathbf{b} = \begin{bmatrix} 1 \\ 3 \end{bmatrix}$$

Clearly, the resultant vector can be found by adding the $x$- and $y$-components:

$$\mathbf{a} + \mathbf{b} = \begin{bmatrix} 4 \\ -1 \end{bmatrix} + \begin{bmatrix} -3 \\ 4 \end{bmatrix} = \begin{bmatrix} 4 + -3 \\ -1 + 4 \end{bmatrix} = \begin{bmatrix} 1 \\ 3 \end{bmatrix}$$

**B2** Given that $\mathbf{c} = \begin{bmatrix} 4 \\ -1 \end{bmatrix}$ and $\mathbf{d} = \begin{bmatrix} 2 \\ -1 \end{bmatrix}$, write $\mathbf{c} + 5\mathbf{d}$ as a column vector.

Subtraction works in a similar way. For example, from the diagram,

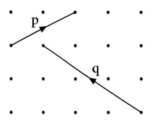

$$\mathbf{p} = \begin{bmatrix} 2 \\ 1 \end{bmatrix}, \quad \mathbf{q} = \begin{bmatrix} -3 \\ 2 \end{bmatrix}$$

and $\mathbf{p} - \mathbf{q} = \mathbf{p} + -\mathbf{q} = \begin{bmatrix} 5 \\ -1 \end{bmatrix}$

Looking at components, $\mathbf{p} - \mathbf{q} = \begin{bmatrix} 2 \\ 1 \end{bmatrix} - \begin{bmatrix} -3 \\ 2 \end{bmatrix} = \begin{bmatrix} 2 - -3 \\ 1 - 2 \end{bmatrix} = \begin{bmatrix} 5 \\ -1 \end{bmatrix}$

Vectors such as $2\mathbf{p} + 3\mathbf{q}$ and $\mathbf{p} - \mathbf{q}$ are called **linear combinations** of vectors $\mathbf{p}$ and $\mathbf{q}$: they are of the form $a\mathbf{p} + b\mathbf{q}$, where $a$ and $b$ are real numbers.

**B3 (a)** Given that $\mathbf{x} = \begin{bmatrix} 4 \\ -1 \end{bmatrix}$ and $\mathbf{y} = \begin{bmatrix} 3 \\ -4 \end{bmatrix}$, write the linear combination $2\mathbf{x} - \mathbf{y}$ as a column vector.

**(b)** Find a linear combination of $\mathbf{x}$ and $\mathbf{y}$ that gives the vector $\begin{bmatrix} 13 \\ -13 \end{bmatrix}$.

We can calculate the magnitude of the vector $\mathbf{p} = \begin{bmatrix} 4 \\ 1 \end{bmatrix}$ using Pythagoras's theorem.

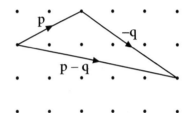

$$|\mathbf{p}| = \sqrt{4^2 + 1^2} = \sqrt{17}$$

This process will give the magnitude of any vector, including a vector with one or more negative components.

For example, for $\mathbf{q} = \begin{bmatrix} -4 \\ 1 \end{bmatrix}$ we have $|\mathbf{q}| = \sqrt{(-4)^2 + 1^2} = \sqrt{17}$.

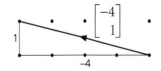

In general, the magnitude of the vector $\begin{bmatrix} a \\ b \end{bmatrix}$ is $\sqrt{a^2 + b^2}$.

**B4** Given that $\mathbf{p} = \begin{bmatrix} 3 \\ -4 \end{bmatrix}$ and $\mathbf{q} = \begin{bmatrix} -5 \\ 12 \end{bmatrix}$, calculate $|\mathbf{p}|$, $|\mathbf{q}|$ and $|\mathbf{p} + \mathbf{q}|$.

Use your results to verify that $|\mathbf{p}| + |\mathbf{q}| \neq |\mathbf{p} + \mathbf{q}|$ in general.

**B5** Points $P$ and $Q$ have coordinates $(3, -1)$ and $(5, 4)$ respectively.

(a) Write $\overrightarrow{PQ}$ as a column vector.

(b) Find the distance between points $P$ and $Q$.

---

**K** Any vector with a magnitude of 1 is a **unit vector**. The unit vectors parallel to the $x$- and $y$-axis are conventionally labelled $\mathbf{i}$ and $\mathbf{j}$.

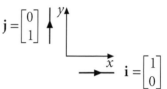

Any vector can be written as a unique linear combination of $\mathbf{i}$ and $\mathbf{j}$.

For example, $\begin{bmatrix} 3 \\ -2 \end{bmatrix} = 3\begin{bmatrix} 1 \\ 0 \end{bmatrix} - 2\begin{bmatrix} 0 \\ 1 \end{bmatrix} = 3\mathbf{i} - 2\mathbf{j}$.

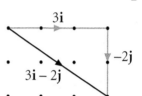

---

**B6** Write $\begin{bmatrix} -4 \\ 3 \end{bmatrix}$ in terms of $\mathbf{i}$ and $\mathbf{j}$.

**B7** Write $4\mathbf{i} + 7\mathbf{j}$ as a column vector.

**B8** Given that $\mathbf{a} = 2\mathbf{i} + 5\mathbf{j}$ and $\mathbf{b} = \mathbf{i} - 3\mathbf{j}$, write these in terms of $\mathbf{i}$ and $\mathbf{j}$.

(a) $\mathbf{a} + \mathbf{b}$        (b) $\mathbf{a} - \mathbf{b}$        (c) $3\mathbf{a} + 5\mathbf{b}$

**B9** What is the magnitude of the vector $8\mathbf{i} - 6\mathbf{j}$?

**B10** Write down any vector parallel to $2\mathbf{i} + 5\mathbf{j}$.

---

**Exercise B** (answers p 172)

**1** Vectors are given by $\mathbf{p} = \begin{bmatrix} 5 \\ 0 \end{bmatrix}$, $\mathbf{q} = \begin{bmatrix} -1 \\ 2 \end{bmatrix}$ and $\mathbf{r} = \begin{bmatrix} -2 \\ -6 \end{bmatrix}$.
Write each of these as column vectors.

(a) $\mathbf{p} + 4\mathbf{q}$        (b) $-\mathbf{p} - 2\mathbf{r}$        (c) $\mathbf{p} + 3\mathbf{q} + \mathbf{r}$

**2** Given that $\mathbf{a} = \begin{bmatrix} -2 \\ -3 \end{bmatrix}$ and $\mathbf{b} = \begin{bmatrix} 1 \\ 1 \end{bmatrix}$, calculate each of these.

(a) $|\mathbf{a}|$       (b) $|\mathbf{a} - \mathbf{b}|$       (c) $|-\mathbf{b}|$       (d) $|3\mathbf{b} - 2\mathbf{a}|$

**3** Points $A$, $B$ and $C$ have coordinates $(3, 9)$, $(1, -3)$ and $(-2, -5)$ respectively.

(a) Write $\overrightarrow{CB}$ as a column vector.

(b) Find the distance between points $A$ and $B$.

**4** Find the magnitude of the vector $3(\mathbf{i} - 5\mathbf{j})$.

**5** Sort these into three pairs of parallel vectors.

$\mathbf{a} = 5\mathbf{i} - 2\mathbf{j}$           $\mathbf{b} = 2\mathbf{i} + \mathbf{j}$           $\mathbf{c} = 10\mathbf{i} - 6\mathbf{j}$

$\mathbf{d} = \frac{5}{8}\mathbf{i} - \frac{3}{8}\mathbf{j}$         $\mathbf{e} = -10\mathbf{i} + 4\mathbf{j}$        $\mathbf{f} = 10\mathbf{i} + 5\mathbf{j}$

**6** If $\mathbf{a} = 4\mathbf{i} + k\mathbf{j}$, where $k$ is a constant, and $|\mathbf{a}| = 2\sqrt{5}$, find the two possible values of $k$.

**7** Write down all the vectors that are parallel to $\begin{bmatrix} 3 \\ 4 \end{bmatrix}$ and have a magnitude of 15.

**8** (a) Show that $\frac{5}{13}\mathbf{i} + \frac{12}{13}\mathbf{j}$ is a unit vector.

    (b) Find a unit vector that is parallel to $3\mathbf{i} - 4\mathbf{j}$.

**9** Vectors $\mathbf{a}$ and $\mathbf{b}$ are given by $\mathbf{a} = k\mathbf{i} + 6\mathbf{j}$ and $\mathbf{b} = 2\mathbf{i} + l\mathbf{j}$, where $k$ and $l$ are constants. If $\mathbf{a} + \mathbf{b} = 3\mathbf{i} + 2\mathbf{j}$, find the values of $k$ and $l$.

**10** $PQRS$ is a trapezium where $PQ$ is parallel to $SR$. The length of $SR$ is twice the length of $PQ$.

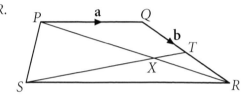

$T$ is the mid-point of $QR$ and the lines $PR$ and $ST$ cross at the point $X$.
$\overrightarrow{PQ} = \mathbf{a}$ and $\overrightarrow{QR} = \mathbf{b}$.

(a) Write each of these in terms of $\mathbf{a}$ and $\mathbf{b}$.

    (i) $\overrightarrow{PR}$        (ii) $\overrightarrow{RS}$        (iii) $\overrightarrow{TR}$        (iv) $\overrightarrow{TS}$        (v) $\overrightarrow{PS}$

(b) (i) Show that $\overrightarrow{PX} = k(\mathbf{a} + \mathbf{b})$ for some number $k$.

    (ii) Show that $\overrightarrow{XS} = l(\frac{1}{2}\mathbf{b} - 2\mathbf{a})$ for some number $l$.

    (iii) Use the vector equation $\overrightarrow{PX} + \overrightarrow{XS} = \overrightarrow{PS}$ to find the values of $k$ and $l$.

## C Vectors in three dimensions (answers p 173)

Many situations where we use vectors are three-dimensional. For example, the velocity of a rocket in space, the displacement of a person on a rollercoaster and the acceleration of a car can all be represented by three-dimensional vectors.

The ideas and techniques in sections A and B can be extended to three dimensions.

**C1** In the diagram, $ABCD$ is a rectangle and $AF$, $BG$, $CH$ and $DE$ are all parallel.

DE is the same length as CH.
AF is the same length as BG.
AF is half the length of DE.
$\overrightarrow{AD} = \mathbf{p}$, $\overrightarrow{DC} = \mathbf{q}$ and $\overrightarrow{CH} = \mathbf{r}$.

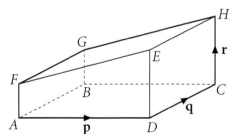

(a) Write these vectors in terms of $\mathbf{p}$, $\mathbf{q}$ and $\mathbf{r}$.

    (i) $\overrightarrow{AF}$        (ii) $\overrightarrow{AC}$        (iii) $\overrightarrow{AE}$        (iv) $\overrightarrow{DB}$

    (v) $\overrightarrow{AH}$       (vi) $\overrightarrow{HB}$       (vii) $\overrightarrow{DG}$       (viii) $\overrightarrow{BF}$

(b) Show that the vectors $\overrightarrow{AG}$ and $\overrightarrow{DH}$ are not parallel.

A coordinate system is needed for vectors in three dimensions.
Conventionally we use coordinate axes that are at right angles to each other
and are labelled $x$, $y$ and $z$ as shown.

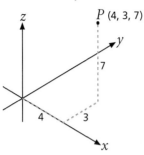

Think of the $x$- and $y$-axes as being drawn
on a horizontal surface (like a table) and
the $z$-axis pointing straight up from it.

The point labelled $P$ has coordinates $(4, 3, 7)$.

*ABCDEFGH* is a cuboid.
The coordinates of $A$, $C$ and $G$ are shown.

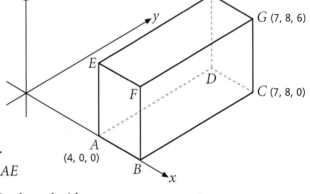

**C2** Write down the coordinates of

(a)  $B$       (b)  $D$

(c)  $F$       (d)  $H$

**C3** Write down the lengths of these edges.

(a)  $AB$       (b)  $AD$       (c)  $AE$

This diagram shows the vectors $\overrightarrow{EC}$ and $\overrightarrow{BC}$ in the cuboid.

The vector from $E$ to $C$ is

- 3 units in the $x$-direction
- 8 units in the $y$-direction
- −6 units in the $z$-direction

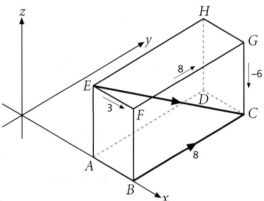

It can be written as a
column vector as $\overrightarrow{EC} = \begin{bmatrix} 3 \\ 8 \\ -6 \end{bmatrix}$  ← $x$-component
 ← $y$-component
 ← $z$-component

The vector from $B$ to $C$ is

- 0 units in the $x$-direction
- 8 units in the $y$-direction
- 0 units in the $z$-direction

and so can be written as $\overrightarrow{BC} = \begin{bmatrix} 0 \\ 8 \\ 0 \end{bmatrix}$.

**C4** Write each of these as a column vector.

(a)  $\overrightarrow{AF}$       (b)  $\overrightarrow{DG}$       (c)  $\overrightarrow{AC}$       (d)  $\overrightarrow{BE}$

(e)  $\overrightarrow{EA}$       (f)  $\overrightarrow{AG}$       (g)  $\overrightarrow{BH}$       (h)  $\overrightarrow{FD}$

**C5** Sort these into two groups of parallel vectors.

$$\begin{bmatrix} 2 \\ -1 \\ 3 \end{bmatrix}, \quad \begin{bmatrix} -6 \\ 3 \\ -9 \end{bmatrix}, \quad \begin{bmatrix} 12 \\ -6 \\ 16 \end{bmatrix}, \quad \begin{bmatrix} 4 \\ -2 \\ 6 \end{bmatrix}, \quad \begin{bmatrix} 6 \\ -3 \\ 8 \end{bmatrix}$$

**C6** This diagram shows the vector $\begin{bmatrix} 1 \\ 3 \\ 2 \end{bmatrix}$ with

the components shown by the dotted lines.
A triangle is shaded.

(a) Show that the shaded triangle
    is a right-angled triangle.

(b) What is the length (in surd form) of
    the hypotenuse of the shaded triangle?

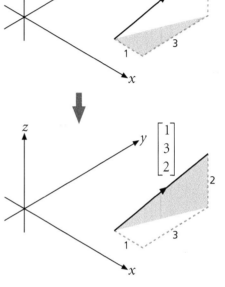

In the next diagram, a second triangle is shaded.

(c) Is the shaded triangle right-angled?

(d) Use this triangle to work out the

magnitude of the vector $\begin{bmatrix} 1 \\ 3 \\ 2 \end{bmatrix}$, giving

your result in surd form.

**C7** Work out the magnitude of the vector $\begin{bmatrix} 5 \\ 12 \\ 3 \end{bmatrix}$.

**D**

**C8** This diagram shows the vector $\begin{bmatrix} 4 \\ -1 \\ -5 \end{bmatrix}$.

The components are shown by the dotted lines.
Work out the magnitude of the vector.

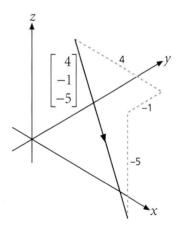

This diagram shows the vector $\begin{bmatrix} a \\ b \\ c \end{bmatrix}$ with

the components shown by the dotted lines.
The shaded triangle is right-angled so, by Pythagoras's
theorem, the length of its hypotenuse is $\sqrt{a^2 + b^2}$.

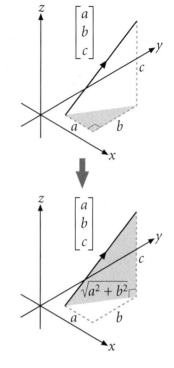

The second shaded triangle is right-angled too so,
using Pythagoras's theorem again, the magnitude

of the vector $\begin{bmatrix} a \\ b \\ c \end{bmatrix}$ is $\sqrt{\left(\sqrt{a^2 + b^2}\right)^2 + c^2} = \sqrt{a^2 + b^2 + c^2}$.

This process will give the magnitude of any vector,
including a vector with one or more negative components.

For example, the magnitude of the vector $\begin{bmatrix} 4 \\ -1 \\ -5 \end{bmatrix}$ is $\sqrt{4^2 + (-1)^2 + (-5)^2} = \sqrt{16 + 1 + 25}$

$$= \sqrt{42}$$

The magnitude of any vector $\begin{bmatrix} a \\ b \\ c \end{bmatrix}$ is $\sqrt{a^2 + b^2 + c^2}$.

**C9** Find the magnitude of each of these vectors.

(a) $\begin{bmatrix} 1 \\ -2 \\ 2 \end{bmatrix}$

(b) $\begin{bmatrix} 3 \\ 1 \\ -5 \end{bmatrix}$

(c) $\begin{bmatrix} 0 \\ -3 \\ -6 \end{bmatrix}$

**C10** *ABCDE* is a square-based pyramid.
The coordinates of points *A* to *E* are shown.

(a) Write each of these as a column vector.

(i) $\overrightarrow{AB}$      (ii) $\overrightarrow{AE}$      (iii) $\overrightarrow{EA}$

(b) By considering the vector addition

$$\overrightarrow{EB} = \overrightarrow{EA} + \overrightarrow{AB}$$

write $\overrightarrow{EB}$ as a column vector.

(c) Write each of these as a column vector.

(i) $\overrightarrow{AC}$      (ii) $\overrightarrow{EC}$      (iii) $\overrightarrow{DE}$

(d) Find $|\overrightarrow{DE}|$.

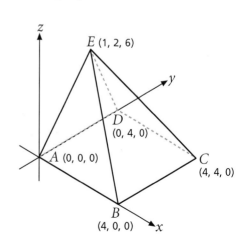

**C11** Vectors are given by $\mathbf{a} = \begin{bmatrix} -2 \\ 3 \\ 0 \end{bmatrix}$, $\mathbf{b} = \begin{bmatrix} 4 \\ -1 \\ 7 \end{bmatrix}$ and $\mathbf{c} = \begin{bmatrix} 2 \\ 0 \\ -4 \end{bmatrix}$.

    (a) Write each of these as a column vector.

        (i) $\mathbf{a} + \mathbf{b}$       (ii) $3\mathbf{c} + 2\mathbf{b}$       (iii) $4\mathbf{b} - \mathbf{c}$       (iv) $\frac{1}{2}\mathbf{c} - 2\mathbf{a}$       (v) $2(\mathbf{a} + 2\mathbf{c})$

    (b) Evaluate $|\mathbf{a} + \mathbf{b} + \mathbf{c}|$.

In three dimensions, unit vectors $\mathbf{i}$, $\mathbf{j}$ and $\mathbf{k}$ are defined as

$$\mathbf{i} = \begin{bmatrix} 1 \\ 0 \\ 0 \end{bmatrix}, \quad \mathbf{j} = \begin{bmatrix} 0 \\ 1 \\ 0 \end{bmatrix}, \quad \mathbf{k} = \begin{bmatrix} 0 \\ 0 \\ 1 \end{bmatrix} \qquad \mathbf{k} = \begin{bmatrix} 0 \\ 0 \\ 1 \end{bmatrix}$$

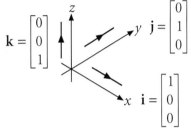

$$\mathbf{j} = \begin{bmatrix} 0 \\ 1 \\ 0 \end{bmatrix} \qquad \mathbf{i} = \begin{bmatrix} 1 \\ 0 \\ 0 \end{bmatrix}$$

Hence any vector can be written as a linear combination of $\mathbf{i}$, $\mathbf{j}$ and $\mathbf{k}$.

For example, $\begin{bmatrix} 4 \\ -1 \\ 7 \end{bmatrix} = 4\begin{bmatrix} 1 \\ 0 \\ 0 \end{bmatrix} - \begin{bmatrix} 0 \\ 1 \\ 0 \end{bmatrix} + 7\begin{bmatrix} 0 \\ 0 \\ 1 \end{bmatrix} = 4\mathbf{i} - \mathbf{j} + 7\mathbf{k}$.

**C12** Write $\begin{bmatrix} 2 \\ 6 \\ -5 \end{bmatrix}$ in terms of $\mathbf{i}$, $\mathbf{j}$ and $\mathbf{k}$.

**C13** Write $3\mathbf{i} - 2\mathbf{j} + 8\mathbf{k}$ as a column vector.

**C14** Vectors $\mathbf{p}$, $\mathbf{q}$ and $\mathbf{r}$ are given by $\mathbf{p} = \mathbf{i} + \mathbf{j} + 4\mathbf{k}$, $\mathbf{q} = -2\mathbf{i} + 5\mathbf{j} + \mathbf{k}$ and $\mathbf{r} = 4\mathbf{i} - \mathbf{k}$.

    (a) Show that $|\mathbf{p}| = 3\sqrt{2}$.

    (b) Write the following in terms of $\mathbf{i}$, $\mathbf{j}$ and $\mathbf{k}$.

        (i) $\mathbf{q} + \mathbf{r}$            (ii) $\mathbf{p} - \mathbf{q}$            (iii) $2\mathbf{q} + \mathbf{r}$

    (c) Evaluate $|\mathbf{q} + \mathbf{r}|$ in surd form.

**C15** Show that the vectors $\mathbf{i} + 2\mathbf{j} - 3\mathbf{k}$ and $2\mathbf{i} + 4\mathbf{j} - 6\mathbf{k}$ are parallel.

**Exercise C** (answers p 173)

  **1** Vectors are given by $\mathbf{a} = \begin{bmatrix} 3 \\ 0 \\ -4 \end{bmatrix}$, $\mathbf{b} = \begin{bmatrix} -1 \\ -5 \\ 2 \end{bmatrix}$ and $\mathbf{c} = \begin{bmatrix} -1 \\ 10 \\ 0 \end{bmatrix}$.

    (a) Write each of these as a column vector.

        (i) $\mathbf{c} - \mathbf{b}$            (ii) $2(\mathbf{a} + 3\mathbf{b})$         (iii) $\mathbf{a} + 2\mathbf{b} + \mathbf{c}$

    (b) Evaluate $|2\mathbf{b} + \mathbf{c}|$.

**2** *ABCDEFGH* is a prism.
The coordinates of points *A* to *D* are shown on the diagram.
Vectors $\overrightarrow{AE}$, $\overrightarrow{BF}$, $\overrightarrow{CG}$ and $\overrightarrow{DH}$ are parallel to the *z*-axis and have magnitude 2.

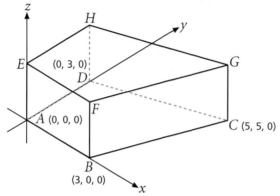

(a) Write each of these as a column vector.

(i) $\overrightarrow{AB}$ (ii) $\overrightarrow{AE}$ (iii) $\overrightarrow{EH}$

(b) By considering the vector addition $\overrightarrow{HB} = \overrightarrow{HE} + \overrightarrow{EA} + \overrightarrow{AB}$, write $\overrightarrow{HB}$ as a column vector.

(c) Write each of these as a column vector.

(i) $\overrightarrow{BG}$ (ii) $\overrightarrow{HC}$ (iii) $\overrightarrow{AG}$ (iv) $\overrightarrow{CE}$

(d) Work out the magnitude of $\overrightarrow{DF}$.

**3** (a) Find the magnitude of the vector $\mathbf{i} + 4\mathbf{j} - 8\mathbf{k}$.

(b) Hence write down the magnitude of the vector $3\mathbf{i} + 12\mathbf{j} - 24\mathbf{k}$.

**4** Sort these into three pairs of parallel vectors.

$$\mathbf{u} = \begin{bmatrix} 1 \\ 3 \\ -4 \end{bmatrix}, \mathbf{v} = \begin{bmatrix} 4 \\ 12 \\ -4 \end{bmatrix}, \mathbf{w} = \begin{bmatrix} 3 \\ 9 \\ 12 \end{bmatrix}, \mathbf{x} = \begin{bmatrix} \frac{1}{2} \\ 1\frac{1}{2} \\ 2 \end{bmatrix}, \mathbf{y} = \begin{bmatrix} 2 \\ 6 \\ -8 \end{bmatrix}, \mathbf{z} = \begin{bmatrix} -1 \\ -3 \\ 1 \end{bmatrix}$$

**5** Vectors **a** and **b** are given by $\mathbf{a} = 2\mathbf{i} - \mathbf{j} + 3\mathbf{k}$ and $\mathbf{b} = \mathbf{i} - 4\mathbf{j} + 4\mathbf{k}$.
Find the vector $4\mathbf{a} - 3\mathbf{b}$ in terms of **i**, **j** and **k**.

**6** Vectors **p** and **q** are parallel.
They are given by $\mathbf{p} = x\mathbf{i} - 9\mathbf{j} + 6\mathbf{k}$ and $\mathbf{q} = 2\mathbf{i} + y\mathbf{j} + 4\mathbf{k}$, where *x* and *y* are constants.
Find the values of *x* and *y*.

**7** The vector $\begin{bmatrix} 5 \\ k \\ 2 \end{bmatrix}$ has a magnitude of $3\sqrt{5}$. Find the two possible values of *k*.

**8** Write down a vector that is parallel to $2\mathbf{i} - 3\mathbf{j} - 6\mathbf{k}$ and has a magnitude of 14.

**\*9** Vectors **a**, **b** and **c** are given by $\mathbf{a} = \mathbf{i} + \mathbf{j} - 2\mathbf{k}$, $\mathbf{b} = 5\mathbf{i} - \mathbf{j} + 3\mathbf{k}$ and $\mathbf{c} = -2\mathbf{i} + \mathbf{j} + \mathbf{k}$.
Show that it is not possible to write **a** as a linear combination of **b** and **c**.

## D Position vectors in two and three dimensions (answers p 174)

For every point $P$ there is associated a unique vector $\overrightarrow{OP}$, where $O$ is the origin.
The vector $\overrightarrow{OP}$ is called the **position vector** of point $P$ and is sometimes written as **p**.

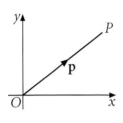
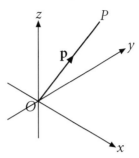

In two dimensions, the point $(x, y)$ has position vector $\begin{bmatrix} x \\ y \end{bmatrix}$ or $x\mathbf{i} + y\mathbf{j}$.

In three dimensions, the point $(x, y, z)$ has position vector $\begin{bmatrix} x \\ y \\ z \end{bmatrix}$ or $x\mathbf{i} + y\mathbf{j} + z\mathbf{k}$.

For example, the point with coordinates $(2, 3)$ has
position vector $\begin{bmatrix} 2 \\ 3 \end{bmatrix}$ or $2\mathbf{i} + 3\mathbf{j}$.

The position vector is fixed with its 'tail'
at the origin as shown.

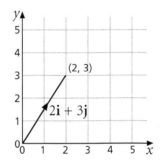

A **free vector** is not fixed to an origin and can be represented by any line of the
correct magnitude and direction.

For example, each of these represents the free vector $2\mathbf{i} + 3\mathbf{j}$.

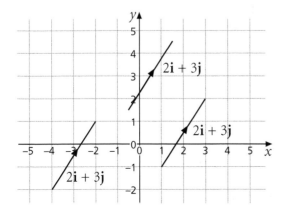

A vector can be used as a position vector or a free vector.

In this diagram point *A* has position vector **a** and point *B* has position vector **b**.
*OAXB* is a parallelogram.

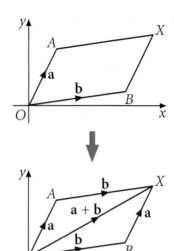

*OAXB* is a parallelogram so $\overrightarrow{BX}$ = **a** and $\overrightarrow{AX}$ = **b**.

The position vector of *X* is $\overrightarrow{OX}$ which is equivalent to $\overrightarrow{OA}$ + $\overrightarrow{AX}$ so the position vector of *X* can be written as **a** + **b**.

**D1** Points *P* and *Q* have position vectors **p** and **q** as shown.

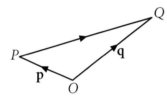

Use the vector addition $\overrightarrow{PQ}$ = $\overrightarrow{PO}$ + $\overrightarrow{OQ}$ to write the vector $\overrightarrow{PQ}$ in terms of **p** and **q**.

The relationship found in D1 is often useful and can be stated as follows.

 If point *A* has position vector **a** (or $\overrightarrow{OA}$) and point *B* has position vector **b** (or $\overrightarrow{OB}$), then $\overrightarrow{AB}$ = **b** − **a** (or $\overrightarrow{OB}$ − $\overrightarrow{OA}$).

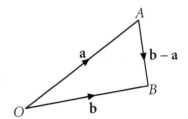

**D2** Two points *X* and *Y* have position vectors **x** = **i** + 6**j** and **y** = 2**i** − 7**j** respectively.

(a) Draw a sketch to show the position of points *X* and *Y*.

(b) What are the coordinates of the point with position vector **x** + **y**?

(c) Use the relationship $\overrightarrow{XY}$ = **y** − **x** to write the vector $\overrightarrow{XY}$ in terms of **i** and **j**.

**D3** Points $M$ and $N$ have position vectors $\mathbf{m}$ and $\mathbf{n}$ as shown.
$P$ is the point on $MN$ such that $MP = \frac{1}{4}MN$.

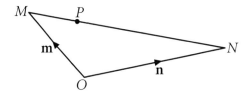

(a) Write $\overrightarrow{MP}$ in terms of $\mathbf{m}$ and $\mathbf{n}$.

(b) Show that the position vector of the point $P$ in terms of $\mathbf{m}$ and $\mathbf{n}$ is $\frac{3}{4}\mathbf{m} + \frac{1}{4}\mathbf{n}$.

**D4** Two points $P$ and $Q$ have position vectors $\mathbf{p} = \begin{bmatrix} 2 \\ -3 \\ 4 \end{bmatrix}$ and $\mathbf{q} = \begin{bmatrix} 0 \\ 5 \\ -2 \end{bmatrix}$.

(a) Write $\overrightarrow{PQ}$ as a column vector.

(b) Calculate the distance between points $P$ and $Q$.

In general, if two points $A$ and $B$ have position vectors $\mathbf{a} = \begin{bmatrix} x_1 \\ y_1 \\ z_1 \end{bmatrix}$ and $\mathbf{b} = \begin{bmatrix} x_2 \\ y_2 \\ z_2 \end{bmatrix}$

then $\overrightarrow{AB} = \mathbf{b} - \mathbf{a} = \begin{bmatrix} x_2 - x_1 \\ y_2 - y_1 \\ z_2 - z_1 \end{bmatrix}$

and $|\overrightarrow{AB}| = \sqrt{(x_2 - x_1)^2 + (y_2 - y_1)^2 + (z_2 - z_1)^2}$

which is the distance between points $A$ and $B$.

---

### Example 2

The points $P$ and $Q$ have position vectors $\mathbf{p} = 2\mathbf{i} - \mathbf{j} - 8\mathbf{k}$ and $\mathbf{q} = 5\mathbf{i} - \mathbf{j} + 4\mathbf{k}$ respectively.
The point $X$ divides $PQ$ such that $PX = \frac{1}{3}PQ$.
Find $|\overrightarrow{OX}|$.

### Solution

$\overrightarrow{PQ} = \mathbf{q} - \mathbf{p} = (5\mathbf{i} - \mathbf{j} + 4\mathbf{k}) - (2\mathbf{i} - \mathbf{j} - 8\mathbf{k})$

$\qquad = 3\mathbf{i} + 12\mathbf{k}$

$\overrightarrow{OX} = \overrightarrow{OP} + \overrightarrow{PX} = \overrightarrow{OP} + \frac{1}{3}\overrightarrow{PQ}$

$\qquad\qquad = (2\mathbf{i} - \mathbf{j} - 8\mathbf{k}) + \frac{1}{3}(3\mathbf{i} + 12\mathbf{k})$

$\qquad\qquad = 2\mathbf{i} - \mathbf{j} - 8\mathbf{k} + \mathbf{i} + 4\mathbf{k}$

$\qquad\qquad = 3\mathbf{i} - \mathbf{j} - 4\mathbf{k}$

So $|\overrightarrow{OX}| = \sqrt{3^2 + (-1)^2 + (-4)^2} = \sqrt{26}$

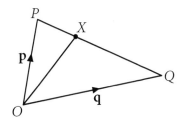

*It is helpful to draw a diagram but it doesn't have to look three-dimensional.*

1 The points $A$ and $B$ have position vectors **a** and **b** respectively.
  The point $P$ divides $AB$ such that $AP = \frac{1}{5}AB$.

  Find, in terms of **a** and **b**, the position vector of $P$.

2 Two points $P$ and $Q$ have position vectors $\mathbf{p} = 2\mathbf{i} - \mathbf{j} - 8\mathbf{k}$ and $\mathbf{q} = 3\mathbf{i} + 4\mathbf{j} - \mathbf{k}$.

  (a) Write $\overrightarrow{PQ}$ as a vector in terms of **i**, **j** and **k**.

  (b) Calculate the distance between $P$ and $Q$.

3 $OABCDEFG$ is a cube with edges of length 4.
  $A$, $C$ and $D$ are points on the $x$-, $y$- and $z$-axes respectively.

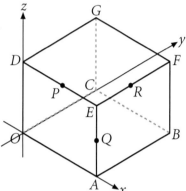

  (a) Using column vector notation, write down
      the position vector of each vertex of the cube.

  (b) Find the vectors $\overrightarrow{AG}$ and $\overrightarrow{BD}$.

  $P$, $Q$ and $R$ are the mid-points of edges $DE$, $AE$ and $EF$.

  (c) Find the position vectors of $P$, $Q$ and $R$.

  (d) (i) Find the vectors $\overrightarrow{PQ}$, $\overrightarrow{QR}$ and $\overrightarrow{RP}$.

      (ii) Calculate the vector addition $\overrightarrow{PQ} + \overrightarrow{QR} + \overrightarrow{RP}$ and comment on your result.

4 Points $A$, $B$, and $C$ have position vectors

  $$\mathbf{a} = 5\mathbf{i} + 5\mathbf{j} + 4\mathbf{k} \qquad \mathbf{b} = 4\mathbf{i} - 7\mathbf{j} + \mathbf{k} \qquad \mathbf{c} = 7\mathbf{i} + 4\mathbf{j} - \mathbf{k}$$

  Show that points $A$, $B$ and $C$ are all on the surface of a sphere whose centre is $(0, 0, 0)$.

5 Points $P$, $Q$, $R$ and $S$ have position vectors

  $$\mathbf{p} = 3\mathbf{i} - \mathbf{j} + 2\mathbf{k} \qquad \mathbf{q} = 2\mathbf{i} + \mathbf{j} + 4\mathbf{k} \qquad \mathbf{r} = 5\mathbf{i} + 2\mathbf{j} - 3\mathbf{k} \qquad \mathbf{s} = 7\mathbf{i} - 2\mathbf{j} - 7\mathbf{k}$$

  Find the vectors $\overrightarrow{PQ}$ and $\overrightarrow{RS}$ and show that they are parallel.

6 Find the distance between each of these pairs of points.

  (a) $A(1, -6, 3)$ and $B(-8, 0, 7)$    (b) $V(5, -4, -7)$ and $W(12, -3, 1)$

7 The points $A$, $B$ and $C$ have position vectors $\mathbf{i} - 2\mathbf{j} + \mathbf{k}$, $10\mathbf{i} + \mathbf{j} + 4\mathbf{k}$ and $4\mathbf{i} - \mathbf{j} + 2\mathbf{k}$ respectively. Prove that $A$, $B$ and $C$ lie on the same straight line.

8 The coordinates of $P$ and $Q$ are $(4, -8, 1)$ and $(2, -2, k)$ respectively.
  Given that $|\overrightarrow{PQ}| = 7$, find the possible values of $k$.

## E The vector equation of a line (answers p 175)

A set of points is defined so that the position vector of each point in the set has the form

$$\begin{bmatrix} x \\ y \end{bmatrix} = \begin{bmatrix} 1 \\ 6 \end{bmatrix} + t \begin{bmatrix} 2 \\ -1 \end{bmatrix} \text{ for all real values of } t$$

For example, when $t = 2$, the position vector is given by $\begin{bmatrix} x \\ y \end{bmatrix} = \begin{bmatrix} 1 \\ 6 \end{bmatrix} + 2 \begin{bmatrix} 2 \\ -1 \end{bmatrix} = \begin{bmatrix} 5 \\ 4 \end{bmatrix}$.

Hence the point with coordinates (5, 4) is in the set.

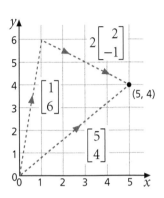

**E1 (a)** Show that $t = 5$ gives the point with position vector $\begin{bmatrix} 11 \\ 1 \end{bmatrix}$.

**(b)** Find the position vector given by each of these values of $t$.

    **(i)** $t = 0$      **(ii)** $t = 1$      **(iii)** $t = -1$      **(iv)** $t = 3$

**(c) (i)** On the same diagram, plot all points defined by the position vectors found so far.

    **(ii)** Explain why all the points lie on a straight line.

    **(iii)** Find the equation of this straight line in the form $ax + by = c$.

All the points given by the expression $\begin{bmatrix} 1 \\ 6 \end{bmatrix} + t \begin{bmatrix} 2 \\ -1 \end{bmatrix}$ lie on a straight line.

Let **r** be the position vector of any point on the line.

Then the equation $\mathbf{r} = \begin{bmatrix} 1 \\ 6 \end{bmatrix} + t \begin{bmatrix} 2 \\ -1 \end{bmatrix}$ is called a **vector equation** of the line.

As $t$ is a number that varies, it is sometimes called a **scalar parameter**.

**E2 (a)** A line has the vector equation $\mathbf{r} = \begin{bmatrix} 3 \\ 5 \end{bmatrix} + s \begin{bmatrix} -2 \\ 1 \end{bmatrix}$, where $s$ is a scalar parameter.

Find the position vector given by each of these values of $s$.

    **(i)** $s = 1$      **(ii)** $s = 0$      **(iii)** $s = -3$      **(iv)** $s = 5$

**(b) (i)** Hence draw the straight line through the points defined by the vector equation.

    **(ii)** Compare this with the line drawn in E1 (c).

    **(iii)** Can you explain what you find?

**K** The vector equation for a straight line is not unique.

For example, both the following diagrams show the straight line with equation $y = x + 3$.

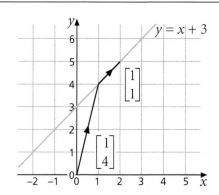

Each point on the line has a position vector that can be written in the form

$$\begin{bmatrix} 1 \\ 4 \end{bmatrix} + s\begin{bmatrix} 1 \\ 1 \end{bmatrix}$$

So $\mathbf{r} = \begin{bmatrix} 1 \\ 4 \end{bmatrix} + s\begin{bmatrix} 1 \\ 1 \end{bmatrix}$ is a vector equation of the line.

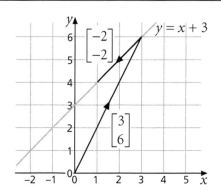

Each point on the line has a position vector that can be written in the form

$$\begin{bmatrix} 3 \\ 6 \end{bmatrix} + t\begin{bmatrix} -2 \\ -2 \end{bmatrix}$$

So $\mathbf{r} = \begin{bmatrix} 3 \\ 6 \end{bmatrix} + t\begin{bmatrix} -2 \\ -2 \end{bmatrix}$ is a vector equation of the line.

**E3** Give a vector equation for each of these lines.

(a) $y = x + 4$         (b) $y = 6 - x$         (c) $y = 2x + 1$

**E4** (a) On the same diagram, sketch the lines $l_1$ and $l_2$ with the following vector equations.

$$l_1: \mathbf{r} = \begin{bmatrix} 1 \\ 3 \end{bmatrix} + \lambda\begin{bmatrix} 1 \\ 2 \end{bmatrix} \qquad l_2: \mathbf{r} = \begin{bmatrix} 5 \\ 2 \end{bmatrix} + \mu\begin{bmatrix} -2 \\ -4 \end{bmatrix}$$

> The Greek letters $\lambda$ (lambda) and $\mu$ (mu) are often used for scalar parameters in vector work.

(b) (i) What do you notice about your lines?

(ii) How could you have predicted this from the vector equations?

**E5** Which of the lines whose vector equations are given below is parallel to the line with vector equation $\mathbf{r} = \begin{bmatrix} 0 \\ 1 \end{bmatrix} + \lambda\begin{bmatrix} 2 \\ 3 \end{bmatrix}$?

$$L_1: \mathbf{r} = \begin{bmatrix} 0 \\ 5 \end{bmatrix} + s\begin{bmatrix} 3 \\ 4 \end{bmatrix} \qquad L_2: \mathbf{r} = \begin{bmatrix} 2 \\ 7 \end{bmatrix} + t\begin{bmatrix} 4 \\ 6 \end{bmatrix} \qquad L_3: \mathbf{r} = \begin{bmatrix} -2 \\ -3 \end{bmatrix} + u\begin{bmatrix} 1 \\ 1 \end{bmatrix}$$

The vector equation of a line in three dimensions is given in a similar way.

The diagram below shows the line with vector equation

$$\mathbf{r} = \begin{bmatrix} 4 \\ 3 \\ 7 \end{bmatrix} + \lambda \begin{bmatrix} 1 \\ 0 \\ -3 \end{bmatrix}$$

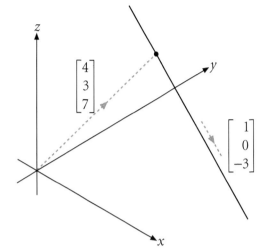

It is more difficult to visualise a line in three dimensions.

**E6** (a) Write down the coordinates of three points on the line above.

(b) The point with position vector $\begin{bmatrix} 9 \\ 3 \\ -8 \end{bmatrix}$ lies on the line.

What value of $\lambda$ gives this position vector?

(c) Show that the point with position vector $\begin{bmatrix} 7 \\ 3 \\ -1 \end{bmatrix}$ does not lie on the line.

We can also use $\mathbf{i}, \mathbf{j}, \mathbf{k}$ notation to write down the vector equation of a line.

For example, we could write the vector equation above in the form

$$\mathbf{r} = 4\mathbf{i} + 3\mathbf{j} + 7\mathbf{k} + \lambda(\mathbf{i} - 3\mathbf{k})$$

**E7** The vector equation of a line is given by

$$\mathbf{r} = \mathbf{i} + 2\mathbf{j} - 3\mathbf{k} + \lambda(2\mathbf{i} - 4\mathbf{j} + \mathbf{k})$$

(a) What position vector is given by $\lambda = 3$?

(b) What value of $\lambda$ gives the position vector $-\mathbf{i} + 6\mathbf{j} - 4\mathbf{k}$?

(c) Show that the point with position vector $3\mathbf{i} - 3\mathbf{j} - 2\mathbf{k}$ does not lie on the line.

**K** The general form of a vector equation of a line is

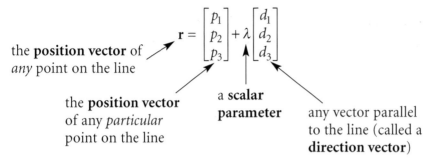

the **position vector** of *any* point on the line

the **position vector** of any *particular* point on the line

a **scalar parameter**

any vector parallel to the line (called a **direction vector**)

Using **i**, **j**, **k** notation this equation is

$$\mathbf{r} = (p_1\mathbf{i} + p_2\mathbf{j} + p_3\mathbf{k}) + \lambda(d_1\mathbf{i} + d_2\mathbf{j} + d_3\mathbf{k})$$

Two lines are parallel if their direction vectors are parallel.

---

## Example 3

Points $A$ and $B$ have position vectors $\begin{bmatrix} 1 \\ 2 \\ -5 \end{bmatrix}$ and $\begin{bmatrix} -5 \\ 6 \\ -3 \end{bmatrix}$ respectively.

Find, in vector form, the equation of the straight line that passes through $A$ and $B$.

## Solution

*The vector $\overrightarrow{AB}$ is a direction vector for the line.*

$$\overrightarrow{AB} = \begin{bmatrix} -5 \\ 6 \\ -3 \end{bmatrix} - \begin{bmatrix} 1 \\ 2 \\ -5 \end{bmatrix}$$   *This is the position vector of B – the position vector of A.*

$$= \begin{bmatrix} -6 \\ 4 \\ 2 \end{bmatrix}$$

$A$ is a point on the line with position vector $\begin{bmatrix} 1 \\ 2 \\ -5 \end{bmatrix}$, so a vector equation is

$$\mathbf{r} = \begin{bmatrix} 1 \\ 2 \\ -5 \end{bmatrix} + \lambda \begin{bmatrix} -6 \\ 4 \\ 2 \end{bmatrix}$$   *You could have written this as* $\mathbf{r} = (\mathbf{i} + 2\mathbf{j} - 5\mathbf{k}) + \lambda(-6\mathbf{i} + 4\mathbf{j} + 2\mathbf{k})$.

*Any scalar multiple of $\overrightarrow{AB}$ is a direction vector for the line so, for example, instead of*

*the direction vector* $\begin{bmatrix} -6 \\ 4 \\ 2 \end{bmatrix}$ *you could have used* $\begin{bmatrix} -3 \\ 2 \\ 1 \end{bmatrix}$ *to obtain* $\mathbf{r} = \begin{bmatrix} 1 \\ 2 \\ -5 \end{bmatrix} + \mu \begin{bmatrix} -3 \\ 2 \\ 1 \end{bmatrix}$.

---

Sometimes it can be useful to write a vector equation in a slightly different form, as the following examples show.

**Example 4**

A line has a vector equation given by $\mathbf{r} = -2\mathbf{i} + \mathbf{j} + 5\mathbf{k} + \lambda(\mathbf{i} - 3\mathbf{j} + 2\mathbf{k})$.

Show that the point $P$ with position vector $3\mathbf{i} - 14\mathbf{j} + 15\mathbf{k}$ is on this line.

**Solution**

*Rewrite the vector equation.*

$$\mathbf{r} = -2\mathbf{i} + \mathbf{j} + 5\mathbf{k} + \lambda(\mathbf{i} - 3\mathbf{j} + 2\mathbf{k})$$
$$= -2\mathbf{i} + \mathbf{j} + 5\mathbf{k} + \lambda\mathbf{i} - 3\lambda\mathbf{j} + 2\lambda\mathbf{k}$$
$$= (-2 + \lambda)\mathbf{i} + (1 - 3\lambda)\mathbf{j} + (5 + 2\lambda)\mathbf{k}$$

We need to find a value of $\lambda$ such that

$$(-2 + \lambda)\mathbf{i} + (1 - 3\lambda)\mathbf{j} + (5 + 2\lambda)\mathbf{k} = 3\mathbf{i} - 14\mathbf{j} + 15\mathbf{k}$$

Equating coefficients of $\mathbf{i}$ gives

$$-2 + \lambda = 3$$
$$\Rightarrow \qquad \lambda = 5$$

This gives $1 - 3\lambda = 1 - 3 \times 5 = -14$ which is the required coefficient of $\mathbf{j}$

and $5 + 2\lambda = 5 + 2 \times 5 = 15$ which is the required coefficient of $\mathbf{k}$

Hence $P$ is on the line.

---

A vector equation of a line can be given in the form $\begin{bmatrix} x \\ y \\ z \end{bmatrix} = \begin{bmatrix} p_1 \\ p_2 \\ p_3 \end{bmatrix} + \lambda \begin{bmatrix} d_1 \\ d_2 \\ d_3 \end{bmatrix}$.

---

**Example 5**

A line has the vector equation $\begin{bmatrix} x \\ y \\ z \end{bmatrix} = \begin{bmatrix} -1 \\ 1 \\ -3 \end{bmatrix} + t \begin{bmatrix} 2 \\ -2 \\ 5 \end{bmatrix}$, where $t$ is a scalar parameter.

The point $P$ lies on this line and has coordinates $(5, a, b)$, where $a$ and $b$ are constants. Find the values of $a$ and $b$.

**Solution**

$$\begin{bmatrix} x \\ y \\ z \end{bmatrix} = \begin{bmatrix} -1 \\ 1 \\ -3 \end{bmatrix} + t \begin{bmatrix} 2 \\ -2 \\ 5 \end{bmatrix} = \begin{bmatrix} -1 + 2t \\ 1 - 2t \\ -3 + 5t \end{bmatrix}$$

$P$ has position vector $\begin{bmatrix} 5 \\ a \\ b \end{bmatrix}$ and lies on the line so $\begin{bmatrix} -1 + 2t \\ 1 - 2t \\ -3 + 5t \end{bmatrix} = \begin{bmatrix} 5 \\ a \\ b \end{bmatrix}$ for some $t$.

Equating the $x$-values, $-1 + 2t = 5$ which gives $t = 3$.

When $t = 3$, $a = 1 - 2t = -5$
$$b = -3 + 5t = 12.$$

Hence $a = -5$ and $b = 12$.

**1** In two dimensions, find vector equations for

(a) the line joining the points $(0, 5)$ and $(1, 9)$

(b) the $x$-axis

(c) the line joining the points with position vectors $\begin{bmatrix} 5 \\ -2 \end{bmatrix}$ and $\begin{bmatrix} 6 \\ -7 \end{bmatrix}$

**2** In three dimensions, find vector equations for

(a) the line through the point $(-1, 3, 5)$, parallel to the vector $\begin{bmatrix} -1 \\ 1 \\ -3 \end{bmatrix}$

(b) the line through the points $(2, 1, 0)$ and $(3, 4, 4)$

(c) the $z$-axis

(d) the line joining the points with position vectors $2\mathbf{i} - 4\mathbf{j} + 7\mathbf{k}$ and $-\mathbf{i} + 2\mathbf{j} - \mathbf{k}$

**3** A line has a vector equation given by $\mathbf{r} = \mathbf{i} - 3\mathbf{j} + 2\mathbf{k} + \lambda(2\mathbf{i} + 4\mathbf{j} - 6\mathbf{k})$.
Show that the point with position vector $2\mathbf{i} - \mathbf{j} - \mathbf{k}$ is on this line.

**4** Points $A$ and $B$ have position vectors $\begin{bmatrix} 3 \\ 1 \\ 2 \end{bmatrix}$ and $\begin{bmatrix} 11 \\ -1 \\ -2 \end{bmatrix}$.

(a) Find, in vector form, an equation of the line that passes through $A$ and $B$.

(b) Show that the line intersects the $x$-axis.

**5** Points $P$ and $Q$ have position vectors $-2\mathbf{i} + \mathbf{j}$ and $4\mathbf{i} + 4\mathbf{k}$.

(a) Find, in vector form, an equation of the line that passes through $P$ and $Q$.

(b) Show that the line does not intersect the $y$-axis.

**6** Referred to a fixed origin $O$ (an airport), the position vector of aircraft $A$,
$t$ minutes after take-off, is given by the vector equation

$$\begin{bmatrix} x \\ y \\ z \end{bmatrix} = t \begin{bmatrix} 1 \\ 5 \\ 0.8 \end{bmatrix}$$

where the position of the aircraft is $x$ km east and $y$ km north, at a height of $z$ km.

(a) Find the position vector of aircraft $A$ after 10 minutes.

The position vector of aircraft $B$ at the same time, $t$ minutes, is given by
the vector equation

$$\begin{bmatrix} x \\ y \\ z \end{bmatrix} = \begin{bmatrix} 5 \\ 0 \\ 4 \end{bmatrix} + t \begin{bmatrix} 0 \\ 5 \\ 0 \end{bmatrix}$$

(b) After 3 minutes, how far is aircraft $B$ from $O$, correct to the nearest 0.1 km?

(c) How far apart are the aircraft after 4 minutes?

(d) How far apart are the aircraft after 5 minutes?
What does this mean?

**7** The points $A$ and $B$ have coordinates $(3, 0, -1)$ and $(-5, 2, 1)$ respectively.
The point $C$ lies on the line through these points and has coordinates $(p, 5, q)$,
where $p$ and $q$ are constants.
Find the values of $p$ and $q$.

**8** A vector equation for a straight line is $\begin{bmatrix} x \\ y \end{bmatrix} = \begin{bmatrix} 4 \\ 7 \end{bmatrix} + \lambda \begin{bmatrix} 1 \\ -2 \end{bmatrix}$.

The line intersects a circle that has centre $(0, 0)$ and radius $5\sqrt{2}$.
Find the coordinates of the points of intersection.

**9** A vector equation for a straight line is $\mathbf{r} = 4\mathbf{i} + \mathbf{j} + 2\mathbf{k} + \lambda(\mathbf{i} + \mathbf{j})$.
The line intersects a hollow sphere that has centre $(0, 0, 0)$ and radius $3$.
Find the coordinates of the points of intersection.

## F Intersecting lines (answers p 176)

In two dimensions, there are three possible relationships between two straight lines.

They are parallel.        They intersect at one point.        They are the same line.

**F1** Two lines are given by these vector equations, where $\lambda$ and $\mu$ are scalar parameters.

$$\begin{bmatrix} x \\ y \end{bmatrix} = \begin{bmatrix} 1 \\ -3 \end{bmatrix} + \lambda \begin{bmatrix} 1 \\ 1 \end{bmatrix} \qquad \begin{bmatrix} x \\ y \end{bmatrix} = \begin{bmatrix} 11 \\ 1 \end{bmatrix} + \mu \begin{bmatrix} 1 \\ -2 \end{bmatrix}$$

(a) Show that, if the lines intersect, there must be values of $\lambda$ and $\mu$ that satisfy
these simultaneous equations.

$$1 + \lambda = 11 + \mu$$
$$-3 + \lambda = 1 - 2\mu$$

(b) Solve the equations to find the values of $\lambda$ and $\mu$.

(c) What is the position vector of the point of intersection?

(d) Why are two different parameters, $\lambda$ and $\mu$, used in the vector equations?

**F2** Two lines are given by these vector equations, where $\lambda$ and $\mu$ are scalar parameters.

$$\mathbf{r} = \begin{bmatrix} 0 \\ 2 \end{bmatrix} + \lambda \begin{bmatrix} 2 \\ 1 \end{bmatrix} \qquad \mathbf{r} = \begin{bmatrix} 3 \\ 1 \end{bmatrix} + \mu \begin{bmatrix} 4 \\ 2 \end{bmatrix}$$

(a) Show that, if the lines intersect, there must be values of $\lambda$ and $\mu$ that satisfy
these simultaneous equations.

$$2\lambda = 3 + 4\mu$$
$$2 + \lambda = 1 + 2\mu$$

(b) What happens if you try to find the values of $\lambda$ and $\mu$?
Can you explain this?

**3** Find the angle between the vectors $\mathbf{i} + 8\mathbf{j} + 5\mathbf{k}$ and $-3\mathbf{i} - \mathbf{j} + 4\mathbf{k}$.

**4** Triangle $PQR$ is defined by points $P(5, -3, 1)$, $Q(-2, 1, 5)$ and $R(9, 5, 0)$.
Find the angles of the triangle.

**5** Show that, for any vector $\mathbf{a} = \begin{bmatrix} a_1 \\ a_2 \\ a_3 \end{bmatrix}$, $\mathbf{a}.\mathbf{a} = |\mathbf{a}|^2$.

**6** Vectors $\mathbf{a}$ and $\mathbf{b}$ are such that $|\mathbf{a}| = 3$, $|\mathbf{b}| = 4$ and $\mathbf{a}.\mathbf{b} = 12$.
What can you say about vectors $\mathbf{a}$ and $\mathbf{b}$?

**7** Show that $(0, 0, 0)$, $(4, -2, 5)$, $(3, 6, 0)$ and $(7, 4, 5)$ are four vertices of a square.

## H The angle between two straight lines (answers p 178)

In two dimensions, the acute angle $\theta$ between two intersecting straight lines is clearly defined as shown.

The obtuse angle between them is $180 - \theta$.

Where two straight line segments in two dimensions do not intersect, the acute angle between them is defined as the angle between the extended lines as shown.

In three dimensions, defining the angles between two straight lines is more complicated.

Where two straight lines intersect, an angle between them is clearly defined.

For example, in the cuboid $ABCDEFGH$ the lines $AG$ and $HB$ intersect and one of the angles between them is $\theta$ as shown.

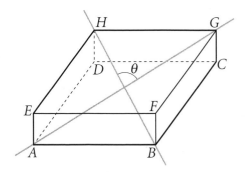

**H1** (a) Do the lines $AC$ and $HB$ intersect?

(b) How would you define an angle between these lines?

**H2** What is the angle between the lines through $EF$ and $GC$?

To find the acute (or obtuse) angle between two skew lines, translate the lines until they intersect and then find the acute (or obtuse) angle between them.

**H3** $PQRSTUVW$ is a cube.
Find the acute angles between these pairs of lines.

(a) $WS$ and $UV$     (b) $TS$ and $QR$

(c) $WP$ and $UR$     (d) $TS$ and $PR$

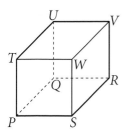

K An angle between two straight lines can be found by finding the angle between any two direction vectors for the lines.

### Example 9

*ABCDEFGH* is a cuboid.
The coordinates of *A*, *F*, *G* and *H* are shown.

Find the acute angle between the line through *A* and *G* and the line through *H* and *F*.

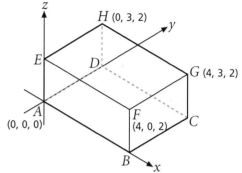

### Solution

$\overrightarrow{AG}$ is a direction vector for the line through *A* and *G*.
$\overrightarrow{HF}$ is a direction vector for the line through *H* and *F*.
Let $\theta$ be the angle between the direction vectors.

$$\overrightarrow{AG} = \begin{bmatrix} 4 \\ 3 \\ 2 \end{bmatrix} \text{ and } \overrightarrow{HF} = \begin{bmatrix} 4 \\ 0 \\ 2 \end{bmatrix} - \begin{bmatrix} 0 \\ 3 \\ 2 \end{bmatrix} = \begin{bmatrix} 4 \\ -3 \\ 0 \end{bmatrix}$$

$$\overrightarrow{AG}.\overrightarrow{HF} = \begin{bmatrix} 4 \\ 3 \\ 2 \end{bmatrix} . \begin{bmatrix} 4 \\ -3 \\ 0 \end{bmatrix} = (4 \times 4) + (3 \times -3) + (2 \times 0) = 7$$

The magnitude of $\overrightarrow{AG}$ is $\sqrt{4^2 + 3^2 + 2^2} = \sqrt{29}$

The magnitude of $\overrightarrow{HF}$ is $\sqrt{4^2 + (-3)^2 + 0^2} = \sqrt{25} = 5$

So $\cos\theta = \dfrac{7}{5\sqrt{29}} = 0.25997...$

So the angle between these direction vectors is 74.9° (correct to 1 d.p.).

Hence the acute angle between the lines is 74.9°.

---

D **H4** The equations of two lines $l_1$ and $l_2$ are given by

$$l_1 : \mathbf{r} = \begin{bmatrix} -2 \\ -11 \\ 17 \end{bmatrix} + \lambda \begin{bmatrix} 3 \\ 5 \\ -1 \end{bmatrix} \qquad l_2 : \mathbf{r} = \begin{bmatrix} 9 \\ 7 \\ 0 \end{bmatrix} + \mu \begin{bmatrix} 1 \\ 2 \\ 13 \end{bmatrix}$$

How can you show that these lines are perpendicular?

## Example 10

The equations of two lines $l_1$ and $l_2$ are given by

$$l_1: \mathbf{r} = \begin{bmatrix} 1 \\ 0 \\ 2 \end{bmatrix} + \lambda \begin{bmatrix} 1 \\ 2 \\ 5 \end{bmatrix} \qquad l_2: \mathbf{r} = \begin{bmatrix} -1 \\ 7 \\ 6 \end{bmatrix} + \mu \begin{bmatrix} 3 \\ -5 \\ 1 \end{bmatrix}$$

Find the acute angle between the two lines.

### Solution

The scalar product of the direction vectors is $\begin{bmatrix} 1 \\ 2 \\ 5 \end{bmatrix} \cdot \begin{bmatrix} 3 \\ -5 \\ 1 \end{bmatrix} = (1 \times 3) + (2 \times -5) + (5 \times 1)$

$$= 3 - 10 + 5$$
$$= -2$$

The magnitude of the direction vector for $l_1$ is $\sqrt{1^2 + 2^2 + 5^2} = \sqrt{30}$

The magnitude of the direction vector for $l_2$ is $\sqrt{3^2 + (-5)^2 + 1^2} = \sqrt{35}$

Let $\theta$ be the angle between the direction vectors.

So $\cos \theta = \dfrac{-2}{\sqrt{30}\sqrt{35}} = -0.0617...$

So the angle between these direction vectors is 93.5° (correct to 1 d.p.)

Hence the acute angle between the lines is $180 - 93.5° = 86.5°$ (correct to 1 d.p.)

## Example 11

The equations of two lines $l_1$ and $l_2$ are given by

$$l_1: \mathbf{r} = 2\mathbf{i} - \mathbf{j} + 6\mathbf{k} + \lambda(-2\mathbf{i} - 4\mathbf{j} + 5\mathbf{k}) \qquad l_2: \mathbf{r} = 6\mathbf{i} + \mathbf{j} - \mathbf{k} + \lambda(-11\mathbf{i} + 3\mathbf{j} - 2\mathbf{k})$$

Show that the lines are perpendicular.

### Solution

The scalar product of the direction vectors is $\quad (-2\mathbf{i} - 4\mathbf{j} + 5\mathbf{k}).(-11\mathbf{i} + 3\mathbf{j} - 2\mathbf{k})$
$$= (-2 \times -11) + (-4 \times 3) + (5 \times -2)$$
$$= 22 - 12 - 10$$
$$= 0$$

Hence the lines are perpendicular.

## Exercise H (answers p 178)

**1** *ABCDEF* is a prism where *ABE* and *CDF* are equilateral triangles and each other face is a square.

Find the acute angles between these pairs of lines.

(a) *AB* and *FC*      (b) *AE* and *FC*

(c) *DB* and *EF*      (d) *AD* and *FC*

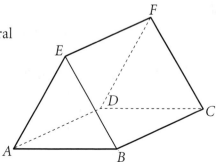

**2** The coordinates of each vertex in the network *PQRST* are shown.

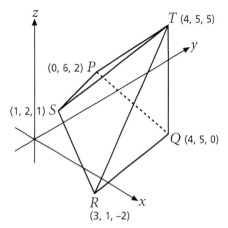

Find the acute angle between the lines *TS* and *QR*.

**3** Show that the following two lines are perpendicular.

$$\mathbf{r} = \begin{bmatrix} 2 \\ 3 \\ -1 \end{bmatrix} + \lambda \begin{bmatrix} 3 \\ -6 \\ 0 \end{bmatrix} \qquad \mathbf{r} = \begin{bmatrix} -2 \\ -7 \\ 6 \end{bmatrix} + \mu \begin{bmatrix} 2 \\ 1 \\ -3 \end{bmatrix}$$

**4** The equations of two lines $l_1$ and $l_2$ are given by

$$l_1: \mathbf{r} = \begin{bmatrix} -3 \\ 0 \\ 2 \end{bmatrix} + \lambda \begin{bmatrix} 2 \\ 3 \\ -1 \end{bmatrix} \qquad l_2: \mathbf{r} = \begin{bmatrix} 4 \\ 8 \\ 1 \end{bmatrix} + \mu \begin{bmatrix} -5 \\ 2 \\ -1 \end{bmatrix}$$

Find the acute angle between the lines.

**5** The equations of two lines $l_1$ and $l_2$ are given by

$$l_1: \mathbf{r} = 7\mathbf{i} + \mathbf{j} + 3\mathbf{k} + \lambda(3\mathbf{i} - 4\mathbf{j} + 2\mathbf{k})$$
$$l_2: \mathbf{r} = -6\mathbf{i} - \mathbf{j} + 3\mathbf{k} + \mu(5\mathbf{i} + 3\mathbf{j} - \mathbf{k})$$

Find the acute angle between the lines.

## I Shortest distance (answers p 179)

**I1** In this diagram, point *A* is fixed and *P* is any point on the straight line. $\theta$ is the angle between *AP* and the line.

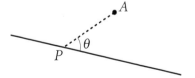

What can you say about $\theta$ when *P* is as close as possible to *A*?

**K** The shortest distance from a point to a line is always the distance along the perpendicular from the point to the line.

It is often useful to be able to find this shortest distance and the coordinates of the **foot** of the perpendicular, that is the point where it intersects the line.

The following example in two dimensions illustrates the technique of using the scalar product to find this shortest distance.

---

### Example 12

Find the shortest distance from the point $A\,(4, 7)$ to the line with equation $\mathbf{r} = \begin{bmatrix} 1 \\ 0 \end{bmatrix} + \lambda \begin{bmatrix} 5 \\ 2 \end{bmatrix}$.

**Solution**

Let $P$ be the point on the line that is closest to $A$.

As $P$ is on the line then there must be some

value of $\lambda$ for which $\overrightarrow{OP} = \begin{bmatrix} 1 + 5\lambda \\ 2\lambda \end{bmatrix}$.

$$\overrightarrow{AP} = \overrightarrow{OP} - \overrightarrow{OA} = \begin{bmatrix} 1 + 5\lambda \\ 2\lambda \end{bmatrix} - \begin{bmatrix} 4 \\ 7 \end{bmatrix} = \begin{bmatrix} 5\lambda - 3 \\ 2\lambda - 7 \end{bmatrix}$$

The direction of the line is given by the vector $\begin{bmatrix} 5 \\ 2 \end{bmatrix}$ and

we know that $\overrightarrow{AP}$ must be perpendicular to this vector. So the scalar product of these vectors must be 0.

$$\begin{bmatrix} 5\lambda - 3 \\ 2\lambda - 7 \end{bmatrix} \cdot \begin{bmatrix} 5 \\ 2 \end{bmatrix} = 0$$

$$\Rightarrow \quad 5(5\lambda - 3) + 2(2\lambda - 7) = 0$$

$$\Rightarrow \quad\quad\quad\quad 29\lambda - 29 = 0$$

$$\Rightarrow \quad\quad\quad\quad\quad\quad \lambda = 1$$

So $\overrightarrow{AP} = \begin{bmatrix} 5 \times 1 - 3 \\ 2 \times 1 - 7 \end{bmatrix} = \begin{bmatrix} 2 \\ -5 \end{bmatrix}$

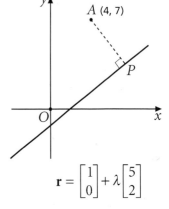

$\mathbf{r} = \begin{bmatrix} 1 \\ 0 \end{bmatrix} + \lambda \begin{bmatrix} 5 \\ 2 \end{bmatrix}$

*A sketch can help you think more clearly about which vectors you need to consider at each stage.*

The shortest distance from $A$ to the line, $|\overrightarrow{AP}|$, is $\sqrt{2^2 + (-5)^2} = \sqrt{29}$.

---

### Example 13

Find the coordinates of the foot of the perpendicular from the point $A\,(10, 9, 11)$ to

the line with equation $\mathbf{r} = \begin{bmatrix} 1 \\ 0 \\ 2 \end{bmatrix} + \lambda \begin{bmatrix} 2 \\ 2 \\ -1 \end{bmatrix}$.

**Solution**

Let $P$ be the foot of the perpendicular from $A$ to the line.

As $P$ is on the line then there must be some value of $\lambda$ for which $\overrightarrow{OP} = \begin{bmatrix} 1 + 2\lambda \\ 2\lambda \\ 2 - \lambda \end{bmatrix}$

where $O$ is the origin $(0, 0, 0)$.

$$\overrightarrow{AP} = \overrightarrow{OP} - \overrightarrow{OA} = \begin{bmatrix} 1 + 2\lambda \\ 2\lambda \\ 2 - \lambda \end{bmatrix} - \begin{bmatrix} 10 \\ 9 \\ 11 \end{bmatrix} = \begin{bmatrix} 2\lambda - 9 \\ 2\lambda - 9 \\ -\lambda - 9 \end{bmatrix}$$

The direction of the line is given by the vector $\begin{bmatrix} 2 \\ 2 \\ -1 \end{bmatrix}$ and we know that $\overrightarrow{AP}$ must be perpendicular to this vector. So the scalar product of these vectors must be 0, that is

$$\begin{bmatrix} 2\lambda - 9 \\ 2\lambda - 9 \\ -\lambda - 9 \end{bmatrix} \cdot \begin{bmatrix} 2 \\ 2 \\ -1 \end{bmatrix} = 0$$

$$\Rightarrow \qquad 2(2\lambda - 9) + 2(2\lambda - 9) - (-\lambda - 9) = 0$$

$$\Rightarrow \qquad\qquad\qquad 9\lambda - 27 = 0$$

$$\Rightarrow \qquad\qquad\qquad\qquad \lambda = 3$$

So $\overrightarrow{OP} = \begin{bmatrix} 1 + 2 \times 3 \\ 2 \times 3 \\ 2 - 3 \end{bmatrix} = \begin{bmatrix} 7 \\ 6 \\ -1 \end{bmatrix}$ and so the coordinates of $P$ are $(7, 6, -1)$.

---

**Exercise I** (answers p 179)

**1** $O$ is the origin $(0, 0)$.
The point $P$ lies on the line $\mathbf{r} = \begin{bmatrix} 5 \\ 4 \end{bmatrix} + \lambda \begin{bmatrix} -1 \\ 3 \end{bmatrix}$ such that $\overrightarrow{OP}$ is perpendicular to the line.
Find the coordinates of $P$.

**2** A line has vector equation $\mathbf{r} = \begin{bmatrix} 6 \\ 1 \end{bmatrix} + t \begin{bmatrix} -2 \\ 1 \end{bmatrix}$.

The point $X$ has coordinates $(-3, 3)$.
Find the coordinates of the foot of the perpendicular from $X$ to the line.

**3** Find the shortest distance from the point $(11, 7)$ to the line $\begin{bmatrix} x \\ y \end{bmatrix} = \begin{bmatrix} 2 \\ 0 \end{bmatrix} + \lambda \begin{bmatrix} 1 \\ 3 \end{bmatrix}$.

**4** $O$ is the origin $(0, 0, 0)$.

The point $M$ lies on the line $\mathbf{r} = \begin{bmatrix} 5 \\ 0 \\ -1 \end{bmatrix} + \lambda \begin{bmatrix} 2 \\ -1 \\ 3 \end{bmatrix}$ such that $\overrightarrow{OM}$ is perpendicular to the line.

Find the coordinates of $M$.

**5** The point $Q$ has coordinates $(9, 3, 12)$.

The point $P$ lies on the line $\mathbf{r} = \begin{bmatrix} 3 \\ 0 \\ 1 \end{bmatrix} + \mu \begin{bmatrix} 0 \\ 3 \\ 1 \end{bmatrix}$ such that $\overrightarrow{QP}$ is perpendicular to the line.

Find the length of $\overrightarrow{QP}$.

**6** A line has vector equation $\mathbf{r} = \begin{bmatrix} -1 \\ 1 \\ 2 \end{bmatrix} + t \begin{bmatrix} 2 \\ 0 \\ 1 \end{bmatrix}$.

The point $A$ has coordinates $(2, -3, 1)$.
Find the coordinates of the foot of the perpendicular from $A$ to the line.

**7** The points $A(2, 0, -3)$, $B(5, 3, 3)$ and $C(3, 1, 2)$ are three vertices of a triangle.

   **(a)** Find a vector equation for the line joining $A$ and $B$.

   **(b)** Find the length $AB$.

   **(c)** Find the shortest distance from $C$ to $AB$, and hence find the area of the triangle.

---

## Key points

- A vector is a quantity that has both magnitude and direction.
  Vectors with the same magnitude and direction are equal.     (pp 98–99)

- The modulus of a vector is its magnitude.
  The modulus of the vector **a** is written $|\mathbf{a}|$.     (p 99)

- Any vector parallel to the vector **a** may be written as $\lambda\mathbf{a}$, where $\lambda$ is a non-zero real number, and is sometimes called a scalar multiple of **a**.
  In particular, $-\mathbf{a}$ has the same magnitude but is in the opposite direction to **a**.     (p 99)

- Vectors can be added and subtracted using the 'triangle law'.

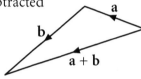

    (pp 99–100)

- Vectors can be written in column vector form such as $\begin{bmatrix} 3 \\ -7 \\ 1 \end{bmatrix}$. $\quad\longleftarrow\quad$ $x$-component, $y$-component, $z$-component     (p 106)

- A unit vector is a vector with a magnitude (or modulus) of 1.
  The vectors **i**, **j** and **k** are unit vectors in the direction of the $x$-, $y$- and $z$-axes respectively.
  As column vectors: $\mathbf{i} = \begin{bmatrix} 1 \\ 0 \\ 0 \end{bmatrix}$, $\mathbf{j} = \begin{bmatrix} 0 \\ 1 \\ 0 \end{bmatrix}$, $\mathbf{k} = \begin{bmatrix} 0 \\ 0 \\ 1 \end{bmatrix}$
  Vectors can be written as linear combinations of these unit vectors.
  For example, $\begin{bmatrix} 3 \\ -7 \\ 1 \end{bmatrix} = 3\mathbf{i} - 7\mathbf{j} + \mathbf{k}$.     (p 109)

- The magnitude (or modulus) of the vector $x\mathbf{i} + y\mathbf{j} + z\mathbf{k}$ is $\sqrt{x^2 + y^2 + z^2}$.
  The distance between two points $(x_1, y_1, z_1)$ and $(x_2, y_2, z_2)$ is
  $$\sqrt{(x_2 - x_1)^2 + (y_2 - y_1)^2 + (z_2 - z_1)^2}.$$     (pp 108, 113)

- For every point $P$ there is associated a unique vector $OP$ (where $O$ is a fixed origin) which is called the **position vector** of the point $P$: it is sometimes written as **p**.

  The point with coordinates $(x, y, z)$ has position vector $\begin{bmatrix} x \\ y \\ z \end{bmatrix}$ or $x\mathbf{i} + y\mathbf{j} + z\mathbf{k}$. (p 111)

- For two points $A$ and $B$ with position vectors $\overrightarrow{OA}$ and $\overrightarrow{OB}$ respectively, the vector $\overrightarrow{AB}$ is given by $\overrightarrow{OB} - \overrightarrow{OA}$. (p 112)

- The general form of a vector equation of a line is

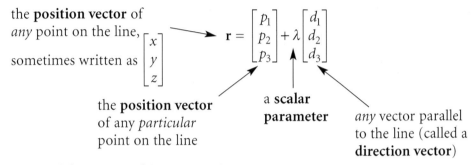

the **position vector** of *any* point on the line, sometimes written as $\begin{bmatrix} x \\ y \\ z \end{bmatrix}$ → $\mathbf{r} = \begin{bmatrix} p_1 \\ p_2 \\ p_3 \end{bmatrix} + \lambda \begin{bmatrix} d_1 \\ d_2 \\ d_3 \end{bmatrix}$

the **position vector** of any *particular* point on the line

a **scalar parameter**

*any* vector parallel to the line (called a **direction vector**)

  Using **i**, **j**, **k** notation this equation is
  $$\mathbf{r} = (p_1\mathbf{i} + p_2\mathbf{j} + p_3\mathbf{k}) + \lambda(d_1\mathbf{i} + d_2\mathbf{j} + d_3\mathbf{k})$$ (p 118)

- Lines are parallel if their direction vectors are parallel. (p 118)

- In three dimensions, a pair of lines may be parallel, intersecting or skew. Skew lines are not parallel but nor do they intersect. (p 122)

- To show that two straight lines intersect, find values of the parameters in their vector equations that produce the same point on each line. If no such values can be found then the lines are skew. (pp 121–123)

- The angle $\theta$ between two vectors is defined as the one formed when the vectors are placed 'tail to tail' or 'head to head' so that $0 \leq \theta \leq 180°$.

(p 125)

- For two vectors $\mathbf{a} = \begin{bmatrix} a_1 \\ a_2 \\ a_3 \end{bmatrix}$ and $\mathbf{b} = \begin{bmatrix} b_1 \\ b_2 \\ b_3 \end{bmatrix}$,

  the scalar product is written as **a.b** and is defined as
  $$\mathbf{a.b} = a_1b_1 + a_2b_2 + a_3b_3$$

  or $\quad \mathbf{a.b} = |\mathbf{a}||\mathbf{b}|\cos\theta$ (where $\theta$ is the angle between the vectors)

  Hence the angle between two vectors is given by $\cos\theta = \dfrac{a_1b_1 + a_2b_2 + a_3b_3}{|\mathbf{a}||\mathbf{b}|}$. (p 126)

- Vectors **a** and **b** are perpendicular if and only if $\mathbf{a.b} = 0$. (p 127)

- One angle between two straight lines is the angle between their direction vectors. (p 129)

## Mixed questions (answers p 179)

**1** The equations of the lines $l_1$ and $l_2$ are given by

$$l_1: \mathbf{r} = \begin{bmatrix} 2 \\ 1 \\ 0 \end{bmatrix} + \lambda \begin{bmatrix} 1 \\ 1 \\ -2 \end{bmatrix} \qquad\qquad l_2: \mathbf{r} = \begin{bmatrix} 5 \\ 2 \\ -1 \end{bmatrix} + \mu \begin{bmatrix} 2 \\ 0 \\ 1 \end{bmatrix}$$

where $\lambda$ and $\mu$ are parameters.

(a) Show that $l_1$ and $l_2$ intersect and find the coordinates of $B$, their point of intersection.

(b) Show that $l_1$ is perpendicular to $l_2$.

(c) Show that the point $A$ with coordinates $(1, 0, 2)$ lies on the line $l_1$.

(d) The point $C$ lies on the line $l_2$ and has coordinates $(1, p, q)$, where $p$ and $q$ are constants. Find the values of $p$ and $q$.

(e) Find, in its simplest form, the exact area of the triangle $ABC$.

**2** The points $A$ and $B$ have coordinates $(1, 1, -2)$ and $(2, -3, 0)$ respectively.

(a) Find, in vector form, an equation of the line $l_1$ that passes through $A$ and $B$.

The line $l_2$ passes through the origin and the point $C$ with coordinates $(7, -3, 8)$.

(b) Using a different scalar parameter from the one used in part (a), find a vector equation for $l_2$.

(c) Show that lines $l_1$ and $l_2$ are skew.

(d) Find the shortest distance from $C$ to $l_1$.

**3** Relative to a fixed origin $O$, points $A$, $B$ and $C$ have position vectors $-4\mathbf{i} - 3\mathbf{j} + 7\mathbf{k}$, $5\mathbf{i} + 4\mathbf{k}$ and $p\mathbf{i} + \mathbf{j} + q\mathbf{k}$ respectively, where $p$ and $q$ are constants.

(a) Find in vector form, an equation of the line $l$ which passes through $A$ and $B$.

The point $C$ lies on $l$.

(b) Find the value of $p$ and the value of $q$.

(c) Calculate, in degrees, the acute angle between $OC$ and $AB$.

Point $D$ lies on $AB$ and is such that $OD$ is perpendicular to $AB$.

(d) Find the position vector of $D$.

**4** (a) Find the vector equation of the line $l_1$ through the points $A\,(2, 1, 1)$ and $B\,(3, 1, 0)$.

(b) The line $l_2$ has equation $\mathbf{r} = \begin{bmatrix} 0 \\ 3 \\ -1 \end{bmatrix} + \mu \begin{bmatrix} -2 \\ 1 \\ 0 \end{bmatrix}$.

Show that $l_1$ and $l_2$ intersect and find the coordinates of their point of intersection.

(c) Show that the point $C\,(-8, 7, -1)$ lies on $l_2$.

(d) Find the coordinates of the point $D$ on $l_1$ such that $CD$ is perpendicular to $l_1$.

**5** Find the acute angle between the two lines that have vector equations given by

$$\mathbf{r} = \mathbf{i} + 2\mathbf{k} + \lambda(-\mathbf{i} + 5\mathbf{j} + 2\mathbf{k}) \quad \text{and} \quad \mathbf{r} = 2\mathbf{i} - \mathbf{j} + 5\mathbf{k} + \mu(3\mathbf{i} - 2\mathbf{j} + 6\mathbf{k})$$

**Test yourself** (answers p 180)

**1** The line $l_1$ has equation $\mathbf{r} = \begin{bmatrix} 1 \\ 0 \\ -2 \end{bmatrix} + \lambda \begin{bmatrix} 1 \\ 4 \\ 3 \end{bmatrix}$.

The line $l_2$ has equation $\mathbf{r} = \begin{bmatrix} 5 \\ 5 \\ 10 \end{bmatrix} + \mu \begin{bmatrix} 2 \\ -3 \\ 6 \end{bmatrix}$.

(a) Show that the lines $l_1$ and $l_2$ intersect at a point $P$ and find the position vector of $P$.

(b) Find the acute angle between the lines $l_1$ and $l_2$, giving your answer to the nearest degree.

(c) The line $l_3$ passes through the point $(0, 0, 0)$ and $(2, 8, 6)$.
Show that $l_1$ and $l_3$ are parallel lines.   AQA 2003

**2** The points $A$, $B$ and $C$ have position vectors $2\mathbf{i} - \mathbf{j} + \mathbf{k}$, $4\mathbf{i} + 3\mathbf{j} + 3\mathbf{k}$ and $\mathbf{i} - 3\mathbf{j}$ respectively, relative to a fixed origin $O$.

(a) Prove that $A$, $B$ and $C$ lie on a straight line $l$.

The point $D$ has position vector $\mathbf{i} + \mathbf{j} - 5\mathbf{k}$.

(b) Show that the cosine of the acute angle between $l$ and the line $OD$ is $\frac{1}{9}\sqrt{2}$.

The point $E$ has position vector $-5\mathbf{j} - \mathbf{k}$.

(c) Prove that $E$ lies on $l$ and that $OE$ is perpendicular to $OD$.

**3** The line $l$ passes through the points $(3, 1, -2)$ and $(-5, 0, 1)$.

(a) Find a vector equation for $l$.

(b) Show that the shortest distance between the point $Q(6, 5, -5)$ and $l$ is $\frac{1}{2}\sqrt{62}$.

**4** $PQR$ is a triangle where point $P$ has position vector $5\mathbf{i} + 2\mathbf{j} - 3\mathbf{k}$, point $Q$ has position vector $3\mathbf{i} + \mathbf{j} - \mathbf{k}$ and point $R$ has position vector $6\mathbf{i} - 5\mathbf{j} + \mathbf{k}$.

(a) (i) Find the cosine of angle $PQR$.

(ii) Hence show that the sine of angle $PQR$ is $\dfrac{5\sqrt{17}}{21}$.

(b) Find the exact value of the area of triangle $PQR$.

**5** The line $l_1$ has equation $\begin{bmatrix} x \\ y \\ z \end{bmatrix} = \begin{bmatrix} 5 \\ 1 \\ -1 \end{bmatrix} + t \begin{bmatrix} 2 \\ 1 \\ 5 \end{bmatrix}$.

The line $l_2$ has equation $\begin{bmatrix} x \\ y \\ z \end{bmatrix} = \begin{bmatrix} 13 \\ -6 \\ 2 \end{bmatrix} + s \begin{bmatrix} -3 \\ 4 \\ 1 \end{bmatrix}$.

(a) Show that $l_1$ and $l_2$ intersect and find the coordinates of their point of intersection.

(b) The point $Q$ has coordinates $(10, 11, 7)$.
Find the coordinates of the foot of the perpendicular from $Q$ to $l_1$.

# Answers

## 1 Rational expressions 1

### A Simplifying (p 6)

**A1** (a) (i) $\frac{1}{2}$    (ii) $\frac{1}{5}$    (iii) $\frac{1}{11}$

(b) (i) $\frac{1}{101}$, following the pattern in part (a)

    (ii) $f(100) = \dfrac{100+3}{100^2 + 4 \times 100 + 3} = \dfrac{103}{10\,403} = \dfrac{1}{101}$

(c) (i) $\dfrac{1}{k+1}$, following the pattern

    (ii) $f(k) = \dfrac{k+3}{k^2+4k+3} = \dfrac{k+3}{(k+1)(k+3)} = \dfrac{1}{k+1}$

(d) $f(n) = \dfrac{1}{n+1}$. For all positive integers $n + 1 \geq 2$

    so $f(n) \leq \frac{1}{2}$.

**A2** (a) (i) $\frac{1}{2}$    (ii) $\frac{4}{5}$    (iii) $\frac{21}{22}$

(b) (i) $\dfrac{k+1}{k+2}$, following the pattern

    (ii) $f(k) = \dfrac{k^2+6k+5}{k^2+7k+10} = \dfrac{(k+1)(k+5)}{(k+2)(k+5)} = \dfrac{k+1}{k+2}$

(c) The fraction will always be in its lowest terms, the numerator being one less than the denominator. No integer $n$ satisfies both $n + 1 = 8$ and $n + 2 = 11$. Hence there is no integer solution to $f(n) = \frac{8}{11}$.

**A3** The fraction $\dfrac{5x+10}{x^2+2x}$ is equivalent to $\dfrac{5(x+2)}{x(x+2)}$

which is equivalent to $\dfrac{5}{x}$. When $x$ is a multiple of 5 then the fraction will simplify to $\dfrac{1}{k}$ where $x = 5k$.

**Exercise A** (p 7)

1 (a) $\dfrac{x}{2}$    (b) $\dfrac{x-3}{x+1}$    (c) 3

   (d) $\frac{1}{5}$    (e) $\dfrac{3n+2}{2n+1}$

2 (a) $\dfrac{14x-4x^2}{x-7} = \dfrac{-2x(x-7)}{x-7} = -2x$

   (b) (i) $-5$    (ii) $-n$

3 (a) $x+3$    (b) $\dfrac{x-1}{2}$    (c) $\dfrac{1}{x+2}$

   (d) $\dfrac{x}{x-5}$    (e) $\dfrac{n}{3n+1}$

4 (a) $g(3) = \frac{1}{2}$, $g(4) = \frac{2}{5}$

(b) $g(n) = \dfrac{2n+18}{n^2+10n+9} = \dfrac{2(n+9)}{(n+1)(n+9)} = \dfrac{2}{n+1}$

When $n$ is odd, $n + 1$ is divisible by 2 and so the fraction will simplify to the unit fraction $\dfrac{1}{k}$ where $k$ is the integer $(n + 1) \div 2$.

(c) $n = 8$

5 (a) $\dfrac{n+4}{n+6}$    (b) $\dfrac{n+7}{n-5}$    (c) $\dfrac{2(n-6)}{n+5}$

   (d) $\dfrac{3n-1}{n+2}$    (e) $\dfrac{n-1}{n+2}$    (f) $\dfrac{2n-1}{3(n-4)}$

   (g) $\dfrac{1}{n-1}$    (h) $\dfrac{n+8}{n(n+3)}$

6 (a) 6    (b) $2x$    (c) $\dfrac{5(x+4)}{x+2}$

   (d) $\dfrac{2(x+5)}{x-2}$    (e) $\dfrac{x+7}{x-1}$    (f) $\dfrac{x-5}{x-1}$

7 (a) $\dfrac{5}{2x}$    (b) $\dfrac{2(x+1)}{x}$ or $2 + \dfrac{2}{x}$

   (c) $x+3$    (d) $\dfrac{3x+2}{2(x-7)}$

8 $\dfrac{1}{x} \div y = \dfrac{1}{x} \div \dfrac{y}{1} = \dfrac{1}{x} \times \dfrac{1}{y} = \dfrac{1}{xy}$

9 (a) $\dfrac{y}{x}$    (b) $\dfrac{1}{3x}$    (c) $2xy$

   (d) $\dfrac{8}{x}$    (e) $\dfrac{1}{50x}$

10 (a) $fg(7) = 18$

(b) $fg(x) = f\left(\dfrac{2}{x-1}\right) = 6 \div \dfrac{2}{x-1} = 6 \times \dfrac{x-1}{2}$

    $= 3(x-1)$

11 (a) (i) $f(2) = \frac{1}{2}$, $g(2) = \frac{1}{8}$    (ii) 4

(b) $\dfrac{f(x)}{g(x)} = \dfrac{6x+8}{3x^2+10x+8} \div \dfrac{2}{x^2+4x+4}$

    $= \dfrac{6x+8}{3x^2+10x+8} \times \dfrac{x^2+4x+4}{2}$

    $= \dfrac{2(3x+4)}{(3x+4)(x+2)} \times \dfrac{(x+2)(x+2)}{2}$

    $= x+2$

Since $x$ is an integer, $x + 2$ is too.

## B Adding and subtracting

### Exercise B (p 10)

**1 (a)** $\dfrac{3(x+1)}{x(2x+3)}$ **(b)** $\dfrac{5}{x(x+5)}$ **(c)** $\dfrac{13x-4}{3x(x-1)}$

**(d)** $\dfrac{2}{x(x-1)}$

**2 (a)** $\dfrac{x^2+5}{x}$ **(b)** $\dfrac{6(x+2)}{2x+1}$ **(c)** $\dfrac{4(5-x)}{x-4}$

**(d)** $\dfrac{3x(1-x)}{3x-2}$

**3 (a)** $\dfrac{a+b}{ab}$ **(b)** $\dfrac{2y-x}{xy}$ **(c)** $\dfrac{ab+3}{b}$

**(d)** $\dfrac{a-bc}{c}$ **(e)** $\dfrac{3b-2a}{6ab}$

**4** $\dfrac{a}{b(b+1)}$

**5 (a)** $\dfrac{2x}{(x+1)(x-1)}$ or $\dfrac{2x}{x^2-1}$

**(b)** $\dfrac{5x-1}{(3x+1)(x+3)}$ **(c)** $\dfrac{x^2-7}{(x-2)(x-5)}$

**(d)** $\dfrac{20}{(x+4)(x-1)}$ **(e)** $\dfrac{3x^2-13}{(x+3)(2x-1)}$

**(f)** $\dfrac{48}{(x+1)(x-7)}$

**6 (a)** $\dfrac{3(2x-7)}{x(x-4)}$ **(b)** $\dfrac{x-3}{(x-1)(x+3)}$

**(c)** $\dfrac{2x+13}{(x+4)(x+7)}$ **(d)** $\dfrac{8}{(x-7)(x+1)(2x-1)}$

**(e)** $\dfrac{c+a}{abc}$ **(f)** $\dfrac{4z^2-3x^2}{12xyz}$

**7 (a)** $\dfrac{4}{(2x+1)(x-1)}+\dfrac{12}{(2x+1)(x+3)}$

**(b)** $\dfrac{4}{(2x+1)(x-1)}+\dfrac{12}{(2x+1)(x+3)}$

$=\dfrac{4(x+3)+12(x-1)}{(2x+1)(x-1)(x+3)}$

$=\dfrac{4x+12+12x-12}{(2x+1)(x-1)(x+3)}$

$=\dfrac{16x}{(2x+1)(x-1)(x+3)}$

**8 (a)** $\dfrac{2(6x+1)}{(x+5)(2x-1)}$ **(b)** $\dfrac{4(x+3)}{x(x+2)(x+4)}$

**(c)** $\dfrac{x+4}{x(x-3)}$ **(d)** $\dfrac{x-3}{(x+1)(x-1)}$ or $\dfrac{x-3}{x^2-1}$

**9** $\dfrac{x-6}{x-5}$

**10 (a)** $f(5)=\frac{6}{5}$

**(b)** First show that $f(x)=\dfrac{x+1}{x}=1+\dfrac{1}{x}$

When $x>0$ then $\dfrac{1}{x}>0$ so $1+\dfrac{1}{x}>1$ giving

$f(x)>1$ as required.

**11** $gh(x)=g\left(\dfrac{3}{x-4}\right)=\dfrac{1}{\dfrac{3}{x-4}-1}$

$=\dfrac{1}{\dfrac{3-(x-4)}{x-4}}=\dfrac{1}{\dfrac{7-x}{x-4}}=\dfrac{x-4}{7-x}$

**12 (a)** $\dfrac{x+2}{2x}$ **(b)** $\dfrac{2x}{x+2}$

## C Extension: Leibniz's harmonic triangle (p 12)

**C1** The $n$th term is the reciprocal of the $n$th triangle
number $\frac{1}{2}n(n+1)$ which is $\dfrac{1}{\frac{1}{2}n(n+1)}=\dfrac{2}{n(n+1)}$
(multiplying top and bottom by 2).

**C2 (a)** $\dfrac{2}{n}-\dfrac{2}{n+1}=\dfrac{2(n+1)-2n}{n(n+1)}=\dfrac{2n+2-2n}{n(n+1)}$

$=\dfrac{2}{n(n+1)}$ as required

**(b)** C1 and C2 (a) show that the $n$th term in the
series can be written as the difference of the
two fractions $\dfrac{2}{n}$ and $\dfrac{2}{n+1}$. So the first term is
$\frac{2}{1}-\frac{2}{2}$, the second term is $\frac{2}{2}-\frac{2}{3}$, the third term
is $\frac{2}{3}-\frac{2}{4}$ and so on. Hence the whole series can
be written as

$\left(\frac{2}{1}-\frac{2}{2}\right)+\left(\frac{2}{2}-\frac{2}{3}\right)+\left(\frac{2}{3}-\frac{2}{4}\right)+\left(\frac{2}{4}-\frac{2}{5}\right)+\ldots+$
$\left(\dfrac{2}{n}-\dfrac{2}{n+1}\right).$

(c) The series can be written with the terms grouped as

$$\tfrac{2}{1} + \left(-\tfrac{2}{2} + \tfrac{2}{2}\right) + \left(-\tfrac{2}{3} + \tfrac{2}{3}\right) + \left(-\tfrac{2}{4} + \tfrac{2}{4}\right) + \left(-\tfrac{2}{5} + \tfrac{2}{5}\right)$$
$$+ \dots + \left(-\tfrac{2}{n} + \tfrac{2}{n}\right) - \tfrac{2}{n+1} \text{ so that the sum of}$$

each bracketed pair is 0. Hence the sum of the whole series is $2 - \dfrac{2}{n+1}$. As a single

fraction this is $\dfrac{2(n+1)-2}{n+1} = \dfrac{2n+2-2}{n+1} = \dfrac{2n}{n+1}$.

(d) The formula gives $\tfrac{10}{6} = \tfrac{5}{3}$.

Adding gives $\tfrac{1}{1} + \tfrac{1}{3} + \tfrac{1}{6} + \tfrac{1}{10} + \tfrac{1}{15}$

$= 1 + \dfrac{10+5+3+2}{30} = 1 + \tfrac{20}{30} = 1\tfrac{2}{3} = \tfrac{5}{3}$ so the

formula gives the correct result.

**C3** In C2 (c) it was shown that the sum of the series is $2 - \dfrac{2}{n+1}$.

As $n$ gets larger and larger, $\dfrac{2}{n+1}$ gets closer and

closer to 0 so the sum $2 - \dfrac{2}{n+1}$ gets closer and

closer to 2.

**Exercise C** (p 12)

**1** $\tfrac{1}{20} + \tfrac{1}{30} = \dfrac{3+2}{60} = \tfrac{5}{60} = \tfrac{1}{12}$

**2** $\tfrac{1}{6}, \tfrac{1}{30}, \tfrac{1}{60}, \tfrac{1}{60}, \tfrac{1}{30}, \tfrac{1}{6}$

**3** $\tfrac{1}{90}$

**4** (a) The first fraction in diagonal 1 can be written as $\tfrac{1}{1}$. We know that the denominators in the first diagonal increase by 1 so the first fraction and its successor are $\tfrac{1}{1}$ and $\tfrac{1}{2}$, the second and its successor are $\tfrac{1}{2}$ and $\tfrac{1}{3}$ and so on giving the $k$th fraction and its successor as $\dfrac{1}{k}$ and $\dfrac{1}{k+1}$.

(b) Each fraction in diagonal 1 is the sum of the two fractions below it. Hence each fraction in diagonal 2 is the difference of the fraction to the left in the row above and the fraction to the left in the same row. So the $n$th fraction in diagonal 2 is the $n$th fraction in diagonal 1 minus the $(n+1)$th fraction in diagonal 1, i.e. $\dfrac{1}{n} - \dfrac{1}{n+1}$.

So in the sum, the first term is $\tfrac{1}{1} - \tfrac{1}{2}$, the second term is $\tfrac{1}{2} - \tfrac{1}{3}$, the third term is $\tfrac{1}{3} - \tfrac{1}{4}$ and so on. Hence the whole series can be written as

$$\left(\tfrac{1}{1} - \tfrac{1}{2}\right) + \left(\tfrac{1}{2} - \tfrac{1}{3}\right) + \left(\tfrac{1}{3} - \tfrac{1}{4}\right) + \left(\tfrac{1}{4} - \tfrac{1}{5}\right) + \dots$$
$$+ \left(\dfrac{1}{n} - \dfrac{1}{n+1}\right).$$

(c) The series can be written with the terms grouped as

$$\tfrac{1}{1} + \left(-\tfrac{1}{2} + \tfrac{1}{2}\right) + \left(-\tfrac{1}{3} + \tfrac{1}{3}\right) + \left(-\tfrac{1}{4} + \tfrac{1}{4}\right) + \left(-\tfrac{1}{5} + \tfrac{1}{5}\right)$$
$$+ \dots + \left(-\tfrac{1}{n} + \tfrac{1}{n}\right) - \tfrac{1}{n+1} \text{ so that the sum}$$

of each bracketed pair is 0. Hence the sum of the whole series is $1 - \dfrac{1}{n+1}$. As a single

fraction this is $\dfrac{(n+1)-1}{n+1} = \dfrac{n}{n+1}$.

(d) The formula gives $\dfrac{4}{4+1} = \tfrac{4}{5}$.

Adding gives $\tfrac{1}{2} + \tfrac{1}{6} + \tfrac{1}{12} + \tfrac{1}{20} = \dfrac{30+10+5+3}{60}$

$= \tfrac{48}{60} = \tfrac{4}{5}$ so the formula gives the correct result.

(e) As $n$ gets larger and larger, the sum converges to 1. From part (c) above we see that the sum can be written as $1 - \dfrac{1}{n+1}$. As $n$ gets larger and

larger $\dfrac{1}{n+1}$ gets closer and closer to 0, so the

sum $1 - \dfrac{1}{n+1}$ gets closer and closer to 1.

(f) From part (b) we know that the $k$th fraction in diagonal 2 is $\dfrac{1}{k} - \dfrac{1}{k+1}$; this is equivalent to

$\dfrac{(k+1)-k}{k(k+1)} = \dfrac{1}{k(k+1)}$ as required.

(g) (i) $\tfrac{1}{420} = \dfrac{1}{20 \times 21}$ and so it is the 20th fraction in diagonal 2.

(ii) Row 21

**5 (a)** From the result of question 4 (f) we know that the $k$th fraction in diagonal 2 is $\dfrac{1}{k(k+1)}$ so its successor in diagonal 2 is the $(k+1)$th, which is $\dfrac{1}{(k+1)((k+1)+1)} = \dfrac{1}{(k+1)(k+2)}$.

**(b)** Each fraction in diagonal 3 is the difference of the fraction to the left in the row above and the fraction to the left in the same row. So the $n$th fraction in diagonal 3 is the $n$th fraction in diagonal 2 minus the $(n+1)$th fraction in diagonal 2.

From part (a) this is $\dfrac{1}{n(n+1)} - \dfrac{1}{(n+1)(n+2)}$.

So the sum of the first $n$ fractions can be written as

$\left(\tfrac{1}{2} - \tfrac{1}{6}\right) + \left(\tfrac{1}{6} - \tfrac{1}{12}\right) + \left(\tfrac{1}{12} - \tfrac{1}{20}\right) + \left(\tfrac{1}{20} - \tfrac{1}{30}\right) + \dots$

$+ \left(\dfrac{1}{n(n+1)} - \dfrac{1}{(n+1)(n+2)}\right)$.

The series can be written with the terms grouped as

$\tfrac{1}{2} + \left(-\tfrac{1}{6} + \tfrac{1}{6}\right) + \left(-\tfrac{1}{12} + \tfrac{1}{12}\right) + \left(-\tfrac{1}{20} + \tfrac{1}{20}\right) + \dots$

$+ \left(-\dfrac{1}{n(n+1)} + \dfrac{1}{n(n+1)}\right) - \dfrac{1}{(n+1)(n+2)}$

so that the sum of each bracketed pair is 0. Hence the sum of the whole series is

$\tfrac{1}{2} - \dfrac{1}{(n+1)(n+2)}$.

**(c)** As $n$ gets larger and larger, the sum converges to $\tfrac{1}{2}$. The sum of the first $n$ fractions is $\tfrac{1}{2} - \dfrac{1}{(n+1)(n+2)}$. As $n$ gets larger and larger $\dfrac{1}{(n+1)(n+2)}$ gets closer and closer to 0 so the sum $\tfrac{1}{2} - \dfrac{1}{(n+1)(n+2)}$ gets closer and closer to $\tfrac{1}{2}$.

**(d) (i)** From part (b) we know that the $k$th fraction in diagonal 3 is

$\dfrac{1}{k(k+1)} - \dfrac{1}{(k+1)(k+2)}$ and this is

equivalent to $\dfrac{(k+2)-k}{k(k+1)(k+2)}$

$= \dfrac{2}{k(k+1)(k+2)}$ as required.

**(ii)** $\dfrac{1}{660}$

**6** Investigations (and proofs) leading to:

- the $n$th fraction in diagonal $m$ is
$$\dfrac{(m-1)!}{n(n+1)(n+2)\dots(n+m-1)}$$

- the sum of the first $n$ fractions in diagonal $m$ is
$$\dfrac{1}{m-1} - \dfrac{(m-2)!}{(n+1)(n+2)\dots(n+m-1)}$$

- as $n$ gets larger and larger the sum of the first $n$ fractions in diagonal $m$ converges to a limit of $\dfrac{1}{m-1}$

**7** One method of proof is as follows. From C1 we know that the reciprocal of the $n$th triangle number $T_n$ can be written as $\dfrac{2}{n(n+1)}$.

Hence the reciprocal of the $(n+1)$th triangle number $T_{n+1}$ can be written as $\dfrac{2}{(n+1)(n+2)}$.

The sum of these reciprocals is

$\dfrac{2}{n(n+1)} + \dfrac{2}{(n+1)(n+2)}$

which is equivalent to

$\dfrac{2(n+2)+2n}{n(n+1)(n+2)}$

$= \dfrac{4n+4}{n(n+1)(n+2)}$

$= \dfrac{4(n+1)}{n(n+1)(n+2)} = \dfrac{4}{n(n+2)}$

We also have

$\dfrac{4}{T_n + T_{n+1} - 1} = \dfrac{4}{\tfrac{1}{2}n(n+1) + \tfrac{1}{2}(n+1)(n+2) - 1}$

$= \dfrac{8}{n(n+1) + (n+1)(n+2) - 2}$

$= \dfrac{8}{n^2 + n + n^2 + 3n + 2 - 2}$

$= \dfrac{8}{2n^2 + 4n} = \dfrac{4}{n(n+2)}$

which is the same as the sum above, as required.

**D Extension: the harmonic mean** (p 14)

**D1** (a) 10    (b) 10    (c) 10

**D2** (a) 9    (b) 12    (c) 7

**D3 (a)** $\dfrac{b-a}{a+b}$

**(b)** Since $k$ is a fraction such that $a + ka = b - kb$ then the harmonic mean of $a$ and $b$ is $a + ka$ (or $b - kb$).

$k = \dfrac{b-a}{a+b}$ so the harmonic mean is

$$a + a\left(\dfrac{b-a}{a+b}\right) = \dfrac{a(a+b) + a(b-a)}{a+b}$$

$$= \dfrac{a^2 + ab + ab - a^2}{a+b} = \dfrac{2ab}{a+b} \text{ as required.}$$

**(c)** $\dfrac{2 \times 10 \times 90}{10 + 90} = \dfrac{1800}{100} = 18$

**D4 (a)** Dividing the numerator and denominator by $ab$ gives

$$\dfrac{2ab}{a+b} = \dfrac{2}{\dfrac{a+b}{ab}} = \dfrac{2}{\dfrac{a}{ab} + \dfrac{b}{ab}} = \dfrac{2}{\dfrac{1}{b} + \dfrac{1}{a}} = \dfrac{2}{\dfrac{1}{a} + \dfrac{1}{b}}$$

as required.

**(b)** The mean of the reciprocals of $a$ and $b$ is $\dfrac{\dfrac{1}{a} + \dfrac{1}{b}}{2}$ so the reciprocal of the mean of the reciprocals is $\dfrac{2}{\dfrac{1}{a} + \dfrac{1}{b}}$ which is the harmonic mean (from part (a)).

**Exercise D** (p 15)

**1 (a)** Let $d$ miles be the distance from Harton to Monyborough. Then the total distance for the return journey is $2d$ miles.

The time for the outward journey is $\dfrac{d}{x}$ and the time for the return journey is $\dfrac{d}{y}$ so the total time is $\dfrac{d}{x} + \dfrac{d}{y} = d\left(\dfrac{1}{x} + \dfrac{1}{y}\right)$. Hence the average speed is $\dfrac{2d}{d\left(\dfrac{1}{x} + \dfrac{1}{y}\right)} = \dfrac{2}{\dfrac{1}{x} + \dfrac{1}{y}}$ which is the harmonic mean of $x$ and $y$ as required.

**(b)** $\dfrac{2}{\dfrac{1}{30} + \dfrac{1}{60}} = \dfrac{2}{\dfrac{1}{20}}$ so the average speed is 40 m.p.h.

**2 (a)** $\dfrac{2 \times 2 \times 6}{2 + 6} = \dfrac{24}{8} = 3$ so 3 is the harmonic mean of 2 and 6.

**(b)** The reciprocals in order are $\tfrac{1}{6}, \tfrac{1}{3}, \tfrac{1}{2}$. Now $\tfrac{1}{3} - \tfrac{1}{6} = \tfrac{1}{6}$ and $\tfrac{1}{2} - \tfrac{1}{3} = \tfrac{1}{6}$ so there is a common difference and hence an arithmetic sequence.

**(c)** $q$ is the harmonic mean of $p$ and $r$ so $q = \dfrac{2pr}{p+r}$. The reciprocals of $r$, $q$ and $p$ are

$\dfrac{1}{r}, \dfrac{p+r}{2pr}$ and $\dfrac{1}{p}$.

Now $\dfrac{p+r}{2pr} - \dfrac{1}{r} = \dfrac{p+r-2p}{2pr} = \dfrac{r-p}{2pr}$ and

$\dfrac{1}{p} - \dfrac{p+r}{2pr} = \dfrac{2r-(p+r)}{2pr} = \dfrac{r-p}{2pr}$ so we have a common difference and hence an arithmetic sequence.

**3** One proof is as follows. The diagram can be labelled as follows with $h$ as the height and $b$ as the length of the base of $\triangle PST$.

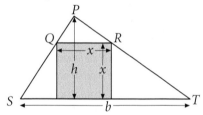

Triangles $PQR$ and $PST$ are similar (they share $\angle QPR$, $\angle PQR = \angle PST$ and $\angle PRQ = \angle PTS$) and the height of $\triangle PQR$ is $h - x$. Hence

$$\dfrac{b}{h} = \dfrac{x}{h-x}$$

$\Rightarrow xh = b(h - x)$

$\Rightarrow xh = bh - bx$

$\Rightarrow xh + bx = bh$

$\Rightarrow x(b + h) = bh$

$\Rightarrow x = \dfrac{bh}{b+h} = \tfrac{1}{2}\left(\dfrac{2bh}{b+h}\right)$

i.e. half the harmonic mean of $b$ and $h$.

**4** One proof is as follows. In diagram 1, $a$ and $c$ are parallel so the two shaded triangles are similar (equal angles are shown). A dotted line is drawn through the point of intersection that is parallel to the left-hand edge of the trapezium and lengths $l_1$ and $l_2$ are labelled on the triangles as shown.

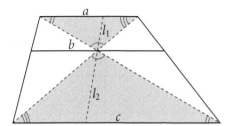

Diagram 1

Since the triangles are similar, $\dfrac{l_2}{l_1} = \dfrac{c}{a}$.

In diagram 2, dotted lines are drawn as shown to be parallel to the left-hand edge of the trapezium. Their lengths are $l_1$ and $l_2$ as before. Again, the two shaded triangles are similar.

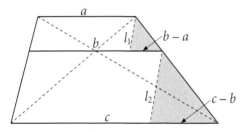

Diagram 2

The base of the smaller shaded triangle is $b - a$ and the base of the larger shaded triangle is $c - b$.

So, again by similar triangles, $\dfrac{l_2}{l_1} = \dfrac{c-b}{b-a}$.

Putting the two results together gives

$$\frac{c}{a} = \frac{c-b}{b-a}$$
$$\Rightarrow c(b-a) = a(c-b)$$
$$\Rightarrow bc - ac = ac - ab$$
$$\Rightarrow ab + bc = 2ac$$
$$\Rightarrow b(a+c) = 2ac$$
$$\Rightarrow b = \frac{2ac}{a+c}$$

which is the harmonic mean of $a$ and $c$.

**Test yourself** (p 16)

**1** $\dfrac{5x}{x-1}$

**2 (a)** $\frac{1}{4}$

**(b)** $f(x) = \dfrac{x+5}{(x+1)(x+5)} = \dfrac{1}{x+1}$

which is a fraction with 1 as its numerator.

**3 (a)** One method is as follows:
$$f(x) = \frac{(x+1)(x+4)}{x(x+4)} = \frac{x+1}{x} = \frac{x}{x} + \frac{1}{x}$$
$$= 1 + \frac{1}{x}$$

**(b)** $0 < x < 1$

**4 (a)** $\dfrac{x+6}{x(x+3)}$   **(b)** $\dfrac{3x}{(x+4)(x-2)}$

**(c)** $\dfrac{x^2 + y^2}{xy}$

**5** $\dfrac{6}{(y-3)(y-1)} - \dfrac{3}{y-3}$

$\equiv \dfrac{6 - 3(y-1)}{(y-3)(y-1)}$

$\equiv \dfrac{6 - 3y + 3}{(y-3)(y-1)}$

$\equiv \dfrac{-3y + 9}{(y-3)(y-1)}$

$\equiv \dfrac{-3(y-3)}{(y-3)(y-1)} \equiv \dfrac{-3}{y-1} \equiv \dfrac{3}{1-y}$

**6** $\dfrac{8}{(x-1)(x+3)}$

**7** $\dfrac{3(x+2)}{(x+1)(x-5)}$

**8** $\dfrac{x-4}{x(x+1)}$

**9** One method is as follows:
$$f(x) = 2x + \frac{1}{x-1} - \frac{5}{x^2 + 3x - 4}$$
$$= 2x + \frac{1}{x-1} - \frac{5}{(x-1)(x+4)}$$
$$= 2x + \frac{x+4-5}{(x-1)(x+4)}$$
$$= 2x + \frac{x-1}{(x-1)(x+4)}$$
$$= 2x + \frac{1}{x+4}$$
$$= \frac{2x(x+4)+1}{x+4}$$
$$= \frac{2x^2 + 8x + 1}{x+4} \text{ as required.}$$

# 2 Rational expressions 2

## A Using the remainder theorem (p 17)

**A1** (a) $g(\frac{1}{2}) = 8 \times (\frac{1}{2})^3 + 4 \times (\frac{1}{2})^2 + 6 \times (\frac{1}{2}) - 11 = -6$
so the remainder is $-6$.

(b) (i) The student's conjecture (which may be $-12$)

(ii) $-6$

(c) The remainders are the same.
A possible proof is:

Let $R_1$ be the remainder after division by $(x - \frac{1}{2})$. Then by the remainder theorem $g(\frac{1}{2}) = R_1$.

Let $R_2$ be the remainder after division by $(2x - 1)$. We can write
$g(x) = (2x - 1)q(x) + R_2$, where $q(x)$ is a polynomial in $x$.

Hence $g(\frac{1}{2}) = 0 \times q(x) + R_2 = R_2$. So $R_1 = R_2$ and the remainders must be the same.

$\left(\text{Clearly, this argument will be valid for any expression that is a 'multiple' of } (x - \frac{1}{2}).\right)$

## Exercise A (p 18)

**1** (a) 53   (b) $-2$   (c) 3   (d) $\frac{1}{2}$   (e) $-\frac{2}{3}$   (f) 0

**2** (a) $p(-2) = (-2)^3 + 2 \times (-2)^2 - 3 \times -2 - 6 = 0$ and
$q(-2) = (-2)^3 + 2 \times (-2)^2 + 5 \times -2 + 10 = 0$
so $(x + 2)$ is a common linear factor.

(b) $\dfrac{p(x)}{q(x)} = \dfrac{(x+2)(x^2-3)}{(x+2)(x^2+5)} = \dfrac{x^2-3}{x^2+5}$

**3** (a) $2 \times (\frac{1}{2})^3 + 7 \times (\frac{1}{2})^2 - 14 \times \frac{1}{2} + 5 = \frac{1}{4} + \frac{7}{4} - 7 + 5$
$= 0$ so $(2x - 1)$ is a factor.

(b) $(x + 5)(x - 1)$

## B Further division (p 19)

**B1** $3 + \dfrac{4}{x+2}$

**B2** $x + 4 + \dfrac{5}{x-1}$

**B3** $x^2 + 3x - 1 - \dfrac{4}{x-5}$

**B4** (a) $A = 1, B = 3$   (b) $x + 1 + \dfrac{3x}{x^2 - 1}$

(c) The remainder theorem refers to division by a linear expression and $x^2 - 1$ is quadratic. However, you can check the statement $x^3 + x^2 + 2x - 1 = (x^2 - 1)(x + 1) + 3x$ by substituting various values for $x$. As $x^2 - 1 = 0$ has solutions $x = \pm 1$, these are the simplest to use.

**B5** $x + 3 + \dfrac{3x - 2}{x^2 + 1}$

## Exercise B (p 21)

**1** (a) $1 + \dfrac{3}{x+2}$   (b) $2 - \dfrac{3}{x^2}$   (c) $2 - \dfrac{1}{x+3}$

(d) $3 - \dfrac{5}{x^2+1}$   (e) $\frac{1}{2} + \dfrac{1}{2x}$

**2** (a) $x + 2 + \dfrac{3}{x+1}$   (b) $x - 4 - \dfrac{3}{x+2}$

(c) $x - 5 + \dfrac{1}{x-4}$   (d) $x - \dfrac{5}{x-2}$

(e) $2x + 3 - \dfrac{1}{x-1}$   (f) $3x - 1 + \dfrac{3}{x+3}$

(g) $x - 2 + \dfrac{9}{2x+1}$   (h) $2x - 5 - \dfrac{2}{3x-2}$

**3** (a) $x^2 + 2x + 3 + \dfrac{6}{x+1}$   (b) $x^2 + 1 - \dfrac{3}{x-5}$

(c) $x^2 - 3x - 2 + \dfrac{1}{2x-1}$   (d) $x + 1 + \dfrac{x+4}{x^2+1}$

(e) $3 + \dfrac{x-10}{x^2+x}$   (f) $3x - 2 - \dfrac{7}{2x^2-1}$

**4** $\dfrac{x^3+1}{x^2-1} \equiv x + \dfrac{x+1}{x^2-1} \equiv x + \dfrac{x+1}{(x+1)(x-1)} \equiv x + \dfrac{1}{x-1}$

or

$\dfrac{x^3+1}{x^2-1} \equiv \dfrac{(x+1)(x^2-x+1)}{(x+1)(x-1)} \equiv \dfrac{x^2-x+1}{x-1} \equiv x + \dfrac{1}{x-1}$

**5** (a) $x - 1 + \dfrac{7}{x+1}$   (b) $x^2 + 3x + 9 + \dfrac{32}{x-3}$

(c) $x^2 - 2x + 5 - \dfrac{10}{x+2}$   (d) $x + \dfrac{5x}{x^2-5}$

## C Further addition and subtraction

**Exercise C** (p 23)

**1** (a) $\dfrac{1}{4x}$  (b) $\dfrac{6x-1}{x^2}$  (c) $\dfrac{5x+3}{3x^2}$  (d) $\dfrac{2x-9}{6x^2}$

**2** (a) $\dfrac{8}{(x+1)(x+3)(x+5)}$  (b) $\dfrac{3(x+32)}{(5+x)(2+x)(x-4)}$

(c) $\dfrac{19-x^2}{(x-1)(3-x)(x+2)}$

**3** (a) $\dfrac{3x-2}{(x-1)^2}$  (b) $\dfrac{x}{(x+2)^2}$

(c) $\dfrac{7x-1}{6(x^2-1)}$ or $\dfrac{7x-1}{6(x-1)(x+1)}$

(d) $\dfrac{8x+5}{10(2x+1)^2}$  (e) $\dfrac{x+1}{(3x+2)^2}$

(f) $\dfrac{3x-5}{(3-x)^2}$

**4** (a) $\dfrac{1}{x+2}-\dfrac{2}{x+4}+\dfrac{x}{(x+4)^2}$

$\equiv \dfrac{(x+4)^2-2(x+2)(x+4)+x(x+2)}{(x+2)(x+4)^2}$

$\equiv \dfrac{x^2+8x+16-2x^2-12x-16+x^2+2x}{(x+2)(x+4)^2}$

$\equiv \dfrac{-2x}{(x+2)(x+4)^2}$

(b) When $x>0$ then $(x+2)(x+4)^2>0$ and $-2x<0$ so $\dfrac{-2x}{(x+2)(x+4)^2}<0$.

**5** (a) $\dfrac{7x+4}{(2-x)(x+1)^2}$  (b) $\dfrac{7}{(2x+1)(x-3)^2}$

(c) $\dfrac{x^2+12x+14}{6(x+1)(x+2)^2}$  (d) $\dfrac{x(x+2)}{(x-1)^3}$

(e) $\dfrac{x+5}{(x+1)(x+3)^2}$  (f) $\dfrac{x^2+x+34}{3(1-x)(2x+1)^2}$

**6** (a) $\dfrac{A}{x+1}+\dfrac{B}{x-1}\equiv\dfrac{A(x-1)+B(x+1)}{(x+1)(x-1)}$

$\equiv\dfrac{Ax-A+Bx+B}{x^2-1}\equiv\dfrac{(A+B)x+(B-A)}{x^2-1}$

(b) $A+B=5$ and $B-A=1$ so $A=2$ and $B=3$, and $\dfrac{5x+1}{x^2-1}\equiv\dfrac{2}{x+1}+\dfrac{3}{x-1}$

**7** (a) $\dfrac{A}{x+2}+\dfrac{B}{(x+2)^2}\equiv\dfrac{A(x+2)+B}{(x+2)^2}$

$\equiv\dfrac{Ax+(2A+B)}{(x+2)^2}$

(b) $A=2$ and $2A+B=3$ so $B=-1$, and $\dfrac{2x+3}{(x+2)^2}\equiv\dfrac{2}{x+2}-\dfrac{1}{(x+2)^2}$

## D Partial fractions (p 24)

**D1** (a) $\dfrac{A}{x+1}+\dfrac{B}{x+3}\equiv\dfrac{A(x+3)+B(x+1)}{(x+1)(x+3)}$

$\equiv\dfrac{Ax+3A+Bx+B}{(x+1)(x+3)}\equiv\dfrac{(A+B)x+(3A+B)}{(x+1)(x+3)}$

(b) The denominators are identical so the numerators are too. The numerator can be written as $0x+4$ so we have $(A+B)x=0x\Rightarrow A+B=0$ and $3A+B=4$.

(c) $A=2$ and $B=-2$

(d) $\dfrac{4}{(x+1)(x+3)}\equiv\dfrac{2}{x+1}+\dfrac{-2}{x+3}$

which is equivalent to $\dfrac{2}{x+1}-\dfrac{2}{x+3}$

**D2** (a) $\dfrac{A}{x-1}+\dfrac{B}{2x+5}\equiv\dfrac{A(2x+5)+B(x-1)}{(x-1)(2x+5)}$

$\equiv\dfrac{2Ax+5A+Bx-B}{(x-1)(2x+5)}\equiv\dfrac{(2A+B)x+(5A-B)}{(x-1)(2x+5)}$

(b) $\dfrac{1}{x-1}+\dfrac{5}{2x+5}$

**D3** (a) $\dfrac{2}{x+2}+\dfrac{1}{2x-1}$

(b) $\dfrac{1}{x-2}-\dfrac{1}{x+3}$

(c) $\dfrac{2}{x-5}-\dfrac{1}{x-2}$

(d) $\dfrac{\frac{1}{2}}{3-2x}+\dfrac{\frac{1}{2}}{3+2x}=\dfrac{1}{2(3-2x)}+\dfrac{1}{2(3+2x)}$

**D4** (a) $\dfrac{2}{x-3} - \dfrac{2}{x+2}$  (b) $\dfrac{1}{x-5} + \dfrac{1}{x+3}$

**D5** (a) $\dfrac{1}{x+2} - \dfrac{1}{x+3}$

(b) $\dfrac{\frac{1}{2}}{x+3} + \dfrac{\frac{1}{2}}{x-3} = \dfrac{1}{2(x+3)} + \dfrac{1}{2(x-3)}$

(c) $\dfrac{1}{x+1} + \dfrac{2}{x-1}$

(d) $\dfrac{5}{x} - \dfrac{3}{x+1}$

**D6** (a) $\dfrac{1}{x-1} + \dfrac{1}{x-2} + \dfrac{1}{x-3}$

(b) $\dfrac{8}{x} + \dfrac{3}{1-x} - \dfrac{5}{x+4}$

**D7** $\dfrac{AC-B}{(C-D)(x+C)} + \dfrac{B-AD}{(C-D)(x+D)}$

$\equiv \dfrac{(x+D)(AC-B)+(x+C)(B-AD)}{(C-D)(x+C)(x+D)}$

$\equiv \dfrac{ACx-Bx+ACD-BD+Bx+BC-ADx-ADC}{(C-D)(x+C)(x+D)}$

$\equiv \dfrac{ACx-ADx-BD+BC}{(C-D)(x+C)(x+D)}$

$\equiv \dfrac{Ax(C-D)+B(C-D)}{(C-D)(x+C)(x+D)}$

$\equiv \dfrac{(Ax+B)(C-D)}{(C-D)(x+C)(x+D)}$

$\equiv \dfrac{Ax+B}{(x+C)(x+D)}$ as required

**Exercise D** (p 27)

**1** (a) $\dfrac{3}{x} + \dfrac{3}{1-x}$  (b) $\dfrac{5}{x} - \dfrac{2}{x+6}$

(c) $\dfrac{1}{x+3} + \dfrac{1}{x+4}$  (d) $\dfrac{2}{x-3} - \dfrac{1}{x+1}$

(e) $\dfrac{3}{3x-1} - \dfrac{2}{2x+1}$  (f) $\dfrac{4}{2-x} + \dfrac{2}{2x-1}$

(g) $\dfrac{1}{2(x+1)} - \dfrac{1}{2(x+5)}$  (h) $\dfrac{1}{4(x-1)} + \dfrac{1}{4(3x+1)}$

(i) $\dfrac{7}{11(x+2)} - \dfrac{2}{11(5x-1)}$

**2** (a) $\dfrac{1}{x-2} - \dfrac{1}{x+2}$  (b) $\dfrac{1}{3x} + \dfrac{2}{3(x+3)}$

(c) $\dfrac{3}{x+1} - \dfrac{7}{3x+2}$  (d) $\dfrac{1}{3(2x-3)} - \dfrac{1}{3(2x+3)}$

**3** (a) $\dfrac{1}{x-1} - \dfrac{9}{x+2} + \dfrac{13}{x+3}$

(b) $-\dfrac{3}{x} + \dfrac{2}{x+1} + \dfrac{1}{x-2}$

(c) $-\dfrac{1}{x+1} + \dfrac{4}{2x+1} - \dfrac{3}{3x+1}$

(d) $\dfrac{1}{2(x-1)} - \dfrac{5}{2(x+1)} + \dfrac{4}{2x+1}$

**4** (a) $A = 3, B = -2, C = 5$

(b) $A = 2, B = -5, C = 4$

(c) $A = 8, B = 9, C = -25$

(d) $A = 2, B = -1, C = -3$

**5** (a) $f(3) = \frac{9}{10}$, $f(4) = \frac{12}{13}$

(b) (i) $\dfrac{1}{3n-2} - \dfrac{1}{3n+1}$

(ii) Part (i) shows that the $n$th term in the series can be written as the difference of the two fractions $\dfrac{1}{3n-2}$ and $\dfrac{1}{3n+1}$.
So the first term is $\frac{1}{1} - \frac{1}{4}$, the second term is $\frac{1}{4} - \frac{1}{7}$, the third term is $\frac{1}{7} - \frac{1}{10}$ and so on. Hence the whole series can be written as $\left(\frac{1}{1} - \frac{1}{4}\right) + \left(\frac{1}{4} - \frac{1}{7}\right) + \left(\frac{1}{7} - \frac{1}{10}\right) + \dots +$ $\left(\dfrac{1}{3n-2} - \dfrac{1}{3n+1}\right)$. The series can be written with the terms grouped as
$\frac{1}{1} + \left(-\frac{1}{4} + \frac{1}{4}\right) + \left(-\frac{1}{7} + \frac{1}{7}\right) + \left(-\frac{1}{10} + \frac{1}{10}\right) + \dots +$
$\left(-\dfrac{1}{3n-2} + \dfrac{1}{3n-2}\right) - \dfrac{1}{3n+1}$ so that the sum of each bracketed pair is 0.
Hence the sum of the whole series is $1 - \dfrac{1}{3n+1}$.
As $f(n) = 1 - \dfrac{1}{3n+1}$ and $n$ is positive then $f(n) < 1$ as required.

**6 (a)** $g(5) = \frac{5}{21}$

**(b) (i)** First show that
$$\frac{1}{n(n+1)(n+2)} \equiv \frac{1}{2n} - \frac{1}{n+1} + \frac{1}{2(n+2)}$$

This shows that each fraction can be written as the sum of three fractions so that the first term is $\frac{1}{2} - \frac{1}{2} + \frac{1}{6}$, the second term is $\frac{1}{4} - \frac{1}{3} + \frac{1}{8}$, the third term is $\frac{1}{6} - \frac{1}{4} + \frac{1}{10}$, the fourth term is $\frac{1}{8} - \frac{1}{5} + \frac{1}{12}$ and so on.

If we write these sums in rows, we obtain three columns $g(n) \equiv$

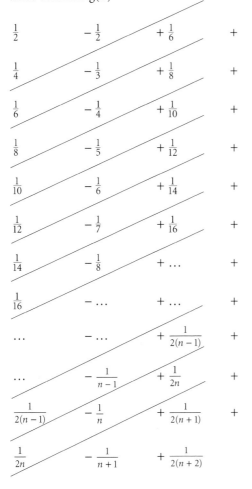

Most of the fractions can be grouped in sets of three as shown above where the sum of each set of three fractions is 0.

Hence $g(n)$ is the sum of the three fractions in the 'upper triangle' and the three fractions in the 'lower triangle' which gives us $g(n) \equiv$

$$\frac{1}{2} - \frac{1}{2} + \frac{1}{4} + \frac{1}{2(n+1)} - \frac{1}{n+1} + \frac{1}{2(n+2)}$$

$$\equiv \frac{1}{4} + \frac{n+2 - 2(n+2) + n+1}{2(n+1)(n+2)}$$

$$\equiv \frac{1}{4} - \frac{1}{2(n+1)(n+2)}$$

**(ii)** Since $g(n) \equiv \frac{1}{4} - \frac{1}{2(n+1)(n+2)}$, as $n$ gets very large, $\frac{1}{2(n+1)(n+2)}$ gets very small and $g(n)$ gets closer and closer to $\frac{1}{4}$.

## E Further partial fractions (p 28)

**E1 (a)** $\dfrac{x^2 + x + 1}{x(x^2+1)}$    **(b)** $\dfrac{x+1}{x(x^2+1)}$

**E2 (a)** $\dfrac{A}{x} + \dfrac{B}{x^2+1} \equiv \dfrac{A(x^2+1) + Bx}{x(x^2+1)}$

$$\equiv \frac{Ax^2 + Bx + A}{x(x^2+1)}$$

So $\dfrac{Ax^2 + Bx + A}{x(x^2+1)} \equiv \dfrac{1 - 2x}{x(x^2+1)}$

$\Rightarrow A = 0$ (from equating coefficients of $x^2$) and $A = 1$ (from equating constants) which is a contradiction so no such identity exists.

**(b)** $A = 1, B = -1, C = -2$

**E3** $\dfrac{x+2}{(x+3)^2}$

**E4** $\dfrac{A}{x-1} + \dfrac{B}{x-1} \equiv \dfrac{A+B}{x-1} \equiv \dfrac{(A+B)(x-1)}{(x-1)^2}$

$$\equiv \frac{(A+B)x - (A+B)}{(x-1)^2}$$

So $\dfrac{x}{(x-1)^2} \equiv \dfrac{A}{x-1} + \dfrac{B}{x-1}$

$\Rightarrow A + B = 1$ (from equating coefficients of $x$) and $A + B = 0$ (from equating constants) which is a contradiction so no such identity exists.

**E5 (a) (i)** $A = 1, B = 1$

**(ii)** $A = 3, B = 1$

**(b) (i)** $\dfrac{A}{x+C} + \dfrac{B-AC}{(x+C)^2} \equiv \dfrac{A(x+C)+B-AC}{(x+C)^2}$

$\equiv \dfrac{Ax+AC+B-AC}{(x+C)^2} \equiv \dfrac{Ax+B}{(x+C)^2}$

as required

**(ii)** $\dfrac{5}{x+3} + \dfrac{1}{(x+3)^2}$

**E6** $\dfrac{7x^2+2x-12}{(2x-5)(x+1)^2}$

**Exercise E** (p 30)

**1 (a)** $\dfrac{1}{x+2} + \dfrac{2}{(x+2)^2}$

**(b)** $\dfrac{2}{x+3} - \dfrac{2}{x+1} + \dfrac{4}{(x+1)^2}$

**(c)** $\dfrac{1}{x-2} + \dfrac{2}{(x-1)^2}$

**(d)** $\dfrac{1}{x-1} - \dfrac{1}{x+3} - \dfrac{1}{(x+3)^2}$

**(e)** $\dfrac{1}{2(x-4)} + \dfrac{1}{2(x+2)} - \dfrac{1}{(x+2)^2}$

**(f)** $-\dfrac{2}{3(x+4)} + \dfrac{2}{3(x-2)} + \dfrac{3}{(x-2)^2}$

**(g)** $\dfrac{3}{x-5} + \dfrac{2}{2-x} - \dfrac{2}{(2-x)^2}$

**(h)** $\dfrac{2}{2x+1} - \dfrac{2}{x+3} + \dfrac{1}{(x+3)^2}$

**(i)** $\dfrac{1}{3(2x-1)} - \dfrac{2}{3(x-5)} - \dfrac{2}{(x-5)^2}$

**(j)** $\dfrac{1}{7(x+2)} - \dfrac{3}{7(3x-1)} + \dfrac{1}{(3x-1)^2}$

**(k)** $\dfrac{3}{x} - \dfrac{12}{4x-1} + \dfrac{16}{(4x-1)^2}$

**(l)** $\dfrac{14}{5(2x+5)} - \dfrac{2}{5x} + \dfrac{1}{x^2}$

**Test yourself** (p 31)

**1 (a)** $p(\tfrac{1}{3}) = 0$ and $q(\tfrac{1}{3}) = 0$ so $(3x-1)$ is a factor of each polynomial.

**(b)** $\dfrac{p(x)}{q(x)} \equiv \dfrac{(3x-1)(x+4)}{(3x-1)(x^2+1)} = \dfrac{x+4}{x^2+1}$

**2** $A = 3, B = -1, C = 6$

**3 (a)** $\dfrac{x^3+8}{x^2-4} \equiv x + \dfrac{4x+8}{x^2-4} \equiv x + \dfrac{4(x+2)}{(x-2)(x+2)}$

$\equiv x + \dfrac{4}{x-2}$ as required

**(b)** $f(x) = x + 4(x-2)^{-1}$ so

$f'(x) = 1 + 4\times-1\times(x-2)^{-2}$

$= 1 - 4(x-2)^{-2}$

$= 1 - \dfrac{4}{(x-2)^2}$ as required

**4** $\dfrac{x^2}{(x+1)(x-1)^2}$

**5** $-\dfrac{2}{x+3} + \dfrac{3}{2x+1}$

**6** $\dfrac{3}{1+5x} + \dfrac{2}{3-x}$

**7** $A = 4, B = 1, C = 2$

**8** $\dfrac{1}{2(2x+3)} - \dfrac{5}{2(2x+3)^2}$

**9** $\dfrac{9}{2-3x} - \dfrac{3}{1-x} - \dfrac{2}{(1-x)^2}$

**10** $\dfrac{1}{x+2} - \dfrac{2}{x-1} + \dfrac{1}{x-4}$

# 3 Parametric equations

## A Coordinates in terms of a third variable
(p 32)

**A1** (a)

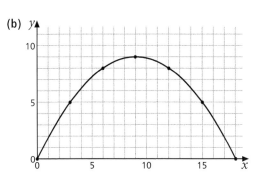

| $t$ | 0 | 1 | 2 | 3 | 4 | 5 | 6 |
|---|---|---|---|---|---|---|---|
| $x$ | 0 | 3 | 6 | 9 | 12 | 15 | 18 |
| $y$ | 0 | 5 | 8 | 9 | 8 | 5 | 0 |

(b)

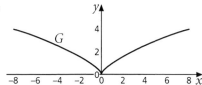

It might represent an object that has been thrown.

**A2** (a) $x = 2t$  (b) $y = t$

**A3** (a) The dot accelerates away from the origin, rather than moving at constant speed.

(b) $x = t^2$

(c) $y = \dfrac{t^2}{2}$

**A4**

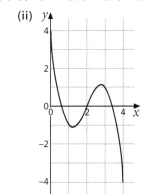

**A5** Plots with the following descriptions

(a) $G$ translated by $\begin{bmatrix} 0 \\ 2 \end{bmatrix}$

(b) $G$ translated by $\begin{bmatrix} -1 \\ 0 \end{bmatrix}$

(c) $G$ stretched by factor 3 in the $x$-direction

(d) $G$ 'stretched' by factor $\frac{1}{2}$ in the $y$-direction

(e) $G$ reflected in the $x$-axis

(f) $G$ translated by $\begin{bmatrix} 4 \\ -1 \end{bmatrix}$

**A6** (a) $x = t^2 + t + 3$, $y = -t$

(b) $x = 2(t^2 + t)$, $y = 1 - t$

### Exercise A (p 34)

**1** $(-\frac{1}{3}, 9)$, $(-\frac{1}{2}, 4)$, $(-1, 1)$, $(1, 1)$, $(\frac{1}{2}, 4)$, $(\frac{1}{3}, 9)$

**2** (a) $x = t$, $y = 3t^2$  (b) $x = t + 2$, $y = t^2 + 1$

**3** (a) (i) $(2, -3)$, $(3, 0)$, $(4, 1)$, $(5, 0)$, $(6, -3)$

(ii)

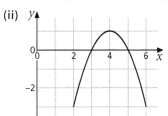

(b) (i) $(4, -4)$, $(3, 1)$, $(2, 0)$, $(1, -1)$, $(0, 4)$

(ii)

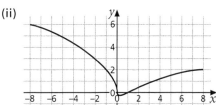

(c) (i) $(-8, 6)$, $(-1, 2)$, $(0, 0)$, $(1, 0)$, $(8, 2)$

(ii)

**4** $(0, 10)$, $(0, -10)$

**5** (a) $(0, 5)$  (b) $(0, 6)$
(c) $(0, -12)$, $(0, -3)$  (d) $(0, \frac{1}{3})$

**6** (a) $(-2.5, 0)$  (b) $(3, 0)$, $(2, 0)$
(c) $(4, 0)$  (d) $(7, 0)$

**7**

$$\frac{t}{t^2-2} = 1$$

$$\Rightarrow \quad t = t^2 - 2$$

$$\Rightarrow \quad t^2 - 2 - t = 0$$

$$\Rightarrow (t+1)(t-2) = 0$$

$$\Rightarrow \quad t = -1, 2$$

When $t = -1$, $x = \sqrt{-1+1} = 0$

When $t = 2$, $x = \sqrt{2+1} = \sqrt{3}$

So the curve meets $y = 1$ at $(0, 1)$ and $(\sqrt{3}, 1)$.

**8** $2(\sqrt{2})^3$ or $4\sqrt{2}$

**9** (a) $x = t^2$, $y = t^2 - t$     (b) $x = t^2 - 2$, $y = t^3 - 3t$

## B Converting between parametric and cartesian equations (p 35)

**B1** (a)

| $t$ | -2 | -1.5 | -1 | -0.5 | 0 | 0.5 | 1 | 1.5 | 2 |
|---|---|---|---|---|---|---|---|---|---|
| $x$ | -5 | -4 | -3 | -2 | -1 | 0 | 1 | 2 | 3 |
| $y$ | -8 | -6 | -4 | -2 | 0 | 2 | 4 | 6 | 8 |

(b) $t = \dfrac{y}{4}$

(c) $\qquad x = 2\left(\dfrac{y}{4}\right) - 1$

$$\Rightarrow \qquad x = \frac{y}{2} - 1$$

$$\Rightarrow \qquad 2x = y - 2$$

$$\Rightarrow 2x - y + 2 = 0$$

(d) A check of the values

(e) A straight line

**B2** (a) $2x - 3y - 8 = 0$     (b) $x + 6y - 5 = 0$

**B3** (a) $t = \dfrac{x}{3}$

(b) $\qquad y = 6\left(\dfrac{x}{3}\right) - \left(\dfrac{x}{3}\right)^2$

$$\Rightarrow y = 2x - \frac{x^2}{9}$$

(c) A check of the table values

**B4** These equations or their equivalents:

(a) $4x - 5y - 15 = 0$     (b) $y^2 = 4x$

(c) $y = \dfrac{x^3}{8}$

**B5** (a) $y = x^4$         (b) $y = -x^2 + 6x - 6$

(c) $y = x^3 - 3x^2 + 2$

## Exercise B (p 38)

**1** These equations or their equivalents:

(a) $y = 20x - 1$

(b) $y = \dfrac{16}{x}$

(c) $x - 9y^2 - 12y = 0$

(d) $2xy = 1$

(e) $y = x^2 - 4x + 8$

(f) $y = 1 - 2x$

(g) $y = x^4 + x^2$

(h) $y = 4 - \dfrac{1}{x}$

(i) $x = y^3 - 6y^2 + 11y - 6$

(j) $y = -x^3 + 5x^2 - 7x + 3$

(k) $y = 4x^2 + 10x + 6$

(l) $x + 4y - 27 = 0$

(m) $y = 5x^2 - x^4$

(n) $y = \dfrac{1}{x^2} + \dfrac{6}{x} + 9$

(o) $y = \dfrac{1}{x^3} + \dfrac{6}{x^2} + \dfrac{12}{x} + 8$

(p) $\dfrac{y}{x} - 3y - 1 = 0$

(q) $y = 17 - 4x$

(r) $y = \dfrac{x}{1-x}$

**2** $x + y = 2t^3$

$x - y = \dfrac{6}{t}$

Hence $(x+y)(x-y)^3 = 2t^3 \times \dfrac{216}{t^3} = 432$ as required.

**3** $x + y = \dfrac{1}{t} + \dfrac{1}{t(t-1)}$

$$= \frac{(t-1)+1}{t(t-1)} = \frac{t}{t(t-1)} = \frac{1}{t-1}$$

$$\frac{y}{x} = \frac{1}{t(t-1)} \div \frac{1}{t} = \frac{1}{t(t-1)} \times \frac{t}{1} = \frac{1}{t-1}$$

Hence $x + y = \dfrac{y}{x}$ is the cartesian equation.

**4**
$$x = \frac{1}{2t-1}$$

$$\Rightarrow \quad 2t-1 = \frac{1}{x}$$

$$\Rightarrow \quad 2t = \frac{1}{x}+1$$

$$\Rightarrow \quad t = \tfrac{1}{2}\left(\frac{1}{x}+1\right)$$

Substituting into the $y$-equation:

$$y = \frac{\tfrac{1}{2}\left(\frac{1}{x}+1\right)}{\frac{1}{x}}$$

$$\Rightarrow \quad y = \tfrac{1}{2}\left(\frac{1}{x}+1\right)\times\frac{x}{1}$$

$$\Rightarrow \quad y = \tfrac{1}{2}+\tfrac{1}{2}x, \text{ which is a straight line.}$$

Alternatively:

$$x = \frac{1}{2t-1} \text{ and } y = \frac{t}{2t-1}$$

Hence $2y-x = \dfrac{2t-1}{2t-1}$

$$\Rightarrow \quad 2y-x = 1$$

## C Circle and ellipse (p 39)

**C1** A check with a graph plotter

**C2** These in fact give

(a) a circle centre $(0,0)$, radius 3 units

(b) a circle centre $(0,0)$, radius 0.5 unit

**C3** (a) $x = \cos\theta,\ y = \sin\theta + 2$

(b) $x = \cos\theta - 3,\ y = \sin\theta$

(c) $x = \cos\theta + 1,\ y = \sin\theta - 6$

(d) $x = 2\cos\theta + 5,\ y = 2\sin\theta + 4$

**C4** (a)  (b)

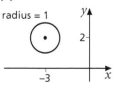

radius = 1

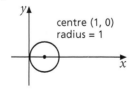

centre (1, 0)
radius = 1

**(c)**

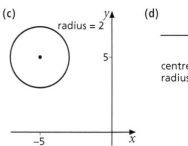

radius = 2

**(d)**

centre (0, −3)
radius = 0.6

**C5** (a) Stretch, factor 2, in the $y$-direction

(b) Stretch, factor 4, in the $x$-direction

(c) 'Stretch', factor 0.6, in the $y$-direction

(d) 'Stretch', factor 0.5, in the $x$-direction and stretch, factor 1.2, in the $y$-direction

**C6** (a) $x = 4\cos\theta,\ y = 2\sin\theta$

(b) $x = 5\cos\theta,\ y = 3\sin\theta$

(c) $x = 2\cos\theta,\ y = 3\sin\theta$

**C7** (a) $x = 2\cos\theta + 3,\ y = \sin\theta$

(b) $x = 2\cos\theta,\ y = \sin\theta - 2$

(c) $x = 2\cos\theta + 1,\ y = \sin\theta + 2$

(d) $x = 2\cos\theta - 1,\ y = 3\sin\theta - 1$

**C8** From the parametric equations,
$$\cos\theta = \frac{x}{a},\ \sin\theta = \frac{y}{b}$$
Substituting into $\cos^2\theta + \sin^2\theta = 1$ gives
$$\frac{x^2}{a^2}+\frac{y^2}{b^2} = 1$$

**C9** $\dfrac{x^2}{2^2}+\dfrac{y^2}{3^2} = 1$
$x = 2\cos\theta,\ y = 3\sin\theta$

**C10** (a) $x = 3\cos\theta,\ y = 6\sin\theta$

(b) $x = 3\cos\theta,\ y = \sin\theta$

(c) $x = \tfrac{1}{2}\cos\theta,\ y = 3\sin\theta$

### Exercise C (p 41)

**1** $(1, \sqrt{3})$

**2** (a) $x = 4\cos\theta,\ y = \sin\theta$  (b) $x = \cos\theta,\ y = 0.7\sin\theta$

**3** $(3,0),\ \left(\dfrac{3\sqrt{2}}{2},2\sqrt{2}\right),\ (0,4),\ (-3,0)$

**4** $4x^2 + 9y^2 = 1$

**5** (a) (i) $x = 2\cos\theta,\ y = \sin\theta$  (ii) $\dfrac{x^2}{4}+y^2 = 1$

(b) (i) $x = \tfrac{1}{2}\cos\theta,\ y = \sin\theta$  (ii) $4x^2 + y^2 = 1$

(c) (i) $x = 2\cos\theta, y = 1.5\sin\theta$  (ii) $\dfrac{x^2}{4} + \dfrac{4y^2}{9} = 1$

**6** (a) $(3, -2)$  (b) 5 units

(c) $x = 5\cos\theta + 3, y = 5\sin\theta - 2$

**7** (a)

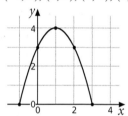

(b) $x^2 - 6x + 4y^2 + 8y + 9 = 0$

**8** $x = 6\cos\theta + 3, y = 6\sin\theta - 4$

**9** (a) $4x^2 - y^2 + 4 = 0$  (b) $9x^2 - 4y^2 - 36 = 0$

## Test yourself (p 44)

**1** $(\frac{1}{9}, -9), (\frac{1}{4}, -6), (1, -3), (1, 3), (\frac{1}{4}, 6), (\frac{1}{9}, 9)$

**2** (a) $(-1, 0), (0, 3), (1, 4), (2, 3), (3, 0)$

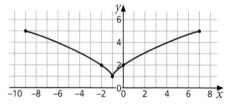

(b) $(-9, 5), (-2, 2), (-1, 1), (0, 2), (7, 5)$

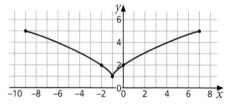

(c) $(4, -6), (3, -1), (2, 0), (1, 3), (0, 14)$

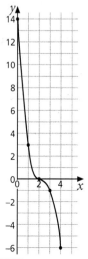

**3** (a) $(-3\frac{1}{3}, 0), (0, 10)$

(b) $(15, 0), (0, 5), (0, 3)$

(c) $(-14, 0), (-4, 0), (0, 14)$

(d) $(\frac{1}{2}, 0), (0, 26)$

**4** $(-6, 1\frac{1}{2}), (-6, 1\frac{1}{3})$

**5** (a) $3x - 4y - 15 = 0$  (b) $x + 6y - 5 = 0$

**6** (a) $y = \dfrac{x^2}{9}$

(b) $x = 8y^3$

(c) $y = x^6$

(d) $y = -x^2 - 2x + 1$

(e) $y = \dfrac{3}{x}$

(f) $x = 16y^2 - 4y$

(g) $y = x^3 - 6x^2 + 14x - 12$

(h) $y = 3 - \dfrac{1}{2x}$

(i) $x + 3y - 17 = 0$

(j) $x = 3y^2 - y^4$

(k) $x = \dfrac{1}{y^2} + \dfrac{4}{y} + 4$

(l) $y = \dfrac{x}{2x - 1}$

(m) $x + 3y - 10 = 0$

(n) $x = \dfrac{y}{5y - 3}$

**7** $(x + y)(x - y)^2 = 32$

**8** (a) Circle, radius 4 units, centre the origin

(b) Ellipse, 2 units wide, 6 units high, centre the origin

(c) Circle, radius 0.6 units, centre the origin

(d) Ellipse, 4 units wide, 6 units high, centre the origin

**9** (a) $x = 2\cos\theta, y = 2\sin\theta$

(b) $x = 2\cos\theta, y = 3\sin\theta$

(c) $x = 4\cos\theta - 1, y = 4\sin\theta - 3$

(d) $x = 3\cos\theta + 4, y = \sin\theta + 2$

**10** $\dfrac{x^2}{9} + \dfrac{y^2}{16} = 1$

**11** (a) $x = 2\cos\theta, y = 4\sin\theta$

(b) $x = 2\cos\theta, y = 5\sin\theta$

**12** $6\sqrt{3}$

# 4 The binomial theorem

## A Reviewing the binomial theorem for positive integers

### Exercise A (p 46)

**1** $1 + 30x + 375x^2 + 2500x^3 + 9375x^4 + 18\,750x^5 + 15\,625x^6$

**2** $1 - 36x + 594x^2 - 5940x^3 + 40\,095x^4$

**3** $16\,384 + 229\,376x + 1\,376\,256x^2$

**4** (a) $1 + 4x + 7x^2 + 7x^3$

(b) $256 + 1024x + 1792x^2 + 1792x^3$

**5** (a) $729 + 1458x + 1215x^2 + 540x^3 + 135x^4 + 18x^5 + x^6$

(b) $743.70$

## B Extending the binomial theorem (p 47)

**B1** (a) The coefficients for the $x^2, x^3$ and $x^4$ terms are

$$\frac{(-2)(-3)}{2!} = \frac{-2 \times -3}{2 \times 1} = \frac{6}{2} = 3$$

$$\frac{(-2)(-3)(-4)}{3!} = \frac{-2 \times -3 \times -4}{3 \times 2 \times 1} = \frac{-24}{6} = -4$$

$$\frac{(-2)(-3)(-4)(-5)}{4!} = \frac{-2 \times -3 \times -4 \times -5}{4 \times 3 \times 2 \times 1} = \frac{120}{24} = 5$$

So the expansion simplifies to
$1 - 2x + 3x^2 - 4x^3 + 5x^4 - \ldots$

(b) $\ldots - 6x^5 + 7x^6 - 8x^7$

(c) If $n$ is negative then the factors in the product $n(n-1)(n-2)(n-3)\ldots$ are all non-zero, no matter how many factors there are. Hence a non-zero coefficient of $x^k$ exists for all values of $k$. The powers of $x$ form the infinite sequence $x^0, x^1, x^2, x^3, x^4, \ldots$ so the expansion can go on for ever. However, if we try to continue the expansion of $(1 + ax)^n$ when $n$ is a positive integer, we will find that after the last term which is $a^n x^n$ the coefficients will all be zero (as $(n - n)$ which is 0 will be a factor of the product $n(n - 1)(n - 2)(n - 3) \ldots$). So the number of terms is finite.

(d) $15x^{14}$

**B2** (a) (i) $0.694\,444$

(ii)

| Expansion | Value |
| --- | --- |
| 1 | 1 |
| $1 - 2x$ | 0.6 |
| $1 - 2x + 3x^2$ | 0.72 |
| $1 - 2x + 3x^2 - 4x^3$ | 0.688 |
| $1 - 2x + 3x^2 - 4x^3 + 5x^4$ | 0.696 |
| $1 - 2x + 3x^2 - 4x^3 + 5x^4 - 6x^5$ | 0.694\,08 |
| $1 - 2x + 3x^2 - 4x^3 + 5x^4 - 6x^5 + 7x^6$ | 0.694\,528 |
| $1 - 2x + 3x^2 - 4x^3 + 5x^4 - 6x^5 + 7x^6 - 8x^7$ | 0.694\,4256 |

(iii) The values appear to be converging towards a limit which looks as though it is the value of $(1 + x)^{-2}$ when $x = 0.2$, i.e. $0.694\,444\ldots$

(b) (i) 1

(ii) Values when $x = -2$ are:
1, 5, 17, 49, 129, 321, 769, 1793
The values are diverging and not converging towards the value of $(1 + x)^{-2}$ when $x = -2$, i.e. 1.

(c) (i) $0.277\,008$

(ii) Values (rounded to 6 d.p. where appropriate) when $x = 0.9$ are:
1, −0.8, 1.63, −1.286, 1.9945, −1.548\,44, 2.171\,647, −1.654\,728
The values do not appear to be converging but it is not possible to deduce from the expansion that values will continue to diverge.

**B3** (a) The expansion does in fact converge to the value of $(1 + x)^{-2}$ when $x = 0.9$, i.e. $0.277\,008$ (to 6 d.p.), though you need to evaluate the sum of many terms in the expansion before you can conjecture this with confidence.

(b) When $-1 < x < 1$, then the expansion will converge. For values close to 0, the convergence is much faster than for those values near −1 or 1.

**B4**

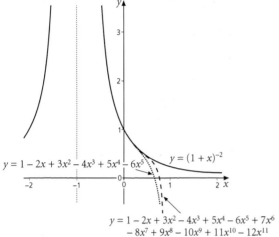

$y = 1 - 2x + 3x^2 - 4x^3 + 5x^4 - 6x^5$

$y = (1 + x)^{-2}$

$y = 1 - 2x + 3x^2 - 4x^3 + 5x^4 - 6x^5 + 7x^6$
$- 8x^7 + 9x^8 - 10x^9 + 11x^{10} - 12x^{11}$

Comments such as:
The graphs of $y = f(x)$ and $y = g(x)$ are very close between about $-0.5$ and $0.5$. The graph of $y = f(x)$ is very close to the graph of $y = h(x)$ over a larger interval between about $-0.7$ and $0.7$.

**B5 (a)** Using the binomial theorem gives

$$(1 - 2x)^{-1} = 1 + (-1)(-2x) + \frac{(-1)(-2)}{2!}(-2x)^2$$

$$+ \frac{(-1)(-2)(-3)}{3!}(-2x)^3 + \frac{(-1)(-2)(-3)(-4)}{4!}(-2x)^4$$

$$+ \frac{(-1)(-2)(-3)(-4)(-5)}{5!}(-2x)^5 + \dots$$

$$= 1 + 2x + 4x^2 + 8x^3 + 16x^4 + 32x^5 + \dots$$

**(b)** $2048x^{11}$

**(c) (i)** $-2.5$

**(ii)** Values when $x = 0.7$ are:
1, 2.4, 4.36, 7.104, 10.9456, … and further rows in the spreadsheet show that the values are diverging and not converging towards the value of $(1 - 2x)^{-1}$ when $x = 0.7$, i.e. $-2.5$.

**(d)** When $-0.5 < x < 0.5$, then the expansion will converge to the value of $(1 - 2x)^{-1}$.

**B6 (a)** The coefficients for $x^2$ and $x^3$ are

$$\frac{\left(\frac{1}{2}\right)\left(-\frac{1}{2}\right)}{2!} = \frac{\frac{1}{2} \times -\frac{1}{2}}{2 \times 1} = \frac{-\frac{1}{4}}{2} = -\frac{1}{8}$$

$$\frac{\left(\frac{1}{2}\right)\left(-\frac{1}{2}\right)\left(-\frac{3}{2}\right)}{3!} = \frac{\frac{1}{2} \times -\frac{1}{2} \times -\frac{3}{2}}{3 \times 2 \times 1} = \frac{\frac{3}{8}}{6} = \frac{3}{48} = \frac{1}{16}$$

So the expansion simplifies to
$1 + \frac{1}{2}x - \frac{1}{8}x^2 + \frac{1}{16}x^3 + \dots$

**(b)** $\dots -\frac{5}{128}x^4 + \frac{7}{256}x^5$

**(c) (i)** 1.341 641 (to 6 d.p.)     **(ii)** 1.352

**(d)**

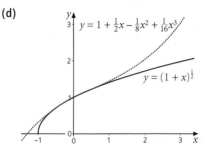

$y = 1 + \frac{1}{2}x - \frac{1}{8}x^2 + \frac{1}{16}x^3$

$y = (1 + x)^{\frac{1}{2}}$

As shown above, between $x = -1$ and $x = 1$ the graphs of $y = (1 + x)^{\frac{1}{2}}$ and $y = 1 + \frac{1}{2}x - \frac{1}{8}x^2 + \frac{1}{16}x^3$ are close.

**B7 (a)** $|2x| < 1 \Rightarrow -1 < 2x < 1$
$\Rightarrow -\frac{1}{2} < x < \frac{1}{2}$
$\Rightarrow |x| < \frac{1}{2}$

**(b)** $|-4x| < 1 \Rightarrow -1 < -4x < 1$
$\Rightarrow 1 > 4x > -1$
$\Rightarrow -1 < 4x < 1$
$\Rightarrow -\frac{1}{4} < x < \frac{1}{4}$
$\Rightarrow |x| < \frac{1}{4}$

**(c)** $\left|\frac{1}{3}x\right| < 1 \Rightarrow -1 < \frac{1}{3}x < 1$
$\Rightarrow -3 < x < 3$
$\Rightarrow |x| < 3$

**(d)** $\left|\frac{3}{4}x\right| < 1 \Rightarrow -1 < \frac{3}{4}x < 1$
$\Rightarrow -\frac{4}{3} < x < \frac{4}{3}$
$\Rightarrow |x| < \frac{4}{3}$

## Exercise B (p 51)

**1 (a)** $1 - x + x^2 - x^3$      $|x| < 1$

**(b)** $1 + 2x + 3x^2 + 4x^3$      $|x| < 1$

**(c)** $1 - 8x + 40x^2 - 160x^3$      $|x| < \frac{1}{2}$

**(d)** $1 - x + \frac{3}{4}x^2 - \frac{1}{2}x^3$      $|x| < 2$

**(e)** $1 - 3x + 9x^2 - 27x^3$      $|x| < \frac{1}{3}$

**(f)** $1 + \frac{2}{3}x + \frac{1}{3}x^2 + \frac{4}{27}x^3$      $|x| < 3$

**(g)** $1 - \frac{1}{2}x - \frac{1}{8}x^2 - \frac{1}{16}x^3$      $|x| < 1$

**(h)** $1 + \frac{1}{8}x - \frac{1}{128}x^2 + \frac{1}{1024}x^3$      $|x| < 4$

**(i)** $1 - x - \frac{3}{2}x^2 - \frac{5}{2}x^3$      $|x| < \frac{1}{2}$

**2 (a)** Using the binomial theorem,

$$(1+3x)^{\frac{1}{3}} = 1 + \left(\tfrac{1}{3}\right)(3x) + \frac{\left(\tfrac{1}{3}\right)\left(-\tfrac{2}{3}\right)}{2!}(3x)^2$$

$$+ \frac{\left(\tfrac{1}{3}\right)\left(-\tfrac{2}{3}\right)\left(-\tfrac{5}{3}\right)}{3!}(3x)^3 + \ldots = 1 + x - x^2 + \tfrac{5}{3}x^3 - \ldots$$

**(b)** $|x| < \tfrac{1}{3}$

**3 (a)** $1 + 2x - 2x^2 + 4x^3 - 10x^4 + 28x^5 - 84x^6$

**(b)** The expansion is valid when $|x| < \tfrac{1}{4}$.
$\sqrt{1.4} = (1 + 4 \times 0.1)^{\frac{1}{2}}$ which is $(1 + 4x)^{\frac{1}{2}}$ when
$x = 0.1$. As $|0.1| < \tfrac{1}{4}$, the expansion will be
valid for this value.

So $\sqrt{1.4} \approx 1 + 2(0.1) - 2(0.1)^2 + 4(0.1)^3$
$- 10(0.1)^4 + 28(0.1)^5 - 84(0.1)^6 = 1 + 0.2$
$- 0.02 + 0.004 - 0.001 + 0.000\,28 - 0.000\,084$.
Now the first six terms give $1.183\,28$ and
subsequent terms will not alter the value of
the first two decimal places. Hence
$\sqrt{1.4} = 1.18$ (to 2 d.p.)

**4 (a)** $1 + 3x + \tfrac{3}{2}x^2$

**(b)** $1.8^{\frac{3}{2}} = (1 + 2 \times 0.4)^{\frac{3}{2}} \approx 1 + 3(0.4) + \tfrac{3}{2}(0.4)^2$
$= 2.44$
Using a calculator gives $1.8^{\frac{3}{2}} = 2.414\,953\,4\ldots$,
which agrees with the approximate value
when both values are rounded to 2 s.f. (to give
2.4). So the approximate value is accurate to
2 s.f.

**5 (a)** $1 + \tfrac{1}{4}x - \tfrac{1}{32}x^2$

**(b) (i)** $4 + x - \tfrac{1}{8}x^2$      **(ii)** $|x| < 2$

**6** $\tfrac{1}{648}$

**7 (a)** $\tfrac{1}{2} - \tfrac{1}{4}x + \tfrac{1}{8}x^2$      $|x| < 2$

**(b)** $\tfrac{1}{64} + \tfrac{3}{256}x + \tfrac{3}{512}x^2$      $|x| < 4$

**(c)** $\tfrac{1}{36} - \tfrac{1}{36}x + \tfrac{1}{48}x^2$      $|x| < 2$

**(d)** $2 + \tfrac{1}{4}x - \tfrac{1}{64}x^2$      $|x| < 4$

**(e)** $\tfrac{1}{3} - \tfrac{2}{9}x + \tfrac{4}{27}x^2$      $|x| < \tfrac{3}{2}$

**(f)** $2 - \tfrac{4}{5}x - \tfrac{16}{25}x^2$      $|x| < \tfrac{1}{2}$

## C Multiplying to obtain expansions

### Exercise C (p 52)

**1 (a)** $5 + 10x + 15x^2 + 20x^3$

**(b)** $x - 3x^2 + 9x^3$

**(c)** $1 + 3x + 8x^2 + 26x^3$

**(d)** $1 + 7x + 36x^2 + 162x^3$

**2 (a) (i)** $(1 - 3x)^{-1} = 1 + (-1)(-3x) + \frac{(-1)(-2)}{2!}(-3x)^2 + \ldots$

$\approx 1 + 3x + 9x^2$

**(ii)** $|x| < \tfrac{1}{3}$

**(b) (i)** $(1 + x)^{-4} = 1 + (-4)x + \frac{(-4)(-5)}{2!}x^2 + \ldots$

$\approx 1 - 4x + 10x^2$

**(ii)** $|x| < 1$

**(c) (i)** $(1 + 3x + 9x^2 + \ldots)(1 - 4x + 10x^2 - \ldots)$
$= 1 - 4x + 10x^2 + \ldots + 3x - 12x^2 + \ldots$
$\quad + 9x^2 + \ldots$
$= 1 - x + 7x^2 + \ldots$
$\approx 1 - x + 7x^2$

**(ii)** The expansion is valid for values of $x$ that
satisfy both $|x| < \tfrac{1}{3}$ and $|x| < 1$, that is,
which satisfy $|x| < \tfrac{1}{3}$.

## D Adding (using partial fractions) to obtain expansions

### Exercise D (p 54)

**1 (a)** $\dfrac{3}{1-x} + \dfrac{1}{1+2x}$

**(b)** $4 + x + 7x^2$

**(c)** $\dfrac{1}{1-x}$ is valid for $|x| < 1$ and $\dfrac{1}{1+2x}$ is valid for
$|x| < \tfrac{1}{2}$ so the expansion for f($x$) is valid for
values of $x$ that satisfy both inequalities, i.e.
for $|x| < \tfrac{1}{2}$.

**2 (a)** $\dfrac{2}{2+x} + \dfrac{3}{1-2x}$

**(b) (i)** $\dfrac{1}{2+x} = (2+x)^{-1} = 2^{-1}\left(1 + \tfrac{1}{2}x\right)^{-1}$

$= \tfrac{1}{2}\left(1 + \tfrac{1}{2}x\right)^{-1}$

$= \tfrac{1}{2}\left(1 + (-1)\left(\tfrac{1}{2}x\right) + \dfrac{(-1)(-2)}{2!}\left(\tfrac{1}{2}x\right)^2 + \ldots\right)$

$= \tfrac{1}{2}\left(1 - \tfrac{1}{2}x + \tfrac{1}{4}x^2 - \ldots\right)$

$= \tfrac{1}{2} - \tfrac{1}{4}x + \tfrac{1}{8}x^2 - \ldots$

so the first three terms are $\tfrac{1}{2} - \tfrac{1}{4}x + \tfrac{1}{8}x^2$.

**(ii)** $1 + 2x + 4x^2$

**(c)** $4 + \tfrac{11}{2}x + \tfrac{49}{4}x^2$

**(d)** $|x| < \tfrac{1}{2}$

**3 (a)** $2 - x + 25x^2 - 37x^3$ $\qquad |x| < \tfrac{1}{4}$

**(b)** $\tfrac{7}{3} - \tfrac{53}{9}x + \tfrac{487}{27}x^2 - \tfrac{4373}{81}x^3$ $\quad |x| < \tfrac{1}{3}$

**(c)** $3 - \tfrac{4}{3}x + \tfrac{22}{9}x^2 - \tfrac{46}{27}x^3$ $\qquad |x| < 1$

**4** $\dfrac{11x - 3}{(4-3x)(1+x)} \equiv \dfrac{A}{4-3x} + \dfrac{B}{1+x}$

$\Rightarrow A(1+x) + B(4-3x) \equiv 11x - 3$

$x = -1 \Rightarrow 7B = -14 \Rightarrow B = -2$

$x = \tfrac{4}{3} \Rightarrow \tfrac{7}{3}A = \tfrac{35}{3} \Rightarrow A = 5$

So $\dfrac{11x - 3}{(4-3x)(1+x)} \equiv \dfrac{5}{4-3x} - \dfrac{2}{1+x}$

$\dfrac{5}{4-3x} = 5(4-3x)^{-1} = \tfrac{5}{4}\left(1 - \tfrac{3}{4}x\right)^{-1}$

$= \tfrac{5}{4}\left(1 + (-1)\left(-\tfrac{3}{4}x\right) + \dfrac{(-1)(-2)}{2!}\left(-\tfrac{3}{4}x\right)^2 + \ldots\right)$

$= \tfrac{5}{4}\left(1 + \tfrac{3}{4}x + \tfrac{9}{16}x^2 + \ldots\right)$

$= \tfrac{5}{4} + \tfrac{15}{16}x + \tfrac{45}{64}x^2 + \ldots$

$\dfrac{2}{1+x} = 2(1+x)^{-1} = 2\left(1 - x + x^2 - \ldots\right)$

$= 2 - 2x + 2x^2 - \ldots$

so $\dfrac{5}{4-3x} - \dfrac{2}{1+x}$

$= \left(\tfrac{5}{4} + \tfrac{15}{16}x + \tfrac{45}{64}x^2 + \ldots\right) - \left(2 - 2x + 2x^2 - \ldots\right)$

$= -\tfrac{3}{4} + \tfrac{47}{16}x - \tfrac{83}{64}x^2 + \ldots$

So the first three terms of the expansion are

$-\tfrac{3}{4} + \tfrac{47}{16}x - \tfrac{83}{64}x^2$ as required.

## Mixed questions (p 54)

**1 (a)** $4 - 24x + 96x^2$ $\qquad$ **(b)** $|x| < \tfrac{1}{2}$

**2 (a)** $10 - 20x - 20x^2 - 40x^3$

**(b) (i)** $x = 0.1$

**(ii)** $\sqrt{60} = 60^{\frac{1}{2}} = (100 - 400 \times 0.1)^{\frac{1}{2}}$

$\approx 10 - 20(0.1) - 20(0.1)^2 - 40(0.1)^3$

$= 7.76$.

**(iii)** From a calculator, $\sqrt{60} = 7.745\,966\,69\ldots$, which agrees with the approximate value when both values are rounded to 1 s.f. (to give 8). So the approximate value is accurate to 1 s.f.

**3** $a = 5$, $n = -2$

**4 (a)** $1 - x + x^2 - x^3$

**(b)** $(1+x)^{-1} = \dfrac{1}{1+x}$; the integral of this is $\ln(1+x)$. The integral of the first four terms of the expansion is $x - \tfrac{1}{2}x^2 + \tfrac{1}{3}x^3 - \tfrac{1}{4}x^4$ so the series expansion for $\ln(1+x)$ as far as the term in $x^4$ is $x - \tfrac{1}{2}x^2 + \tfrac{1}{3}x^3 - \tfrac{1}{4}x^4$.

**(c)** No, $\ln(1+x) = \ln 3$ when $x = 2$ and the expansion is only valid for $|x| < 1$.

**5 (a)** $1 + 2x + 4x^2 + 8x^3$

**(b)** $\dfrac{1-x}{1-2x} = (1-x)(1-2x)^{-1}$

$= (1-x)(1 + 2x + 4x^2 + 8x^3 + \ldots)$

$= 1 + 2x + 4x^2 + 8x^3 + \ldots - x - 2x^2 - 4x^3 - \ldots$

$= 1 + x + 2x^2 + 4x^3 + \ldots$

So the first four terms in the expansion are $1 + x + 2x^2 + 4x^3$.

**(c)** $\dfrac{99}{98} = \dfrac{0.99}{0.98} = \dfrac{1 - 0.01}{1 - 0.02} = \dfrac{1-x}{1-2x}$ when $x = 0.01$.

So $\dfrac{99}{98} \approx 1 + (0.01) + 2(0.01)^2 + 4(0.01)^3$

$= 1 + 0.01 + 0.0002 + 0.000\,004$

$= 1.010\,20$ (to 5 d.p.)

**(d)** $0.010\,20$

## Test yourself (p 55)

**1** (a) $p = 24$, $q = 80$     (b) $1 + 3x + 6x^2$

**2** (a) $\dfrac{3}{1+3x} + \dfrac{2}{2-x}$

  (b) $1 - 3x + 9x^2$

  (c) Using the binomial theorem,

$$(2-x)^{-1} = 2^{-1}\left(1 - \tfrac{1}{2}x\right)^{-1} = \tfrac{1}{2}\left(1 - \tfrac{1}{2}x\right)^{-1}$$

$$= \tfrac{1}{2}\left(1 + (-1)\left(-\tfrac{1}{2}x\right) + \frac{(-1)(-2)}{2!}\left(-\tfrac{1}{2}x\right)^2 + \ldots\right)$$

$$= \tfrac{1}{2}\left(1 + \tfrac{1}{2}x + \tfrac{1}{4}x^2 + \ldots\right)$$

$$= \tfrac{1}{2} + \tfrac{1}{4}x + \tfrac{1}{8}x^2 + \ldots$$

So the first three terms of the expansion are $\tfrac{1}{2} + \tfrac{1}{4}x + \tfrac{1}{8}x^2$.

  (d) $4 - \dfrac{17}{2}x + \dfrac{109}{4}x^2$

  (e) $|x| < \tfrac{1}{3}$

**3** (a) $1 + \tfrac{1}{2}x - \tfrac{1}{8}x^2$

  (b) (i) $2 + \tfrac{1}{2}x - \tfrac{1}{16}x^2$    (ii) $|x| < 2$

**4** (a) $1 - 2x - 8x^2 - 48x^3$

  (b) $(1 - 10 \times 0.001)^{\frac{1}{5}} = 0.99^{\frac{1}{5}}$

$$\approx 1 - (2 \times 0.001) - (8 \times 0.001^2) - (48 \times 0.001^3)$$

$$= 0.997\,991\,952$$

So $\sqrt[5]{0.99} = 0.997\,99$ to 5 s.f. (further terms in the expansion will not affect the value of the fifth significant figure).

Hence $\sqrt[5]{99\,000} = \sqrt[5]{0.99 \times 100\,000}$

$$= \sqrt[5]{0.99} \times \sqrt[5]{100\,000}$$

$$= 10 \times \sqrt[5]{0.99}$$

$$= 10 \times 0.997\,99 \text{ (to 5 s.f.)}$$

$$= 9.9799 \text{ (to 5 s.f.)}$$

**5** $\dfrac{5}{32}$

# 5 Trigonometric formulae

## A Addition formulae (p 56)

**A1** (a) $\cos B$

  (b) $\cos B \sin A$

  (c) $\angle RPO = 90° - A$

$$\angle QPT = 180° - (90° + \angle RPO)$$
$$= 180° - (90° + 90° - A) = A$$
$$PT = PQ \cos \angle QPT$$

In $\triangle OPQ$, $PQ = \sin B$, so $PT = \sin B \cos \angle QPT$
$$= \sin B \cos A$$

  (d) $\cos B \sin A + \sin B \cos A$

  (e) $QH = \sin (A + B) = RP + PT$

Hence $\sin (A + B) = \cos B \sin A + \sin B \cos A$
$$= \sin A \cos B + \cos A \sin B$$

**A2** $OH = OR - HR = OR - QT$
$$\cos (A + B) = OP \cos A - PQ \sin A$$
$$= \cos B \cos A - \sin B \sin A$$
$$= \cos A \cos B - \sin A \sin B$$

**A3** $\sin (A + B) = \sin A \cos B + \cos A \sin B$
$$\Rightarrow \sin (A + (-B)) = \sin A \cos (-B) + \cos A \sin (-B)$$
$$= \sin A \cos B + \cos A (-\sin B)$$
$$\Rightarrow \quad \sin (A - B) = \sin A \cos B - \cos A \sin B$$

$$\cos (A + B) = \cos A \cos B - \sin A \sin B$$
$$\Rightarrow \cos (A + (-B)) = \cos A \cos (-B) - \sin A \sin (-B)$$
$$= \cos A \cos B - \sin A (-\sin B)$$
$$\Rightarrow \quad \cos (A + B) = \cos A \cos B + \sin A \sin B$$

**A4** $\sin (A + A) = \sin A \cos A + \cos A \sin A$
$$\Rightarrow \sin 2A = 2 \sin A \cos A$$

**A5** (a) $\cos (A + A) = \cos A \cos A - \sin A \sin A$
$$\Rightarrow \quad \cos 2A = \cos^2 A - \sin^2 A$$
$$= \cos^2 A - (1 - \cos^2 A)$$
$$= \cos^2 A - 1 + \cos^2 A$$
$$= 2 \cos^2 A - 1$$

  (b) $\cos 2A = \cos^2 A - \sin^2 A$
$$= 1 - \sin^2 A - \sin^2 A$$
$$= 1 - 2 \sin^2 A$$

**A6** Given that $\sin A = \tfrac{1}{4}$, if $A$ is acute, then $0° < A < 45°$, so $0° < 2A < 90°$.

In this case $\sin 2A$ and $\cos 2A$ are both $> 0$.

But for $\sin A = \tfrac{1}{4}$, $A$ might be obtuse, with $135° < A < 180°$, giving $270° < 2A < 360°$.

In this case $\sin 2A < 0$ but again $\cos 2A > 0$. Hence there is one value for $\cos 2A$ but two for $\sin 2A$.

**A7** (a) $\dfrac{\sin(A+B)}{\cos(A+B)}$

(b) $\dfrac{\sin(A+B)}{\cos(A+B)} = \dfrac{\sin A \cos B + \cos A \sin B}{\cos A \cos B - \sin A \sin B}$

(c) $\dfrac{\dfrac{\sin A \cos B}{\cos A \cos B} + \dfrac{\cos A \sin B}{\cos A \cos B}}{\dfrac{\cos A \cos B - \sin A \sin B}{\cos A \cos B}}$

$= \dfrac{\dfrac{\sin A}{\cos A} + \dfrac{\sin B}{\cos B}}{1 - \dfrac{\sin A \sin B}{\cos A \cos B}}$

$= \dfrac{\tan A + \tan B}{1 - \tan A \tan B}$

**A8** (a) $\tan(A + (-B)) = \dfrac{\tan A + \tan(-B)}{1 - \tan A \tan(-B)}$

$= \dfrac{\tan A + (-\tan B)}{1 - \tan A(-\tan B)}$

$\Rightarrow \tan(A - B) = \dfrac{\tan A - \tan B}{1 + \tan A \tan B}$

(b) $\tan 2A = \tan(A + A)$

$= \dfrac{\tan A + \tan A}{1 - \tan A \tan A} = \dfrac{2\tan A}{1 - \tan^2 A}$

**Exercise A** (p 60)

**1** $\sin(x + 180)° = \sin x° \cos 180° + \cos x° \sin 180°$

$= \sin x° \times (-1) + \cos x° \times 0$

$= -\sin x°$

The graph of $y = \sin(x + 180)°$ is that of $y = \sin x°$ translated by $\begin{bmatrix} -180° \\ 0 \end{bmatrix}$.

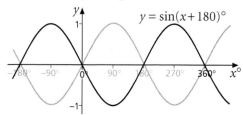

$y = \sin(x+180)°$

The resulting graph is the same as the reflection of $y = \sin x°$ in the $x$-axis, i.e. $y = -\sin x°$.

**2** (a) $\sin 75° = \sin(45° + 30°)$

$= \sin 45° \cos 30° + \cos 45° \sin 30°$

$= \dfrac{1}{\sqrt{2}} \times \dfrac{\sqrt{3}}{2} + \dfrac{1}{\sqrt{2}} \times \dfrac{1}{2}$

$= \dfrac{\sqrt{3} + 1}{2\sqrt{2}}$

(b) $\sin 15° = \sin(45° - 30°)$

$= \sin 45° \cos 30° - \cos 45° \sin 30°$

$= \dfrac{1}{\sqrt{2}} \times \dfrac{\sqrt{3}}{2} - \dfrac{1}{\sqrt{2}} \times \dfrac{1}{2}$

$= \dfrac{\sqrt{3} - 1}{2\sqrt{2}}$

**3** (a) $\sin^2 A = 1 - \cos^2 A = 1 - \left(\dfrac{4}{5}\right)^2 = 1 - \dfrac{16}{25} = \dfrac{9}{25}$

So $\sin A = \pm\dfrac{3}{5}$

Since $A$ is acute, $\sin A > 0$, so $\sin A = \dfrac{3}{5}$

(b) $\sin 2A = 2\sin A \cos A = 2 \times \dfrac{3}{5} \times \dfrac{4}{5} = \dfrac{24}{25}$

(c) $\cos 2A = 1 - 2\sin^2 A = 1 - 2 \times \dfrac{9}{25} = \dfrac{7}{25}$

(d) $\operatorname{cosec} 2A = \dfrac{1}{\sin 2A} = \dfrac{1}{\frac{24}{25}} = \dfrac{25}{24}$

**4** (a) $\tan(A + B) = \dfrac{\tan A + \tan B}{1 - \tan A \tan B} = \dfrac{\frac{1}{2} + \frac{1}{3}}{1 - \frac{1}{2} \times \frac{1}{3}}$

$= \dfrac{\frac{5}{6}}{1 - \frac{1}{6}} = \dfrac{\frac{5}{6}}{\frac{5}{6}} = 1$

(b) $\tan 2C = \dfrac{3}{4} \Rightarrow \dfrac{2\tan C}{1 + \tan^2 C} = \dfrac{3}{4}$

$\Rightarrow 4 \times 2\tan C = 3 \times (1 - \tan^2 C)$

$\Rightarrow 8\tan C = 3 - 3\tan^2 C$

$\Rightarrow 3\tan^2 C + 8\tan C - 3 = 0$

$\Rightarrow (3\tan C - 1)(\tan C + 3) = 0$

$\Rightarrow \tan C = \dfrac{1}{3}$ or $-3$

**5** (a) $\cos(A + B) + \cos(A - B)$

$= (\cos A \cos B - \sin A \sin B)$

$\quad + (\cos A \cos B + \sin A \sin B)$

$= 2\cos A \cos B$

(b) $\cos(A - B) - \cos(A + B)$

$= (\cos A \cos B + \sin A \sin B)$

$\quad - (\cos A \cos B - \sin A \sin B)$

$= 2\sin A \sin B$

**6 (a)** $\cos 2A \cos A - \sin 2A \sin A$
$= \cos(2A + A) = \cos 3A$

**(b)** $\cos(A + B)\cos A + \sin(A + B)\sin A$
$= \cos((A + B) - A) = \cos B$

**(c)** $2 \sin 3C \cos 3C = \sin(2 \times 3C) = \sin 6C$

**(d)** $\sin 3D \cos 2D + \cos 3D \sin 2D$
$= \sin(3D + 2D) = \sin 5D$

**7 (a)** $(\cos A + \sin A)(\cos B + \sin B)$
$= \cos A \cos B + \sin A \sin B$
$\quad + \cos A \sin B + \sin A \cos B$
$= \cos(A - B) + \sin(A + B)$

**(b)** $(\cos A + \sin A)^2$
$= \cos^2 A + 2 \sin A \cos A + \sin^2 A$
$= \cos^2 A + \sin^2 A + 2 \sin A \cos A$
$= 1 + 2 \sin A \cos A = 1 + \sin 2A$

**(c)** $\sin 3A = \sin(2A + A)$
$= \sin 2A \cos A + \cos 2A \sin A$
$= (2 \sin A \cos A) \times \cos A + (1 - 2 \sin^2 A) \times \sin A$
$= 2 \sin A \cos^2 A + \sin A - 2 \sin^3 A$
$= 2 \sin A (1 - \sin^2 A) + \sin A - 2 \sin^3 A$
$= 2 \sin A - 2 \sin^3 A + \sin A - 2 \sin^3 A$
$= 3 \sin A - 4 \sin^3 A$

**(d)** $(\sin A + \cos B)^2 + (\cos A - \sin B)^2$
$= (\sin^2 A + 2 \sin A \cos B + \cos^2 B)$
$\quad + (\cos^2 A - 2 \cos A \sin B + \sin^2 B)$
$= \sin^2 A + \cos^2 A + 2 \sin A \cos B - 2 \cos A \sin B$
$\quad + \cos^2 B + \sin^2 B$
$= 1 + 2(\sin A \cos B - \cos A \sin B) + 1$
$= 2 + 2 \times \sin(A - B) = 2(1 + \sin(A - B))$

**8** $\cot 2x + \operatorname{cosec} 2x = \dfrac{\cos 2x}{\sin 2x} + \dfrac{1}{\sin 2x}$

$= \dfrac{\cos 2x + 1}{\sin 2x} = \dfrac{\cos 2x + 1}{2 \sin x \cos x} = \dfrac{(2\cos^2 x - 1) + 1}{2 \sin x \cos x}$

$= \dfrac{2 \cos^2 x}{2 \sin x \cos x} = \dfrac{\cos x}{\sin x} = \cot x$

**9** $\dfrac{\cos \theta}{1 - \sqrt{2} \sin \theta} - \dfrac{\cos \theta}{1 + \sqrt{2} \sin \theta}$

$= \dfrac{\cos \theta(1 + \sqrt{2} \sin \theta) - \cos \theta(1 - \sqrt{2} \sin \theta)}{(1 - \sqrt{2} \sin \theta)(1 + \sqrt{2} \sin \theta)}$

$= \dfrac{\cos \theta + \sqrt{2} \cos \theta \sin \theta - \cos \theta + \sqrt{2} \cos \theta \sin \theta}{1 - 2 \sin^2 \theta}$

$= \dfrac{2\sqrt{2} \cos \theta \sin \theta}{1 - 2 \sin^2 \theta} = \dfrac{\sqrt{2} \sin 2\theta}{\cos 2\theta}$

$= \sqrt{2} \tan 2\theta$

**10** $\dfrac{\tan a}{\sec a - 1} = \dfrac{\dfrac{\sin a}{\cos a}}{\dfrac{1}{\cos a} - 1} = \dfrac{\sin a}{1 - \cos a}$

$= \dfrac{2 \sin \frac{1}{2}a \cos \frac{1}{2}a}{1 - \left(1 - 2 \sin^2 \frac{1}{2}a\right)} = \dfrac{2 \sin \frac{1}{2}a \cos \frac{1}{2}a}{2 \sin^2 \frac{1}{2}a} = \dfrac{\cos \frac{1}{2}a}{\sin \frac{1}{2}a}$

$= \cot \frac{1}{2}a$

**11 (a)** $\dfrac{2t}{1 + t^2} = \dfrac{2 \tan \frac{1}{2}\theta}{1 + \tan^2 \frac{1}{2}\theta} = \dfrac{\dfrac{2 \sin \frac{1}{2}\theta}{\cos \frac{1}{2}\theta}}{1 + \dfrac{\sin^2 \frac{1}{2}\theta}{\cos^2 \frac{1}{2}\theta}}$

$= \dfrac{\cos^2 \frac{1}{2}\theta \times \dfrac{2 \sin \frac{1}{2}\theta}{\cos \frac{1}{2}\theta}}{\cos^2 \frac{1}{2}\theta + \sin^2 \frac{1}{2}\theta} = \dfrac{\cos \frac{1}{2}\theta \times 2 \sin \frac{1}{2}\theta}{1}$

$= 2 \cos \frac{1}{2}\theta \sin \frac{1}{2}\theta = \sin \theta$

**(b)** $\dfrac{1 - t^2}{1 + t^2} = \dfrac{1 - \tan^2 \frac{1}{2}\theta}{1 + \tan^2 \frac{1}{2}\theta} = \dfrac{1 - \dfrac{\sin^2 \frac{1}{2}\theta}{\cos^2 \frac{1}{2}\theta}}{1 + \dfrac{\sin^2 \frac{1}{2}\theta}{\cos^2 \frac{1}{2}\theta}}$

$= \dfrac{\cos^2 \frac{1}{2}\theta - \sin^2 \frac{1}{2}\theta}{\cos^2 \frac{1}{2}\theta + \sin^2 \frac{1}{2}\theta} = \dfrac{\cos^2 \frac{1}{2}\theta - \sin^2 \frac{1}{2}\theta}{1}$

$= \cos \theta$

**12 (a)** $\sin 2x° = \cos x°$
$\Rightarrow 2 \sin x° \cos x° = \cos x°$
$\Rightarrow 2 \sin x° \cos x° - \cos x° = 0$
$\Rightarrow \cos x°(2 \sin x° - 1) = 0$
$\Rightarrow \cos x° = 0$ or $\sin x° = \frac{1}{2}$
$\cos x° = 0$ gives $x° = 90°$ or $270°$
$\sin x° = \frac{1}{2}$ gives $x° = 30°$ or $150°$
So $x° = 30°, 90°, 150°$ or $270°$

**(b)** $\sin x° + \cos 2x° = 0$
$\Rightarrow \sin x° + (1 - 2 \sin^2 x°) = 0$
$\Rightarrow 2 \sin^2 x° - \sin x° - 1 = 0$
$\Rightarrow (2 \sin x° + 1)(\sin x° - 1) = 0$
$\Rightarrow 2 \sin x° + 1 = 0$ or $\sin x° - 1 = 0$
$\Rightarrow \sin x° = -\frac{1}{2}$ or $\sin x° = 1$
$\sin x° = -\frac{1}{2}$ gives $x° = 210°$ or $330°$
$\sin x° = 1$ gives $x° = 90°$
So $x° = 90°, 210°$ or $330°$

(c) $\cos 2x° = 7\cos x° + 3$
$\Rightarrow 2\cos^2 x° - 1 = 7\cos x° + 3$
$\Rightarrow 2\cos^2 x° - 7\cos x° - 4 = 0$
$\Rightarrow (2\cos x° + 1)(\cos x° - 4) = 0$
$\Rightarrow 2\cos x° + 1 = 0$ or $\cos x° - 4 = 0$
$\Rightarrow \cos x° = -\frac{1}{2}$ or $\cos x° = 4$ (no solution)
So $x° = 120°$ or $240°$

(d) $\cos 2x° = 1 + \sin x°$
$\Rightarrow 1 - 2\sin^2 x° = 1 + \sin x°$
$\Rightarrow -2\sin^2 x° = \sin x°$
$\Rightarrow 2\sin^2 x° + \sin x° = 0$
$\Rightarrow \sin x° (2\sin x° + 1) = 0$
$\Rightarrow \sin x° = 0$ or
$\quad 2\sin x° + 1 = 0 \left(\text{so } \sin x° = -\frac{1}{2}\right)$
$\sin x° = 0$ gives $x° = 0°$, $180°$ or $360°$
$\sin x° = -\frac{1}{2}$ gives $x° = 210°$ or $330°$
So $x° = 0°, 180°, 210°, 330°$ or $360°$

(e) $\sin 2x° = \tan x°$
$\Rightarrow 2\sin x° \cos x° = \dfrac{\sin x°}{\cos x°}$
$\Rightarrow \cos x° \times 2\sin x° \cos x° = \sin x°$
$\Rightarrow 2\cos^2 x° \sin x° - \sin x° = 0$
$\Rightarrow \sin x° (2\cos^2 x° - 1) = 0$
$\Rightarrow \sin x° = 0$ or
$\quad 2\cos^2 x° - 1 = 0 \left(\text{so } \cos x° = \pm\dfrac{1}{\sqrt{2}}\right)$
$\sin x° = 0$ gives $x° = 0°$, $180°$ or $360°$
$\cos x° = \pm\dfrac{1}{\sqrt{2}}$ gives $x° = 45°, 135°, 225°$ or $315°$
$\Rightarrow x° = 0°, 45°, 135°, 180°, 225°, 315°$ or $360°$

13 (a) $\sin(\theta + \phi) + \sin(\theta - \phi)$
$= \sin\theta\cos\phi + \cos\theta\sin\phi$
$\quad + \sin\theta\cos\phi - \cos\theta\sin\phi$
$= 2\sin\theta\cos\phi$

(b) $\sin(\theta + \phi) - \sin(\theta - \phi)$
$= \sin\theta\cos\phi + \cos\theta\sin\phi$
$\quad - (\sin\theta\cos\phi - \cos\theta\sin\phi)$
$= \sin\theta\cos\phi + \cos\theta\sin\phi$
$\quad - \sin\theta\cos\phi + \cos\theta\sin\phi$
$= 2\cos\theta\sin\phi$

14 (a) $\dfrac{\cot^2\theta}{1+\cot^2\theta} = \dfrac{\dfrac{\cos^2\theta}{\sin^2\theta}}{1+\dfrac{\cos^2\theta}{\sin^2\theta}}$

$= \dfrac{\cos^2\theta}{\sin^2\theta + \cos^2\theta} = \cos^2\theta$

(b) $\dfrac{\cot^2\theta}{1+\cot^2\theta} = 2\sin 2\theta$
$\Rightarrow \cos^2\theta = 2\sin 2\theta$
$\Rightarrow \cos^2\theta = 2 \times 2\sin\theta\cos\theta$
$\Rightarrow \cos^2\theta - 4\sin\theta\cos\theta = 0$
$\Rightarrow \cos\theta (\cos\theta - 4\sin\theta) = 0$
$\Rightarrow \cos\theta = 0$ or $\tan\theta = \frac{1}{4}$
$\cos\theta = 0$ gives $\theta = 90°$ or $270°$
$\tan\theta = \frac{1}{4}$ gives $\theta = 14°$ or $194°$
So $\theta = 14°, 90°, 194°$ or $270°$ (nearest degree)

## B Equivalent expressions (p 61)

B1 (a) $x° = 0°$ or $120°$ or $360°$
(b) $x° = 2°$ or $98°$
(c) $x° = 143°$ or $323°$

B2 You cannot solve it using methods used in B1.
Dividing by (say) $\cos x°$ gives an equation
involving $\tan x°$ and $\text{cosec}\,x°$.

B3 (a)

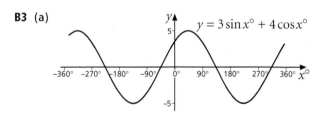

(b) (i) Period = $360°$   (ii) Amplitude = 5

B4 (a) Period = $360°$, amplitude = 13
(b) Period = $360°$, amplitude = 25
(c) Period = $360°$, amplitude = $1.41$ $\left(\text{in fact } \sqrt{2}\right)$

B5 (a) $360°$
(b) $\sqrt{13} = 3.61$ (to 2 d.p.)

**(c)**

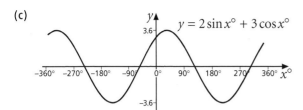

$y = 2\sin x° + 3\cos x°$

**(d)** Period 360°, amplitude $\sqrt{a^2 + b^2}$

**B6 (a)**

$y = \sin x° + \cos x°$

$y = \sin x°$

**(b)** $y = \sqrt{2}\sin(x + 45)°$

**(c)** $y = \sqrt{2}\sin(x + 45)°$
$$= \sqrt{2}(\sin x° \cos 45° + \cos x° \sin 45°)$$
$$= \sqrt{2}\left(\sin x° \frac{1}{\sqrt{2}} + \cos x° \frac{1}{\sqrt{2}}\right)$$
$$= \sin x° + \cos x°$$

**B7** Taking $r = -\sqrt{13}$ we have

$\cos \alpha° = -\dfrac{2}{\sqrt{13}}$ and $\sin \alpha° = -\dfrac{3}{\sqrt{13}}$

$\Rightarrow \tan \alpha° = \frac{3}{2}$ (and $\alpha$ is in the third quadrant)

$\Rightarrow \alpha° = 236°$ (to the nearest degree)

Hence $2\sin x° + 3\cos x° = -\sqrt{13}\sin(x + 236)°$

This has a maximum when $\sin(x + 236)° = -1$,
i.e. when $(x + 236)° = 270°$, giving $x° = 34°$.

**B8 (a)** $r\sin x° \cos \alpha° - r\cos x° \sin \alpha°$

**(b)** $4\sin x° - 3\cos x° = r\sin(x - \alpha)°$
$\Rightarrow r\cos \alpha° = 4$ and $r\sin \alpha° = 3$
$\Rightarrow r^2 = 4^2 + 3^2 = 25 \ (r > 0)$, so $r = 5$

**(c)** $\tan \alpha° = \dfrac{r\sin \alpha°}{r\cos \alpha°} = \frac{3}{4} = 0.75$, so $\alpha° = 37°$

**(d)** $4\sin x° - 3\cos x° = 5\sin(x - 37)°$

**(e) (i)** $-5$

**(ii)** The minimum occurs when
$\sin(x - 37)° = -1$, i.e. $(x - 37)° = 270°$,
$x° = 307°$.

**(f)** A check with a graph plotter

**Exercise B** (p 65)

Angles in these answers are given to the nearest
degree unless stated otherwise.

**1 (a)** $3\sin(\theta + 30)°$ **(b)** $3\cos(\theta - 60)°$
**(c)** $3\sin(\theta - 330)°$ **(d)** $3\cos(\theta + 300)°$

**2 (a)** $\sqrt{29}\sin(\theta + 22)° \approx 5.4\sin(\theta + 22)°$
**(b)** Maximum $= \sqrt{29} \approx 5.4$ when $\theta° = 68°$

**3 (a)** $\sqrt{5}\sin(\theta + 63)° \approx 2.2\sin(\theta + 63)°$
**(b)** $\sqrt{5}\cos(\theta - 27)° \approx 2.2\cos(\theta - 27)°$
**(c)** $\sqrt{5}\cos(\theta - 27)° = \sqrt{5}\sin(90 - (\theta - 27))°$
$= \sqrt{5}\sin(117 - \theta)° = -\sqrt{5}\sin(\theta - 117)°$
$= \sqrt{5}\sin(\theta - 117 + 180)° = \sqrt{5}\sin(\theta + 63)°$

**4 (a)** $\sqrt{13}\sin(\theta - 56)°$ **(b)** $-\sqrt{13}\cos(\theta + 34)°$
**(c)** $\theta = 72°$

**5 (a)** $x° = 84°, 346°$ **(b)** $x° = 77°, 210°$
**(c)** $x° = 38°, 264°$

**6** $\cos(x + 45)° = 2\cos(x - 45)°$
$\Rightarrow \cos x° \cos 45° - \sin x° \sin 45°$
$= 2(\cos x° \cos 45° + \sin x° \sin 45°)$
$\Rightarrow \cos x° \dfrac{1}{\sqrt{2}} - \sin x° \dfrac{1}{\sqrt{2}} = 2\left(\cos x° \dfrac{1}{\sqrt{2}} + \sin x° \dfrac{1}{\sqrt{2}}\right)$
$\Rightarrow \cos x° - \sin x° = 2(\cos x° + \sin x°)$
$\Rightarrow \cos x° - \sin x° = 2\cos x° + 2\sin x°$
$\Rightarrow -3\sin x° = \cos x°$
$\Rightarrow \dfrac{\sin x°}{\cos x°} = -\frac{1}{3}$, i.e. $\tan x° = -\frac{1}{3}$

**7 (a)** $2\sin\left(\theta - \dfrac{\pi}{6}\right)$ **(b)** $\theta = \dfrac{\pi}{3}$ or $\pi$

**8 (a)** $\tan(\theta - 45°) = \dfrac{\tan \theta° - \tan 45°}{1 + \tan \theta° \tan 45°}$
$= \dfrac{\tan \theta° - 1}{1 + \tan \theta° \times 1} = \dfrac{\tan \theta° - 1}{1 + \tan \theta°}$

**(b)** $2 - \sqrt{3}$

**9 (a)** $\frac{12}{13}$ **(b)** $-\frac{16}{65}$

**10 (a)** $\dfrac{\cos 2x}{\cos x - \sin x} = \dfrac{\cos^2 x - \sin^2 x}{\cos x - \sin x}$
$= \dfrac{(\cos x + \sin x)(\cos x - \sin x)}{\cos x - \sin x} = \cos x + \sin x$

**(b)** $\dfrac{\cos 2x}{\cos x - \sin x} = \dfrac{1}{2}$

$\Rightarrow \cos x + \sin x = \dfrac{1}{2}$

$\Rightarrow \sqrt{2}\sin(x + 45°) = \dfrac{1}{2}$

$\Rightarrow \sin(x + 45°) = 0.353\,55\ldots$

$\Rightarrow (x + 45°) = 20.7°$ or $159.3°$ or $380.7°$

$\Rightarrow x = 114°$ or $336°$ (to the nearest degree)

## Test yourself (p 66)

**1** $\sin(x + 90)° = \sin x° \cos 90° + \cos x° \sin 90° = \cos x°$

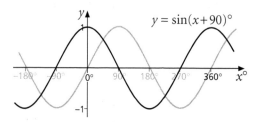

$y = \sin(x+90)°$

The graph of $y = \sin(x + 90)°$ is a translation of $y = \sin x°$ (shown in grey above) by $\begin{bmatrix} -90° \\ 0 \end{bmatrix}$ and is clearly the same as $y = \cos x°$.

**2 (a)** $2\sin(\theta + 345)°$     **(b)** $2\cos(\theta - 105)°$

   **(c)** $2\sin(\theta - 15)°$     **(d)** $2\cos(\theta + 255)°$

**3 (a)** $\cos 105° = \cos(60 + 45)°$

$= \cos 60° \cos 45° - \sin 60° \sin 45°$

$= \dfrac{1}{2} \times \dfrac{1}{\sqrt{2}} - \dfrac{\sqrt{3}}{2} \times \dfrac{1}{\sqrt{2}} = \dfrac{1 - \sqrt{3}}{2\sqrt{2}}$

   **(b)** $\sin 105° = \sin(60 + 45)°$

$= \sin 60° \cos 45° + \cos 60° \sin 45°$

$= \dfrac{\sqrt{3}}{2} \times \dfrac{1}{\sqrt{2}} + \dfrac{1}{2} \times \dfrac{1}{\sqrt{2}} = \dfrac{\sqrt{3} - 1}{2\sqrt{2}}$

**4 (a)** $\dfrac{4}{5}$    **(b)** $\dfrac{7}{25}$    **(c)** $\dfrac{24}{25}$    **(d)** $\dfrac{24}{7}$

**5 (a)** $-\dfrac{5}{13}$    **(b)** $-\dfrac{119}{169}$    **(c)** $-\dfrac{169}{120}$    **(d)** $\dfrac{119}{120}$

**6** $-\dfrac{1}{3} + \dfrac{\sqrt{10}}{3}$ or $-\dfrac{1}{3} - \dfrac{\sqrt{10}}{3}$

**7** $\theta° = 27°, 90°, 207°$ or $270°$

**8 (a)** $x = \dfrac{\pi}{2}$ or $\dfrac{3\pi}{2}$     **(b)** $x = 0, \dfrac{3\pi}{4}, \pi, \dfrac{7\pi}{4}$ or $2\pi$

   **(c)** $x = 2.33$ or $3.96$ (to 2 d.p.)

**9** $\cot\dfrac{\theta}{2} - \tan\dfrac{\theta}{2} = \dfrac{1}{\tan\dfrac{\theta}{2}} - \tan\dfrac{\theta}{2} = \dfrac{1 - \tan^2\dfrac{\theta}{2}}{\tan\dfrac{\theta}{2}}$

$= 2\left(\dfrac{1 - \tan^2\dfrac{\theta}{2}}{2\tan\dfrac{\theta}{2}}\right) = 2\left(\dfrac{1}{\tan\left(2 \times \dfrac{\theta}{2}\right)}\right) = \dfrac{2}{\tan\theta} = 2\cot\theta$

**10** $\tan(A + B) + \tan(A - B)$

$= \dfrac{\tan A + \tan B}{1 - \tan A \tan B} + \dfrac{\tan A - \tan B}{1 + \tan A \tan B}$

$= \dfrac{(\tan A + \tan B)(1 + \tan A \tan B) + (\tan A - \tan B)(1 - \tan A \tan B)}{(1 - \tan A \tan B)(1 + \tan A \tan B)}$

$= \dfrac{2\tan A + 2\tan A \tan^2 B}{1 - \tan^2 A \tan^2 B}$

$= 2\tan A \dfrac{1 + \tan^2 B}{\tan^2 A \left(\dfrac{1}{\tan^2 A} - \tan^2 B\right)}$

$= \dfrac{2\tan A}{\tan^2 A} \times \dfrac{\sec^2 B}{\cot^2 A - \tan^2 B}$

$= 2\cot A \dfrac{\sec^2 B}{\cot^2 A - \tan^2 B}$

**11 (a)** $\cos\left(x + \dfrac{5\pi}{6}\right) = \sin x$

$\Rightarrow \cos x \cos\dfrac{5\pi}{6} - \sin x \sin\dfrac{5\pi}{6} = \sin x$

$\Rightarrow \cos x \times \left(-\dfrac{\sqrt{3}}{2}\right) - \sin x \times \dfrac{1}{2} = \sin x$

$\Rightarrow -\sqrt{3}\cos x - \sin x = 2\sin x$

$\Rightarrow -\sqrt{3}\cos x - 3\sin x = 0$

$\Rightarrow \sqrt{3}\cos x + \sqrt{3} \times \sqrt{3}\sin x = 0$

$\Rightarrow \cos x + \sqrt{3}\sin x = 0$

   **(b)** $\cos\left(x + \dfrac{5\pi}{6}\right) = \sin x$

$\Rightarrow \cos x + \sqrt{3}\sin x = 0$

$\Rightarrow 1 + \sqrt{3}\dfrac{\sin x}{\cos x} = 0$

$\Rightarrow 1 + \sqrt{3}\tan x = 0$

$\Rightarrow \tan x = -\dfrac{1}{\sqrt{3}}$

$\Rightarrow x = \dfrac{5\pi}{6}$ or $\dfrac{11\pi}{6}$

**12 (a)** 1.176

**(b)** $26 \sin(\theta + 1.176)$

**(c) (i)** 26

**(ii)** One angle is $\frac{\pi}{2} - 1.176 = 0.395$

**13 (a)** $5 \sin(x + 53)°$

**(b)** Maximum $= \frac{2}{3}$ when $x° = 217°$

Minimum $= \frac{1}{4}$ when $x° = 37°$

**14 (a) (i)** $\sqrt{41} \sin(\theta - 39)°$

**(ii)** $\theta° = 67°$ or $191°$

**(b) (i)** $\sqrt{41} \cos(\theta + 51)°$

**(ii)** $\theta° = 67°$ or $191°$

**(c)** The answers are identical because the two equations being solved in (a) and (b) are equivalent.

**15 (a)** 1.00 or 5.77

**(b)** 2.14 or 3.65

**(c)** 1.19 or 4.45

**(d)** 1.57 or 5.76 $\left( \frac{\pi}{2} \text{ or } \frac{11\pi}{6} \right)$

**(e)** 1.57 $\left( \frac{\pi}{2} \right)$ or 5.94

**(f)** 0.50 or 5.10

# 6 Differential equations

## A Integration revisited

### Exercise A (p 68)

**1 (a)** $\frac{1}{3}t^3 + c$      **(b)** $\frac{1}{4}y^4 + c$

**(c)** $\frac{1}{4}e^{4s} + c$      **(d)** $\frac{1}{2}\sin 2\theta + c$

**2 (a)** $\frac{2}{3}u^{\frac{3}{2}} + c$      **(b)** $\frac{1}{2}\ln|2P - 1| + c$

**(c)** $2(q + 1)^{\frac{1}{2}} + c$      **(d)** $\frac{1}{2}\ln|v^2 - 1| + c$

## B Forming a differential equation (p 69)

**B1** $\dfrac{dP}{dt} = 0.05P^2$

**B2** $\dfrac{dT}{dt} = 2t + 0.01t^2$

**B3** The differential equation, $\dfrac{dP}{dt} = 0.1Pt$, tells us that $P$ is increasing at the rate $0.1Pt$. It should be $\dfrac{dP}{dt} = -0.1Pt$.

**B4** $\dfrac{ds}{dt} = -0.02s$

**B5 (a)** $\dfrac{dN}{dt} = kN(20\,000 - N)$

**(b)** The increase in sales stops when $\dfrac{dN}{dt} = 0$, i.e. when $N = 20\,000$.

When $N > 20\,000$, $\dfrac{dN}{dt} < 0$ and total sales would then decrease. As this cannot happen in practice, the model breaks down at this point.

## C Solving by separating variables (p 70)

**C1** $\dfrac{dP}{dt} = 0.1Ae^{0.1t} = 0.1P$

**C2 (a) (i)** $P\,dP = 5\,dt$

**(ii)** $\int P\,dP = \int 5\,dt \Rightarrow \frac{1}{2}P^2 = 5t + c$

$P^2 = 10t + 2c$

If $A = 2c$ then $P^2 = 10t + A$

**(b)** $\dfrac{dP}{dt} = \frac{1}{2} \times 10(10t + A)^{-\frac{1}{2}} = \dfrac{5}{\sqrt{10t + A}} = \dfrac{5}{P}$

**(c)** Substituting $P = 6$ and $t = 0$ in $P^2 = 10t + A$ gives $36 = 10 \times 0 + A \Rightarrow A = 36$

**(d)** $P^2 = 10 \times 10.8 + 36 = 108 + 36 = 144$

$P = 12 \ (P > 0)$

**C3 (a) (i)** $\frac{1}{P^2}\,dP = 0.01\,dt$

**(ii)** $\int \frac{1}{P^2}\,dP = \int 0.01\,dt \Rightarrow -\frac{1}{P} = 0.01t + c$

Rearranging gives $P = -\dfrac{1}{0.01t + c}$.

**(b)** Substituting $P = 10$ and $t = 0$ in $P = -\dfrac{1}{0.01t + c}$

gives $10 = -\dfrac{1}{0.01 \times 0 + c} = -\dfrac{1}{c}$ so $c = -0.1$.

Hence $P = -\dfrac{1}{0.01t - 0.1} \Rightarrow P = \dfrac{100}{10 - t}$

**(c)** $P = \dfrac{100}{10 - t}$

As $t$ gets closer to 10, $10 - t$ gets closer to 0 and $P$ gets larger.

**C4 (a)** You cannot integrate $y^2$ with respect to $x$. The student should have rearranged the equation so there in only one variable on each side.

**(b)** $dy = 3y^2\,dx$

$\int \frac{1}{y^2}\,dy = \int 3\,dx$

$-\frac{1}{y} = 3x + c$

Rearranging this gives $y = -\dfrac{1}{3x + c}$.

**Exercise C** (p 72)

**1 (a)** Separating the variables, $y\,dy = x^3\,dx$

Integrating both sides, $\int y\,dy = \int x^3\,dx$

$\Rightarrow \frac{1}{2}y^2 = \frac{1}{4}x^4 + c \Rightarrow y^2 = \frac{1}{2}x^4 + A$

(where $A = 2c$)

**(b)** $y^2 = \frac{1}{2}x^4 + 16$

**2 (a)** Separating the variables, $y\,dy = (1 + x)\,dx$

Integrating both sides, $\int y\,dy = \int (1 + x)\,dx$

$\Rightarrow \frac{1}{2}y^2 = x + \frac{1}{2}x^2 + c \Rightarrow y^2 = x^2 + 2x + A$

(where $A = 2c$)

**(b)** 6

**3 (a)** Separating the variables, $\frac{1}{y}\,dy = x\,dx$

Integrating both sides, $\int \frac{1}{y}\,dy = \int x\,dx$

$\Rightarrow \log y = \frac{1}{2}x^2 + c \Rightarrow y = e^{\frac{1}{2}x^2 + c} = Ae^{\frac{1}{2}x^2}$

(where $A = e^c$)

**(b)** 6

**4** $y = 6e^x - 1$

**5 (a)** Separating the variables, $\dfrac{dy}{\sqrt{y}} = 2x\,dx$

Integrating both sides, $\int \dfrac{dy}{\sqrt{y}} = \int 2x\,dx$

$\Rightarrow 2\sqrt{y} = x^2 + c$

$\Rightarrow \sqrt{y} = \frac{1}{2}x^2 + A$ (where $A = \frac{1}{2}c$)

**(b)** 2 **(c)** 2.22

**6 (a)** $\dfrac{dP}{dt} = -kP$

**(b)** Separating the variables, $\dfrac{dP}{P} = -k\,dt$

Integrating both sides, $\int \dfrac{dP}{P} = -\int k\,dt$

$\Rightarrow \ln P = -kt + c$

$\Rightarrow P = e^{-kt + c} = Ae^{-kt}$ (where $A = e^c$)

**(c)** 20 000 **(d)** 0.0693

**(e)** 43.2 (to 3 s.f.)

**7 (a)** $y = Ae^{-\frac{1}{x}}$ **(b)** $y = e^2 e^{-\frac{1}{x}} = e^{2 - \frac{1}{x}}$

**8** $y = \dfrac{2}{2 - x^2}$

**9** $y = \dfrac{1}{2 - \ln x}$

**10 (a)** $\frac{1}{2}\ln(x^2 + 1) + c$

**(b) (i)** Separating the variables, $\dfrac{dy}{y} = \dfrac{x\,dx}{x^2 + 1}$

$\Rightarrow \ln y = \frac{1}{2}\ln(x^2 + 1) + c$

$\ln y = \ln \sqrt{x^2 + 1} + \ln A = \ln\left(A\sqrt{x^2 + 1}\right)$

(where $\ln A = c$)

$\Rightarrow y = A\sqrt{x^2 + 1}$

**(ii)** $\dfrac{10}{\sqrt{2}}$, or $5\sqrt{2}$

**(c) (i)** $\dfrac{1}{y} = c - \frac{1}{2}\ln(x^2 + 1)$ $\left(y = \dfrac{1}{c - \frac{1}{2}\ln(x^2 + 1)}\right)$

**(ii)** $1 = c - \frac{1}{2}\ln 1 \Rightarrow c = 1$

$\Rightarrow \dfrac{1}{y} = 1 - \frac{1}{2}\ln(x^2 + 1)$

$\Rightarrow y = \dfrac{1}{1 - \frac{1}{2}\ln(x^2 + 1)}$

**11 (a)** $\dfrac{\mathrm{d}T}{\mathrm{d}t} = -k(T - A)$  $(T - A > 0,\ k > 0)$

**(b)** Separating the variables, $\dfrac{\mathrm{d}T}{T - A} = -k\,\mathrm{d}t$

$\Rightarrow \ln(T - A) = -kt + c$

$T - A = e^{-kt + c} = Be^{-kt}$ (where $B = e^c$)

$T = A + Be^{-kt}$

## D  Exponential growth and decay (p 74)

**D1 (a)** 4.05  **(b)** 6.93  **(c)** −2.88

**D2 (a) (i)** 1.02  **(ii)** 1.83  **(iii)** −0.365

**(b)** $P$ gets closer and closer to 0.

**D3 (a)** 50

**(b)** As $t \to \infty$, $e^{-2t} \to 0$, so the limiting value is 40.

**(c)**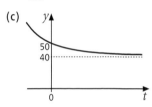

**D4 (a)** As $t \to \infty$, $e^{-bt} \to 0$ so $T \to c + a(0) = c$
This will be the temperature of the surrounding atmosphere, so $c = 20$.

**(b)** When $t = 0$, $80 = 20 + a$ so $a = 60$

**(c)** When $t = 10$, $35 = 20 + 60e^{-10b}$

$60e^{-10b} = 15$

$e^{-10b} = 0.25$

$-10b = \ln(0.25)$

$b = 0.139$ (to 3 s.f.)

**(d)** $\dfrac{\mathrm{d}T}{\mathrm{d}t} = 60 \times (-0.139e^{-0.139t}) = -8.34e^{-1.39}$

$= -2.08$ degrees per minute (to 3 s.f.)

### Exercise D (p 76)

**1 (a)** 5000  **(b)** 11 128  **(c)** 445

**2 (a)** 40  **(b)** 50

**3 (a)** 800

**(b)** $500 = 800e^{-5k} \Rightarrow e^{-5k} = 0.625$
$k = -\tfrac{1}{5}\ln 0.625 = 0.0940$ (to 3 s.f.)

**(c) (i)** 549  **(ii)** 7.37

**4 (a)** 185  **(b)** $T \to 200$  **(c)** 0.0615

---

**5** $N = \tfrac{1}{2}N_0 = N_0 e^{-0.04t}$

$e^{-0.04t} = 0.5$

$-0.04t = \ln(0.5) \Rightarrow t = \dfrac{\ln(0.5)}{-0.04} = 17.3$

## E  Further exponential functions (p 76)

**E1 (a)** $5^x = (e^{\ln 5})^x = e^{(\ln 5)x} = e^{1.61x}$

**(b)** $e^{(\ln 8)x} = e^{2.08x}$

**(c)** $e^{0.693x}$  **(d)** $e^{(\ln a)x}$

**E2** $\dfrac{\mathrm{d}(a^x)}{\mathrm{d}x} = \dfrac{\mathrm{d}}{\mathrm{d}x}(e^{(\ln a)x}) = (\ln a)e^{(\ln a)x} = (\ln a)a^x$

**E3 (a)** £20 000

**(b)** £8874

**(c)** $t = \dfrac{\ln 0.4}{\ln 0.85} = 5.64$

**(d)** $20\,000 \times \ln 0.85 \times 0.85^5 = -1440$ (to 3 s.f.)

**E4 (a)** 1.2  **(b)** $8000 \times 1.2^t$

**E5 (a)** 0.8  **(b)** $8000 \times 0.8^t$

### Exercise E (p 78)

**1 (a)** 5.69 years  **(b)** 11 012 per year

**2 (a)** 3.11 years  **(b)** £2856 per year

**3** $\dfrac{\mathrm{d}y}{\mathrm{d}x} = qa^x \ln a = (y - p)\ln a$

### Mixed questions (p 78)

**1 (a)** $\tan^{-1} y + c$  **(b)** $y = \tan\!\left(x + \dfrac{\pi}{4}\right)$

**2 (a)** $\dfrac{\mathrm{d}h}{\mathrm{d}t} = \dfrac{k}{h^2}$

**(b)** Separating the variables, $h^2\,\mathrm{d}h = k\,\mathrm{d}t$
Integrating both sides,
$\int h^2\,\mathrm{d}h = \int k\,\mathrm{d}t \Rightarrow \tfrac{1}{3}h^3 = kt + c$
$h^3 = 3kt + 3c$
so $h^3 = At + B$  $(A = 3k,\ B = 3c)$

**(c)** $A = 61$, $B = 64$

**3 (a)** Separating the variables and integrating,
$-\ln(50 - r) = \tfrac{1}{2}t + c$
$\ln(50 - r) = -\tfrac{1}{2}t - c$
$50 - r = e^{-\frac{1}{2}t - c}$
$r = 50 - e^{-\frac{1}{2}t - c} = 50 - Ae^{-\frac{1}{2}t}$  (where $A = e^{-c}$)

**(b)** $r \to 50$  **(c)** 30  **(d)** 2.20

**1 (a)** $y = (3x + c)^{\frac{1}{3}}$  **(b)** $y = (3x - 4)^{\frac{1}{3}}$

**2 (a) (i)** 50  **(ii)** 100

**(b)** 2.8 minutes

**3 (a)** Separating the variables, $\dfrac{dv}{10 - 5v} = dt$

$\Rightarrow -\frac{1}{5}\ln(10 - 5v) = t + c$

When $v = 0$ and $t = 0$, $c = -\frac{1}{5}\ln 10$

So $-\frac{1}{5}\ln(10 - 5v) = t - \frac{1}{5}\ln 10$

$\Rightarrow t = \frac{1}{5}(\ln 10 - \ln(10 - 5v)) = \frac{1}{5}\ln\left(\dfrac{10}{10 - 5v}\right)$

$= \frac{1}{5}\ln\left(\dfrac{2}{2 - v}\right)$

**(b)** $1.8\,\mathrm{m\,s^{-1}}$

**4 (a)** $y = 3 + Ae^{\frac{1}{2}x}$  **(b)** $y = 3 - e^{\frac{1}{2}x}$

**5** Separating the variables, $\dfrac{dy}{y + 1} = x\,dx$

$\Rightarrow \ln(y + 1) = \frac{1}{2}x^2 + c$

$\Rightarrow y + 1 = e^{\frac{1}{2}x^2 + c}$

$\Rightarrow y = e^{\frac{1}{2}x^2 + c} - 1 = Ae^{\frac{1}{2}x^2} - 1$  (where $A = e^c$)

# 7 Differentiation

## A Functions defined parametrically (p 80)

**A1** $\frac{3}{2}t$

**A2 (a)** $t + \frac{1}{2}$  **(b)** $-\dfrac{1}{3t^2}$  **(c)** $-\cot t$

**A3** $y - y_1 = m(x - x_1)$, $(x_1, y_1) = (6, 5)$, $m = \frac{4}{3}$

So $y - 5 = \frac{4}{3}(x - 6)$

$\Rightarrow y - 5 = \frac{4}{3}x - 8$

$\Rightarrow \quad y = \frac{4}{3}x - 3$

**A4** $y - 5 = -\frac{3}{4}(x - 6)$

$\Rightarrow y - 5 = -\frac{3}{4}x + \frac{9}{2}$

$\Rightarrow \quad y = -\frac{3}{4}x + \frac{19}{2}$

**A5 (a)** $-\dfrac{1}{2t^2}$

**(b)** $\left(8, \frac{1}{4}\right)$

**(c)** Gradient $= m = -\dfrac{1}{2 \times 4^2} = -\frac{1}{32}$

Using $y - y_1 = m(x - x_1)$

$y - \frac{1}{4} = -\frac{1}{32}(x - 8)$

$\Rightarrow \quad y - \frac{1}{4} = -\frac{1}{32}x + \frac{1}{4}$

$\Rightarrow \quad y = -\frac{1}{32}x + \frac{1}{2}$

**(d)** $x + 32y = 16$

**A6 (a)** $\dfrac{2}{3t}$  **(b)** $y = -3x + 28$

### Exercise A (p 83)

**1 (a)** $\dfrac{dy}{dt} = 3t^2$, $\dfrac{dx}{dt} = 2t$

$\dfrac{dy}{dx} = \dfrac{\frac{dy}{dt}}{\frac{dx}{dt}} = \dfrac{3t^2}{2t} = \frac{3}{2}t$

**(b) (i)** $(16, 64)$  **(ii)** $y = 6x - 32$

**(iii)** $y = -\frac{1}{6}x + \frac{200}{6}$

**2** (a) $\dfrac{1}{4\sqrt{t}}$

(b) When $t = 1$, $x = 2$, $y = 2$, $m = \frac{1}{4}$

Tangent: $y - 2 = \frac{1}{4}(x - 2)$

$\Rightarrow \qquad y - 2 = \frac{1}{4}x - \frac{1}{2}$

$\Rightarrow \qquad y = \frac{1}{4}x + \frac{3}{2}$

(c) $y = -4x + 10$

**3** (a) $-\dfrac{1}{t^2}$

(b) When $t = 2$, $x = 5$, $y = 2$, $m = -\frac{1}{4}$

Tangent: $y - 2 = -\frac{1}{4}(x - 5)$

$\Rightarrow \qquad 4y - 8 = -x + 5$

$\Rightarrow \qquad x + 4y = 13$

(c) $4x - y = 18$

**4** (a) $\dfrac{dy}{d\theta} = 2\cos\theta$, $\dfrac{dx}{d\theta} = -\sin\theta$

$\dfrac{dy}{dx} = \dfrac{\dfrac{dy}{d\theta}}{\dfrac{dx}{d\theta}} = \dfrac{2\cos\theta}{-\sin\theta} = -\dfrac{2}{\tan\theta}$

(b) $\left(\dfrac{1}{\sqrt{2}}, \sqrt{2}\right)$

(c) $m = -\dfrac{2}{\tan\dfrac{\pi}{4}} = -2$

$y - \sqrt{2} = -2\left(x - \dfrac{1}{\sqrt{2}}\right)$

$\Rightarrow y - \sqrt{2} = -2x + \sqrt{2}$

$\Rightarrow \quad 2x + y = 2\sqrt{2}$

**5** (a) $3x + y - 6 = 0$      (b) $x - 3y - 2 = 0$

**6** (a) $\dfrac{2t}{1 + \dfrac{1}{t^2}} = \dfrac{2t^3}{t^2 + 1}$

(b) (i) $4x - 20y + 11 = 0$

(ii) $20x + 4y + 29 = 0$

## B Functions defined implicitly (p 84)

**B1** (a) $\dfrac{d}{dx}(\ln x) = \dfrac{1}{x}$

(b) $\dfrac{d}{dx}(x + \sin 3x) = 1 + 3\cos 3x$

**B2** (a) $2\dfrac{dy}{dx} + 3 + \dfrac{dy}{dx} = 0$

$3\dfrac{dy}{dx} + 3 = 0$   so   $\dfrac{dy}{dx} = -1$

(b) $\quad x\dfrac{dy}{dx} + y + \dfrac{dy}{dx} = 0$

$\Rightarrow (x + 1)\dfrac{dy}{dx} + y = 0$

$\Rightarrow \qquad (x + 1)\dfrac{dy}{dx} = -y$

$\Rightarrow \qquad \dfrac{dy}{dx} = -\dfrac{y}{x + 1}$

**B3** (a) $3x^2 + \dfrac{dy}{dx}$   (b) $4x^3 - \dfrac{dy}{dx}$   (c) $-\dfrac{1}{x^2} + 2\dfrac{dy}{dx}$

**B4** (a) $x^3\dfrac{dy}{dx} + 3x^2y$   (b) $x^4\dfrac{dy}{dx} + 4x^3y$   (c) $e^x\dfrac{dy}{dx} + e^xy$

**B5** (a) Differentiate with respect to $x$:

$x^2\dfrac{dy}{dx} + 2xy + 1 + \dfrac{dy}{dx} = 0$

$\Rightarrow (x^2 + 1)\dfrac{dy}{dx} + 2xy + 1 = 0$

(b) $x^2y + x + y = (1)^2 \times 4 + 1 + 4 = 4 + 1 + 4 = 9$

Gradient: $-\frac{9}{2}$

**B6** (a) $3y^2\dfrac{dy}{dx}$    (b) $4y^3\dfrac{dy}{dx}$    (c) $3(y - 2)^2\dfrac{dy}{dx}$

(d) $4(2y + 1)\dfrac{dy}{dx}$   (e) $-2y^{-3}\dfrac{dy}{dx}$

**B7** (a) $3xy^2\dfrac{dy}{dx} + y^3$       (b) $2x^2y\dfrac{dy}{dx} + 2xy^2$

(c) $4x^3y^3\dfrac{dy}{dx} + 3x^2y^4$   (d) $2x(y - 1)\dfrac{dy}{dx} + (y - 1)^2$

**B8** (a) Differentiating with respect to $x$:

$2y\dfrac{dy}{dx} + 1 + \dfrac{dy}{dx} = 0 \Rightarrow (2y + 1)\dfrac{dy}{dx} + 1 = 0$

(b) $2^2 + 1 + 2 = 7$ so $(1, 2)$ lies on the curve.

At $(1, 2)$, $\dfrac{dy}{dx} = -\frac{1}{5}$

**B9** (a) $x(2y)\dfrac{dy}{dx} + y^2 + \dfrac{dy}{dx} = 0$

$(2xy + 1)\dfrac{dy}{dx} + y^2 = 0$

(b) $1 \times (2)^2 + 2 = 6$ so $(1, 2)$ lies on the curve.

At $(1, 2)$, $\dfrac{dy}{dx} = -\frac{4}{5}$

### Exercise B (p 87)

**1** Tangent: $5x + 3y - 13 = 0$

Normal: $3x - 5y - 1 = 0$

**2** (a) (i) $2x - y - 1 = 0$

(ii) $x + 2y - 3 = 0$

**(b) (i)** $13x + 3y - 29 = 0$

**(ii)** $3x - 13y + 7 = 0$

**(c) (i)** $5x - 3y - 13 = 0$

**(ii)** $3x + 5y - 35 = 0$

**(d) (i)** $7x + 15y - 36 = 0$

**(ii)** $15x - 7y - 38 = 0$

**(e) (i)** $6x + y - 13 = 0$

**(ii)** $x - 6y + 4 = 0$

**(f) (i)** $x + 3y - 13 = 0$

**(ii)** $3x - y - 9 = 0$

**3 (a)** $(1, 2), \ (1, 5)$    **(b)** $\frac{4}{3}, \ -\frac{7}{3}$

**4 (a)** $(3, 1), \ (-4, 1)$    **(b)** $-\frac{7}{5}, \ -\frac{7}{2}$

**(c)** $7x + 5y - 26 = 0, \ 7x + 2y + 26 = 0$

## Mixed questions (p 88)

**1 (a) (i)** $-\dfrac{1}{2t^2}$    **(ii)** $-\frac{1}{8}$

**(b)** $\left(5, \frac{3}{2}\right)$

**(c) (i)** $2t = x - 1$ so $t = \frac{1}{2}(x - 1)$

$$y = 1 + \frac{1}{\frac{1}{2}(x-1)}$$

$$\Rightarrow \tfrac{1}{2}(x-1)y = \tfrac{1}{2}(x-1) + 1$$

$$\Rightarrow (x-1)y = (x-1) + 2$$

$$\Rightarrow xy - y = x + 1 \ \text{ so } \ xy - x - y = 1$$

**(ii)** $-\frac{1}{8}$

**(d)** (a) (ii) and (c) (ii) have the same answer.

**2 (a)**

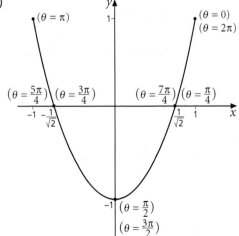

**(b)** The curve repeats itself because
$\cos(\theta + 2\pi) = \cos\theta$ and $\cos(2\theta + 2\pi) = \cos 2\theta$.

**(c)** $\cos 2\theta = 2\cos^2\theta - 1$, so $y = 2x^2 - 1$

The graph is only part of $y = 2x^2 - 1$ because
$x = \cos\theta$, so $-1 \le x \le 1$.

**(d)** $\dfrac{2\sin 2\theta}{\sin\theta} = 4\cos\theta$

**(e)** $2\sqrt{2}x - y - 2 = 0$    **(f)** $\sqrt{2}x + 4y - 1 = 0$

**3 (a)** $(3, 2), \ (3, 1)$

**(b) (i)** $8x - y = 22, \ 7x + y = 22$

**(ii)** $x + 8y = 19, \ x - 7y = -4$

**4 (a)** $(5, -1), \ (5, 7)$    **(b)** $\frac{3}{4}, \ -\frac{3}{4}$

**(c)** $4x + 3y = 17, \ 4x - 3y = -1$

**(d)** $4(2) + 3(3) = 17, \ 4(2) - 3(3) = -1$

**5 (a)** $x^{\frac{1}{2}} + y^{\frac{1}{2}} = 5$

$$\tfrac{1}{2}x^{-\frac{1}{2}} + \tfrac{1}{2}y^{-\frac{1}{2}}\dfrac{dy}{dx} = 0$$

$$\Rightarrow \dfrac{dy}{dx} = -\dfrac{x^{-\frac{1}{2}}}{y^{-\frac{1}{2}}} = -\dfrac{y^{\frac{1}{2}}}{x^{\frac{1}{2}}} = -\sqrt{\dfrac{y}{x}}$$

**(b)** $2x + 3y = 30$

**6 (a)** Differentiating with respect to $x$,

$$(x^2 - 1)\dfrac{dy}{dx} + 2xy = 2x$$

$$\Rightarrow (x^2 - 1)\dfrac{dy}{dx} = 2x - 2xy = 2x(1 - y)$$

**(b)** When $x = 2$, $y = \frac{5}{3}$ and the gradient is $-\frac{8}{9}$.

## Test yourself (p 89)

**1 (a)** $-\dfrac{1}{3t^2}$    **(b)** $3x - y = 5$

**2 (a)** $\dfrac{dx}{dt} = 3\cos t, \ \dfrac{dy}{dt} = -\sin t$

$$\dfrac{dy}{dx} = \dfrac{\frac{dy}{dt}}{\frac{dx}{dt}} = -\dfrac{\sin t}{3\cos t} = -\tfrac{1}{3}\tan t$$

When $t = \frac{1}{4}\pi$, $\dfrac{dy}{dx} = -\tfrac{1}{3}\tan\tfrac{1}{4}\pi = -\tfrac{1}{3}(1) = -\tfrac{1}{3}$

**(b)** $y = -\tfrac{1}{3}x + \sqrt{2}$

**3** Tangent: $7x + 10y - 24 = 0$
Normal: $10x - 7y - 13 = 0$

**4 (a)** $\left(3, \frac{7}{3}\right), \ \left(3, -\frac{1}{3}\right)$

**(b)** 1 at $\left(3, \frac{7}{3}\right)$ and $-1$ at $\left(3, -\frac{1}{3}\right)$

# 8 Integration

## A Using partial fractions (p 90)

**A1** (a) $\dfrac{2}{x-2} + \dfrac{3}{x+1}$  (b) $\dfrac{3}{x-2} - \dfrac{4}{2x+1}$

(c) $\dfrac{7}{4(x-3)} - \dfrac{7}{4(x+1)} - \dfrac{2}{(x+1)^2}$

**A2** (a) $1 + \dfrac{4}{x+1} - \dfrac{7}{x+2}$  (b) $1 + \dfrac{4}{5(x-2)} - \dfrac{9}{5(x+3)}$

(c) $-2 + \dfrac{5}{3(2-x)} - \dfrac{1}{3(x+1)}$

**A3** $2\ln|x-2| + 3\ln|x+1| + c$

**A4** $3\ln|x-2| - 2\ln|2x+1| + c$

**A5** (a) $-\dfrac{3}{x} + \dfrac{4}{x+2}$

(b) $-3\ln|x| + 4\ln|x+2| + c$

**A6** (a) $x + 4\ln|x+1| - 7\ln|x+2| + c$

(b) $x + \tfrac{4}{5}\ln|x-2| - \tfrac{9}{5}\ln|x+3| + c$

(c) $-2x + \tfrac{5}{3}\ln|2-x| - \tfrac{1}{3}\ln|x+1| + c$

**A7** $2\ln|x-1| + 4\ln|x+1| + \dfrac{3}{x+1} + c$

**A8** $\tfrac{7}{4}\ln|x-3| - \tfrac{7}{4}\ln|x+1| + \dfrac{2}{x+1} + c$

### Exercise A (p 94)

**1** (a) $-\ln|x| + \ln|x-1| + c$

(b) $\ln|x-1| - \ln|x+2| + c$

(c) $\tfrac{1}{4}\ln|x-1| + \tfrac{3}{4}\ln|x+3| + c$

(d) $\tfrac{6}{5}\ln|x-1| - \tfrac{1}{5}\ln|x+4| + c$

(e) $\tfrac{3}{2}\ln|2x-1| - \ln|x+2| + c$

(f) $-2\ln|1-x| - \tfrac{1}{2}\ln|2x+1| + c$

**2** (a) $x + \ln|x+1| - 4\ln|x+2| + c$

(b) $x - \ln|x| + 4\ln|x-3| + c$

(c) $x - \tfrac{1}{3}\ln|x+2| - \tfrac{2}{3}\ln|x-1| + c$

**3** (a) $\tfrac{2}{9}\ln|x-2| - \tfrac{2}{9}\ln|x+1| - \dfrac{1}{3(x+1)} + c$

(b) $\tfrac{1}{2}\ln|x+1| - \tfrac{1}{2}\ln|x-1| - \dfrac{2}{x-1} + c$

(c) $\ln|2x-1| - \ln|x-1| - \dfrac{1}{x-1} + c$

(d) $2\ln|x| + \dfrac{1}{x} - 2\ln|x+1| + c$

(e) $\ln|x+2| - \dfrac{1}{x+2} - \ln|2x+3| + c$

(f) $-\tfrac{1}{16}\ln|x| + \tfrac{1}{16}\ln|x-4| - \dfrac{3}{4(x-4)} + c$

## B Definite integrals

### Exercise B (p 95)

**1** (a) $\ln\tfrac{4}{3}$

(b) $\tfrac{1}{3}\ln\tfrac{16}{7}$

(c) $-\tfrac{7}{5}\ln 4$

(d) $\tfrac{1}{4}\ln 2 + \tfrac{3}{4}\ln\tfrac{6}{5}$

(e) $\tfrac{5}{3}\ln 2 - \tfrac{7}{6}\ln\tfrac{7}{5}$

(f) $-\ln 2 - \tfrac{3}{2}\ln 3$

**2** (a) $1 + 7\ln 2 - 4\ln 3 = 1 + \ln\tfrac{128}{81}$

(b) $3 + \tfrac{5}{3}\ln 4 - \tfrac{4}{3}\ln 7$

(c) $2 + 9\ln 2 - \tfrac{15}{2}\ln 3$

(d) $2 - \tfrac{25}{8}\ln\tfrac{7}{5} - \tfrac{9}{8}\ln 3$

(e) $-2 + 3\ln 5 - 2\ln 3 = -2 + \ln\tfrac{125}{9}$

(f) $1 - \ln 3$

**3** (a) $\tfrac{1}{2} - \tfrac{1}{8}\ln 3$

(b) $\tfrac{4}{9}\ln 4 - \tfrac{2}{9}\ln 7 + \tfrac{1}{28}$

(c) $\tfrac{4}{3} - \ln 3 + \tfrac{1}{2}\ln 5$

(d) $4\ln 2 - 2\ln 3 - \tfrac{1}{2} = \ln\tfrac{16}{9} - \tfrac{1}{2}$

(e) $3\ln 5 - 3\ln 3 - \tfrac{2}{3} = \ln\tfrac{125}{27} - \tfrac{2}{3}$

(f) $2\ln 5 - 3\ln 3 + \tfrac{2}{15} = \ln\tfrac{25}{27} + \tfrac{2}{15}$

## C Using trigonometrical identities (p 95)

**C1** (a) $\sin x \cos x = \tfrac{1}{2}\sin 2x$

(b) $\int \tfrac{1}{2}\sin 2x \, dx = -\tfrac{1}{4}\cos 2x + c$

**C2** (a) $\tfrac{1}{2}(\cos 2x + 1)$

(b) $\int \tfrac{1}{2}(\cos 2x + 1) \, dx = \tfrac{1}{4}\sin 2x + \tfrac{1}{2}x + c$

**C3** $\int \tfrac{1}{2}(1 - \cos 2x) \, dx = \tfrac{1}{2}x - \tfrac{1}{4}\sin 2x + c$

**C4 (a)** $\cos 2x = 1 - 2\sin^2 x$

Replace $x$ by $\tfrac{1}{2}x$: $\cos x = 1 - 2\sin^2 \tfrac{1}{2}x$

Rearrange: $2\sin^2 \tfrac{1}{2}x = 1 - \cos x$

So $\sin^2 \tfrac{1}{2}x = \tfrac{1}{2}(1 - \cos x)$

**(b) (i)** $\int \tfrac{1}{2}(1 - \cos x)\,dx = \tfrac{1}{2}x - \tfrac{1}{2}\sin x + c$

**(ii)** $\int_0^{\frac{\pi}{2}} \tfrac{1}{2}(1 - \cos x)\,dx = \tfrac{1}{2}[x - \sin x]_0^{\frac{\pi}{2}} = \dfrac{\pi}{4} - \dfrac{1}{2}$

**C5 (a)** $\cos 3x = \cos(2x + x)$
$$= \cos 2x \cos x - \sin 2x \sin x$$

**(b)** Using $\cos 2x = 2\cos^2 x - 1$
and $\sin 2x = 2\sin x \cos x$:
$$\cos 3x = (2\cos^2 x - 1)\cos x - (2\sin x \cos x)\sin x$$
$$= 2\cos^3 x - \cos x - 2\sin^2 x \cos x$$
$$= 2\cos^3 x - \cos x - 2(1 - \cos^2 x)\cos x$$
$$= 2\cos^3 x - \cos x - 2\cos x + 2\cos^3 x$$
$$= 4\cos^3 x - 3\cos x$$

**(c)** $4\cos^3 x = \cos 3x + 3\cos x$
So $\cos^3 x = \tfrac{1}{4}(\cos 3x + 3\cos x)$

**(d)** $\int \cos^3 x\,dx = \int \tfrac{1}{4}(\cos 3x + 3\cos x)\,dx$
$$= \tfrac{1}{4}\left(\tfrac{1}{3}\sin 3x + 3\sin x\right) + c$$

## Exercise C (p 96)

**1 (a)** $\dfrac{\pi}{2}$

**(b)** $\dfrac{\sqrt{3}}{8} + \dfrac{\pi}{12} = 0.478$ (to 3 s.f.)

**(c)** $\dfrac{\sqrt{3}}{4} + \dfrac{\pi}{6} = 0.957$ (to 3 s.f.)

**2** Volume $= \displaystyle\int_0^{\frac{\pi}{2}} \pi \cos^2 x\,dx$
$$= \pi \int_0^{\frac{\pi}{2}} \tfrac{1}{2}(\cos 2x + 1)\,dx$$
$$= \dfrac{\pi}{2}\left[\tfrac{1}{2}\sin 2x + x\right]_0^{\frac{\pi}{2}}$$
$$= \dfrac{\pi}{2}\left(\tfrac{1}{2}\sin \pi + \dfrac{\pi}{2}\right) - 0$$
$$= \dfrac{\pi}{2} \times \dfrac{\pi}{2}$$
$$= \dfrac{\pi^2}{4}$$

**3 (a)** $(1 + \cos x)^2 = 1 + 2\cos x + \cos^2 x$
$$= 1 + 2\cos x + \tfrac{1}{2}(\cos 2x + 1)$$
$$= 1 + 2\cos x + \tfrac{1}{2}\cos 2x + \tfrac{1}{2}$$
$$= \tfrac{3}{2} + 2\cos x + \tfrac{1}{2}\cos 2x$$

**(b)** $\int (1 + \cos x)^2\,dx = \int \left(\tfrac{3}{2} + 2\cos x + \tfrac{1}{2}\cos 2x\right) dx$
$$= \tfrac{3}{2}x + 2\sin x + \tfrac{1}{4}\sin 2x + c$$

**(c)** $(1 + \sin x)^2 = 1 + 2\sin x + \sin^2 x$
$$= 1 + 2\sin x + \tfrac{1}{2}(1 - \cos 2x)$$
$$= \tfrac{3}{2} + 2\sin x - \tfrac{1}{2}\cos 2x$$
$$\int (1 + \sin x)^2\,dx = \int \left(\tfrac{3}{2} + 2\sin x - \tfrac{1}{2}\cos 2x\right) dx$$
$$= \tfrac{3}{2}x - 2\cos x - \tfrac{1}{4}\sin 2x + c$$

**4 (a)** $(\cos\theta + \sin\theta)^2 = \cos^2\theta + 2\sin\theta\cos\theta + \sin^2\theta$
$$= (\cos^2 + \sin^2\theta) + 2\sin\theta\cos\theta$$
$$= 1 + \sin 2\theta$$
$$\int (\cos\theta + \sin\theta)^2\,d\theta = \int (1 + \sin 2\theta)\,d\theta$$
$$= \theta - \tfrac{1}{2}\cos 2\theta + c$$

**(b)** $\displaystyle\int_0^{\frac{\pi}{2}} (\cos\theta - \sin\theta)^2\,d\theta = \int_0^{\frac{\pi}{2}} (1 - \sin 2\theta)\,d\theta$
$$= \dfrac{\pi}{2} - 1$$

## Mixed questions (p 97)

**1 (a)** $\dfrac{2}{1 + 2x} + \dfrac{1}{4 - x}$

**(b) (i)** $\dfrac{1}{4 - x} = \dfrac{1}{4\left(1 - \dfrac{x}{4}\right)} = \tfrac{1}{4}\left(1 - \dfrac{x}{4}\right)^{-1}$
$$= \tfrac{1}{4}\left(1 - \left(-\dfrac{x}{4}\right) + \left(-\dfrac{x}{4}\right)^2 - \cdots\right)$$
$$= \tfrac{1}{4}\left(1 + \dfrac{x}{4} + \dfrac{x^2}{16} + \cdots\right)$$
$$= \tfrac{1}{4} + \dfrac{x}{16} + \dfrac{x^2}{64} + \cdots$$

**(ii)** $\dfrac{1}{1 + 2x} = (1 + 2x)^{-1}$
$$= 1 - 2x + (2x)^2 - \cdots$$
$$= 1 - 2x + 4x^2 - \cdots$$

**(iii)** $f(x) = \dfrac{2}{1 + 2x} + \dfrac{1}{4 - x}$
$$= 2(1 - 2x + 4x^2) + \tfrac{1}{4} + \dfrac{x}{16} + \dfrac{x^2}{64} + \cdots$$
$$= 2 - 4x + 8x^2 + \tfrac{1}{4} + \dfrac{x}{16} + \dfrac{x^2}{64} + \cdots$$
$$= \tfrac{9}{4} - \dfrac{63x}{16} + \dfrac{513x^2}{64} + \cdots$$

**(iv)** $-\tfrac{1}{2} < x < \tfrac{1}{2}$

(c) (i) $\ln|1 + 2x| - \ln|4 - x| + c$

   (ii) $\int_0^{0.25} f(x)\,dx = \left[\ln|1 + 2x| - \ln|4 - x|\right]_0^{0.25}$

         $= 0.4700$ (to 4 s.f.)

         $\int_0^{0.25}\left(\dfrac{9}{4} - \dfrac{63x}{16} + \dfrac{513x^2}{64}\right)dx$

         $= \left[\dfrac{9x}{4} - \dfrac{63x^2}{32} + \dfrac{513x^3}{192}\right]_0^{0.25} = 0.4812$ (to 4 s.f.)

         Error $= 0.4812 - 0.4700$

         $= 0.0112 = 0.011$ (to 2 s.f.)

**2** (a) $(\cos x + 2\sin x)^2 = \cos^2 x + 4\cos x \sin x + 4\sin^2 x$

        $= (\cos^2 x + \sin^2 x) + 3\sin^2 x + 2(2\sin x \cos x)$

        $= 1 + \frac{3}{2}(1 - \cos 2x) + 2\sin 2x$

        $= \frac{5}{2} - \frac{3}{2}\cos 2x + 2\sin 2x$

  (b) $\dfrac{5\pi}{4} + 2$

### Test yourself (p 97)

**1** (a) $\frac{1}{2}\ln|x| - \frac{1}{6}\ln|3x + 2| + c$

  (b) $\frac{1}{3}x + \frac{1}{2}\ln|x| - \frac{13}{18}\ln|3x + 2| + c$

  (c) $-\frac{1}{4}\ln|x| - \dfrac{1}{2x} + \frac{1}{4}\ln|3x + 2| + c$

  (d) $\frac{1}{12}\ln 5 + \frac{1}{4}\ln 3 - \frac{1}{3}\ln 2 = 0.178$ (to 3 s.f.)

  (e) $\frac{1}{3} + \frac{1}{36}\ln 5 - \frac{1}{4}\ln 3 + \frac{2}{9}\ln 2 = 0.257$ (to 3 s.f.)

  (f) $\frac{1}{12} - \frac{1}{8}\ln 5 + \frac{1}{8}\ln 3 = 0.0195$ (to 3 s.f.)

**2** (a) $\dfrac{\pi}{8} - \dfrac{1}{4}$      (b) $\dfrac{3\pi}{4} - 2$      (c) $\dfrac{\pi}{2}$

# 9 Vectors

## A Vectors in two dimensions (p 98)

**A1** No

**A2** (a) 105°        (b) 55.9 km

**A3** (a)     (b)     (c)

  (d)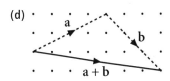

  (e) 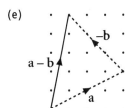        (f)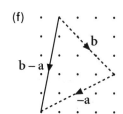

  (g)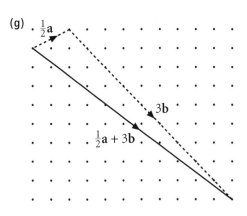

  (h)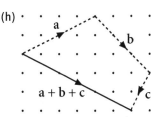

**A4** Any two non-parallel vectors **x** and **y** can be used to form a parallelogram as follows.

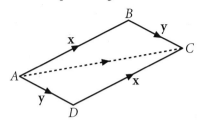

$\overrightarrow{AB} + \overrightarrow{BC} = \overrightarrow{AC}$ and $\overrightarrow{AD} + \overrightarrow{DC} = \overrightarrow{AC}$, showing that **x** + **y** = **y** + **x**.

If **x** and **y** are parallel then clearly it holds that **x** + **y** = **y** + **x**.

**A5** (a) **a** + 5**b**  (b) 5**a** − 4**b**

**A6** 2**p** + 4**q** = 2(**p** + 2**q**) so the vectors **p** + 2**q** and 2**p** + 4**q** are parallel.

**A7** B (6**x** − 3**y**), D (**y** − 2**x**) and E $(\mathbf{x} - \frac{1}{2}\mathbf{y})$

**Exercise A** (p 101)

**1** (a) 3**x** + **y**  (b) 4**y** − **x**  (c) $\frac{1}{2}\mathbf{y}$

**2** A (2**p** − 6**q**) and D $(\mathbf{q} - \frac{1}{3}\mathbf{p})$

**3** (a) **a** + **b**  (b) **a** + **b** + **c**  (c) −**c**
  (d) 3**b** − **c**  (e) **a** − 2**b** + **c**

**4** (a) (i) 2**p**  (ii) **p**  (iii) **q** − **p**  (iv) **q** − **p**
  (b) $\overrightarrow{AB} = \overrightarrow{DM} = \mathbf{p}$ and $\overrightarrow{AD} = \overrightarrow{BM} = \mathbf{q} - \mathbf{p}$
  Hence *ABMD* is a parallelogram.

**5** (a) (i) $\overrightarrow{PR} = \overrightarrow{PQ} + \overrightarrow{QR} = \mathbf{a} + \mathbf{b}$ and
    $\overrightarrow{WX} = \frac{1}{2}\mathbf{a} + \frac{1}{2}\mathbf{b} = \frac{1}{2}(\mathbf{a} + \mathbf{b})$
    so *WX* is parallel to *PR*.
  (ii) $\overrightarrow{PR} = \overrightarrow{PS} + \overrightarrow{SR} = -\mathbf{d} - \mathbf{c}$ and
    $\overrightarrow{ZY} = -\frac{1}{2}\mathbf{d} - \frac{1}{2}\mathbf{c} = \frac{1}{2}(-\mathbf{d} - \mathbf{c})$
    so *ZY* is parallel to *PR*.
  (iii) Since *WX* and *ZY* are both parallel to *PR*, they must be parallel to each other.
  (b) $\overrightarrow{QS} = \overrightarrow{QR} + \overrightarrow{RS} = \mathbf{b} + \mathbf{c}$ and $\overrightarrow{XY} = \frac{1}{2}\mathbf{b} + \frac{1}{2}\mathbf{c}$
    $= \frac{1}{2}(\mathbf{b} + \mathbf{c})$ so *XY* is parallel to *QS*.
    $\overrightarrow{QS} = \overrightarrow{QP} + \overrightarrow{PS} = -\mathbf{a} - \mathbf{d}$ and $\overrightarrow{WZ} = -\frac{1}{2}\mathbf{a} - \frac{1}{2}\mathbf{d}$
    $= \frac{1}{2}(-\mathbf{a} - \mathbf{d})$ so *WZ* is parallel to *QS*.
    Since *XY* and *WZ* are both parallel to *QS*, they must be parallel to each other.
  (c) It is a parallelogram, whatever the shape of the given quadrilateral.

## B Components in two dimensions (p 102)

**B1** B $\begin{bmatrix} 8 \\ -4 \end{bmatrix}$, C $\begin{bmatrix} 2 \\ -1 \end{bmatrix}$ and D $\begin{bmatrix} -16 \\ 8 \end{bmatrix}$

**B2** $\begin{bmatrix} 14 \\ -6 \end{bmatrix}$

**B3** (a) $\begin{bmatrix} 5 \\ 2 \end{bmatrix}$  (b) **x** + 3**y**

**B4** |**p**| = 5, |**q**| = 13 and |**p** + **q**| = √68 or 2√17.
  |**p**| + |**q**| = 5 + 13 = 18 ≠ √68 = |**p** + **q**| so this verifies the fact that |**p**| + |**q**| ≠ |**p** + **q**| in general.

**B5** (a) $\begin{bmatrix} 2 \\ 5 \end{bmatrix}$  (b) √29

**B6** −4**i** + 3**j**

**B7** $\begin{bmatrix} 4 \\ 7 \end{bmatrix}$

**B8** (a) 3**i** + 2**j**  (b) **i** + 8**j**  (c) 11**i**

**B9** 10

**B10** Any multiple of 2**i** + 5**j**, e.g. 4**i** + 10**j**

**Exercise B** (p 104)

**1** (a) $\begin{bmatrix} 1 \\ 8 \end{bmatrix}$  (b) $\begin{bmatrix} -1 \\ 12 \end{bmatrix}$  (c) $\begin{bmatrix} 0 \\ 0 \end{bmatrix}$

**2** (a) √13  (b) 5
  (c) √2  (d) √130

**3** (a) $\begin{bmatrix} 3 \\ 2 \end{bmatrix}$  (b) √148 or 2√37

**4** 3√26

**5** **a** and **e**, **b** and **f**, **c** and **d**

**6** ±2

**7** $\begin{bmatrix} 9 \\ 12 \end{bmatrix}$ and $\begin{bmatrix} -9 \\ -12 \end{bmatrix}$

**8** (a) $\left(\frac{5}{13}\right)^2 + \left(\frac{12}{13}\right)^2 = \frac{25}{169} + \frac{144}{169} = 1$ so the
    magnitude of the vector is √1 which is 1.
    Hence the vector is a unit vector.
  (b) $\frac{3}{5}\mathbf{i} - \frac{4}{5}\mathbf{j}$

**9** $k = 1, l = -4$

**10** (a) (i) **a** + **b**  (ii) −2**a**  (iii) $\frac{1}{2}\mathbf{b}$
    (iv) $\frac{1}{2}\mathbf{b} - 2\mathbf{a}$  (v) **b** − **a**

**(b) (i)** $\overrightarrow{PX}$ and $\overrightarrow{PR}$ are parallel and $\overrightarrow{PR} = \mathbf{a} + \mathbf{b}$.
Hence $\overrightarrow{PX} = k(\mathbf{a} + \mathbf{b})$ for some number $k$.

**(ii)** $\overrightarrow{XS}$ and $\overrightarrow{TS}$ are parallel and $\overrightarrow{TS} = \frac{1}{2}\mathbf{b} - 2\mathbf{a}$.
Hence $\overrightarrow{XS} = l(\frac{1}{2}\mathbf{b} - 2\mathbf{a})$ for some number $l$.

**(iii)** $k = \frac{3}{5}, l = \frac{4}{5}$

## C Vectors in three dimensions (p 105)

**C1 (a) (i)** $\frac{1}{2}\mathbf{r}$      **(ii)** $\mathbf{p} + \mathbf{q}$      **(iii)** $\mathbf{p} + \mathbf{r}$
**(iv)** $\mathbf{q} - \mathbf{p}$      **(v)** $\mathbf{p} + \mathbf{q} + \mathbf{r}$      **(vi)** $-\mathbf{r} - \mathbf{p}$
**(vii)** $\mathbf{q} - \mathbf{p} + \frac{1}{2}\mathbf{r}$      **(viii)** $\frac{1}{2}\mathbf{r} - \mathbf{q}$

**(b)** $\overrightarrow{AG} = \mathbf{q} + \frac{1}{2}\mathbf{r}$ and $\overrightarrow{DH} = \mathbf{q} + \mathbf{r}$.
$\mathbf{q} + \frac{1}{2}\mathbf{r}$ and $\mathbf{q} + \mathbf{r}$ are not multiples of each other and so the vectors are not parallel.

**C2 (a)** $(7, 0, 0)$      **(b)** $(4, 8, 0)$
**(c)** $(7, 0, 6)$      **(d)** $(4, 8, 6)$

**C3 (a)** 3      **(b)** 8      **(c)** 6

**C4 (a)** $\begin{bmatrix} 3 \\ 0 \\ 6 \end{bmatrix}$   **(b)** $\begin{bmatrix} 3 \\ 0 \\ 6 \end{bmatrix}$   **(c)** $\begin{bmatrix} 3 \\ 8 \\ 0 \end{bmatrix}$   **(d)** $\begin{bmatrix} -3 \\ 0 \\ 6 \end{bmatrix}$

**(e)** $\begin{bmatrix} 0 \\ 0 \\ -6 \end{bmatrix}$   **(f)** $\begin{bmatrix} 3 \\ 8 \\ 6 \end{bmatrix}$   **(g)** $\begin{bmatrix} -3 \\ 8 \\ 6 \end{bmatrix}$   **(h)** $\begin{bmatrix} -3 \\ 8 \\ -6 \end{bmatrix}$

**C5** $\begin{bmatrix} 2 \\ -1 \\ 3 \end{bmatrix}, \begin{bmatrix} -6 \\ 3 \\ -9 \end{bmatrix}$ and $\begin{bmatrix} 4 \\ -2 \\ 6 \end{bmatrix}; \begin{bmatrix} 12 \\ -6 \\ 16 \end{bmatrix}$ and $\begin{bmatrix} 6 \\ -3 \\ 8 \end{bmatrix}$

**C6 (a)** The dotted lines that represent the $x$- and $y$-components 1 and 3 are parallel to the $x$- and $y$-axes respectively. The $x$- and $y$-axes are at right angles to each other so the dotted lines must be too. Hence the shaded triangle is a right-angled triangle.

**(b)** $\sqrt{10}$      **(c)** Yes      **(d)** $\sqrt{14}$

**C7** $\sqrt{178}$

**C8** $\sqrt{42}$

**C9 (a)** 3      **(b)** $\sqrt{35}$
**(c)** $\sqrt{45}$, or $3\sqrt{5}$

**C10 (a) (i)** $\begin{bmatrix} 4 \\ 0 \\ 0 \end{bmatrix}$   **(ii)** $\begin{bmatrix} 1 \\ 2 \\ 6 \end{bmatrix}$   **(iii)** $\begin{bmatrix} -1 \\ -2 \\ -6 \end{bmatrix}$

**(b)** $\overrightarrow{EB} = \overrightarrow{EA} + \overrightarrow{AB} = \begin{bmatrix} -1 \\ -2 \\ -6 \end{bmatrix} + \begin{bmatrix} 4 \\ 0 \\ 0 \end{bmatrix} = \begin{bmatrix} 3 \\ -2 \\ -6 \end{bmatrix}$

**(c) (i)** $\begin{bmatrix} 4 \\ 4 \\ 0 \end{bmatrix}$   **(ii)** $\begin{bmatrix} 3 \\ 2 \\ -6 \end{bmatrix}$   **(iii)** $\begin{bmatrix} 1 \\ -2 \\ 6 \end{bmatrix}$

**(d)** $\sqrt{41}$

**C11 (a) (i)** $\begin{bmatrix} 2 \\ 2 \\ 7 \end{bmatrix}$   **(ii)** $\begin{bmatrix} 14 \\ -2 \\ 2 \end{bmatrix}$   **(iii)** $\begin{bmatrix} 14 \\ -4 \\ 32 \end{bmatrix}$

**(iv)** $\begin{bmatrix} 5 \\ -6 \\ -2 \end{bmatrix}$   **(v)** $\begin{bmatrix} 4 \\ 6 \\ -16 \end{bmatrix}$

**(b)** $\sqrt{29}$

**C12** $2\mathbf{i} + 6\mathbf{j} - 5\mathbf{k}$

**C13** $\begin{bmatrix} 3 \\ -2 \\ 8 \end{bmatrix}$

**C14 (a)** $|\mathbf{p}| = \sqrt{1^2 + 1^2 + 4^2} = \sqrt{18} = \sqrt{9} \times \sqrt{2} = 3\sqrt{2}$
**(b) (i)** $2\mathbf{i} + 5\mathbf{j}$      **(ii)** $3\mathbf{i} - 4\mathbf{j} + 3\mathbf{k}$
**(iii)** $10\mathbf{j} + \mathbf{k}$
**(c)** $\sqrt{29}$

**C15** $2\mathbf{i} + 4\mathbf{j} - 6\mathbf{k} = 2(\mathbf{i} + 2\mathbf{j} - 3\mathbf{k})$ so the vectors $2\mathbf{i} + 4\mathbf{j} - 6\mathbf{k}$ and $\mathbf{i} + 2\mathbf{j} - 3\mathbf{k}$ are parallel.

### Exercise C (p 109)

**1 (a) (i)** $\begin{bmatrix} 0 \\ 15 \\ -2 \end{bmatrix}$   **(ii)** $\begin{bmatrix} 0 \\ -30 \\ 4 \end{bmatrix}$   **(iii)** $\begin{bmatrix} 0 \\ 0 \\ 0 \end{bmatrix}$

**(b)** 5

**2 (a) (i)** $\begin{bmatrix} 3 \\ 0 \\ 0 \end{bmatrix}$   **(ii)** $\begin{bmatrix} 0 \\ 0 \\ 2 \end{bmatrix}$   **(iii)** $\begin{bmatrix} 0 \\ 3 \\ 0 \end{bmatrix}$

**(b)** $\overrightarrow{HB} = \overrightarrow{HE} + \overrightarrow{EA} + \overrightarrow{AB} = \begin{bmatrix} 0 \\ -3 \\ 0 \end{bmatrix} + \begin{bmatrix} 0 \\ 0 \\ -2 \end{bmatrix} + \begin{bmatrix} 3 \\ 0 \\ 0 \end{bmatrix}$

$= \begin{bmatrix} 3 \\ -3 \\ -2 \end{bmatrix}$

**(c) (i)** $\begin{bmatrix} 2 \\ 5 \\ 2 \end{bmatrix}$ **(ii)** $\begin{bmatrix} 5 \\ 2 \\ -2 \end{bmatrix}$ **(iii)** $\begin{bmatrix} 5 \\ 5 \\ 2 \end{bmatrix}$ **(iv)** $\begin{bmatrix} -5 \\ -5 \\ 2 \end{bmatrix}$

**(d)** $\sqrt{22}$

**3 (a)** 9        **(b)** 27

**4** **u** and **y**, **v** and **z**, **w** and **x**

**5** $5\mathbf{i} + 8\mathbf{j}$

**6** $x = 3, y = -6$

**7** $\pm 4$

**8** $4\mathbf{i} - 6\mathbf{j} - 12\mathbf{k}$ or $-4\mathbf{i} + 6\mathbf{j} + 12\mathbf{k}$

**9** You can use a proof by contradiction as follows.
Assume that it is possible to write **a** as a linear
combination of **b** and **c**. Then there must exist
numbers $t$ and $s$ such that $\mathbf{a} = t\mathbf{b} + s\mathbf{c}$.
So $\mathbf{i} + \mathbf{j} - 2\mathbf{k} = t(5\mathbf{i} - \mathbf{j} + 3\mathbf{k}) + s(-2\mathbf{i} + \mathbf{j} + \mathbf{k})$
which gives the equations $5t - 2s = 1$, $-t + s = 1$
and $3t + s = -2$. The first two equations have the
solution $t = 1, s = 2$. This gives $3t + s = 5$ which
contradicts the fact that $3t + s = -2$. Hence the
original assumption that it is possible to write **a** as
a linear combination of **b** and **c** must be false.

## D Position vectors in two and three dimensions (p 111)

**D1** $\mathbf{q} - \mathbf{p}$

**D2 (a)** A sketch showing $X\,(1, 6)$ and $Y\,(2, -7)$

    **(b)** $(3, -1)$

    **(c)** $\mathbf{i} - 13\mathbf{j}$

**D3 (a)** $\frac{1}{4}(\mathbf{n} - \mathbf{m})$

    **(b)** The position vector of point $P$ is $\overrightarrow{OP}$.
$\overrightarrow{OP} = \overrightarrow{OM} + \overrightarrow{MP} = \mathbf{m} + \frac{1}{4}(\mathbf{n} - \mathbf{m})$
$= \mathbf{m} + \frac{1}{4}\mathbf{n} - \frac{1}{4}\mathbf{m} = \frac{3}{4}\mathbf{m} + \frac{1}{4}\mathbf{n}$ as required.

**D4 (a)** $\begin{bmatrix} -2 \\ 8 \\ -6 \end{bmatrix}$     **(b)** $\sqrt{104}$ or $2\sqrt{26}$

### Exercise D (p 114)

**1** $\frac{4}{5}\mathbf{a} + \frac{1}{5}\mathbf{b}$

**2 (a)** $\mathbf{i} + 5\mathbf{j} + 7\mathbf{k}$     **(b)** $\sqrt{75}$ or $5\sqrt{3}$

**3 (a)** $O\begin{bmatrix} 0 \\ 0 \\ 0 \end{bmatrix}, A\begin{bmatrix} 4 \\ 0 \\ 0 \end{bmatrix}, B\begin{bmatrix} 4 \\ 4 \\ 0 \end{bmatrix}, C\begin{bmatrix} 0 \\ 4 \\ 0 \end{bmatrix}, D\begin{bmatrix} 0 \\ 0 \\ 4 \end{bmatrix}, E\begin{bmatrix} 4 \\ 0 \\ 4 \end{bmatrix},$
$F\begin{bmatrix} 4 \\ 4 \\ 4 \end{bmatrix}, G\begin{bmatrix} 0 \\ 4 \\ 4 \end{bmatrix}$

    **(b)** $\overrightarrow{AG} = \begin{bmatrix} -4 \\ 4 \\ 4 \end{bmatrix}, \overrightarrow{BD} = \begin{bmatrix} -4 \\ -4 \\ 4 \end{bmatrix}$

    **(c)** $P\begin{bmatrix} 2 \\ 0 \\ 4 \end{bmatrix}, Q\begin{bmatrix} 4 \\ 0 \\ 2 \end{bmatrix}, R\begin{bmatrix} 4 \\ 2 \\ 4 \end{bmatrix}$

    **(d) (i)** $\overrightarrow{PQ} = \begin{bmatrix} 2 \\ 0 \\ -2 \end{bmatrix}, \overrightarrow{QR} = \begin{bmatrix} 0 \\ 2 \\ 2 \end{bmatrix}, \overrightarrow{RP} = \begin{bmatrix} -2 \\ -2 \\ 0 \end{bmatrix}$

    **(ii)** $\overrightarrow{PQ} + \overrightarrow{QR} + \overrightarrow{RP} = \begin{bmatrix} 0 \\ 0 \\ 0 \end{bmatrix}$ which is to be
expected as $PQ$, $QR$ and $RP$ form the
edges of a triangle.

**4** $|\mathbf{a}| = \sqrt{5^2 + 5^2 + 4^2} = \sqrt{66}$,
$|\mathbf{b}| = \sqrt{4^2 + (-7)^2 + 1^2} = \sqrt{66}$ and
$|\mathbf{c}| = \sqrt{7^2 + 4^2 + (-1)^2} = \sqrt{66}$.
So points $A$, $B$ and $C$ are all the same distance
from $(0, 0, 0)$ and hence on the surface of a
sphere with centre $(0, 0, 0)$.

**5** $\overrightarrow{PQ} = \mathbf{q} - \mathbf{p} = -\mathbf{i} + 2\mathbf{j} + 2\mathbf{k}$ and
$\overrightarrow{RS} = \mathbf{s} - \mathbf{r} = 2\mathbf{i} - 4\mathbf{j} - 4\mathbf{k}$.
$2\mathbf{i} - 4\mathbf{j} - 4\mathbf{k} = -2(-\mathbf{i} + 2\mathbf{j} + 2\mathbf{k})$ so $\overrightarrow{RS} = -2\overrightarrow{PQ}$
and hence the vectors are parallel.

**6 (a)** $\sqrt{133}$       **(b)** $\sqrt{114}$

**7** One way is to argue that, since $\overrightarrow{AB} = 9\mathbf{i} + 3\mathbf{j} + 3\mathbf{k}$
and $\overrightarrow{BC} = -6\mathbf{i} - 2\mathbf{j} - 2\mathbf{k}$, then $\overrightarrow{BC} = -\frac{2}{3}\overrightarrow{AB}$. Hence
$BC$ is parallel to $AB$. So $A$, $B$ and $C$ are in a
straight line.

**8** $4, -2$

## E The vector equation of a line (p 115)

**E1** (a) When $t = 5$, $\begin{bmatrix} x \\ y \end{bmatrix} = \begin{bmatrix} 1 \\ 6 \end{bmatrix} + 5\begin{bmatrix} 2 \\ -1 \end{bmatrix}$

$= \begin{bmatrix} 1 \\ 6 \end{bmatrix} + \begin{bmatrix} 10 \\ -5 \end{bmatrix} = \begin{bmatrix} 11 \\ 1 \end{bmatrix}$ as required.

(b) (i) $\begin{bmatrix} 1 \\ 6 \end{bmatrix}$  (ii) $\begin{bmatrix} 3 \\ 5 \end{bmatrix}$  (iii) $\begin{bmatrix} -1 \\ 7 \end{bmatrix}$  (iv) $\begin{bmatrix} 7 \\ 3 \end{bmatrix}$

(c) (i) A diagram with these points plotted:
$(-1, 7)$, $(1, 6)$, $(3, 5)$, $(7, 3)$ and $(11, 1)$.

(ii) Let $P$ be the point $(1, 6)$. For any point $Q$ with position vector given by the rule we have $\overrightarrow{PQ} = t\begin{bmatrix} 2 \\ -1 \end{bmatrix}$ for some $t$.

So all possible vectors $\overrightarrow{PQ}$ are parallel and hence all possible points $Q$ are on the same straight line through $P$ parallel to the vector $\begin{bmatrix} 2 \\ -1 \end{bmatrix}$.

(iii) $x + 2y = 13$

**E2** (a) (i) $\begin{bmatrix} 1 \\ 6 \end{bmatrix}$  (ii) $\begin{bmatrix} 3 \\ 5 \end{bmatrix}$  (iii) $\begin{bmatrix} 9 \\ 2 \end{bmatrix}$  (iv) $\begin{bmatrix} -7 \\ 10 \end{bmatrix}$

(b) (i) A straight line through the points $(-7, 10)$, $(1, 6)$, $(3, 5)$ and $(9, 2)$

(ii) It is the same line.

(iii) The point $(3, 5)$ is on the line found in E1 and the vector $\begin{bmatrix} -2 \\ 1 \end{bmatrix}$ is parallel to the vector $\begin{bmatrix} 2 \\ -1 \end{bmatrix}$. Hence the lines will be the same.

**E3** Examples of equations are

(a) $\mathbf{r} = \begin{bmatrix} 0 \\ 4 \end{bmatrix} + t\begin{bmatrix} 1 \\ 1 \end{bmatrix}$  (b) $\mathbf{r} = \begin{bmatrix} 0 \\ 6 \end{bmatrix} + t\begin{bmatrix} 1 \\ -1 \end{bmatrix}$

(c) $\mathbf{r} = \begin{bmatrix} 0 \\ 1 \end{bmatrix} + t\begin{bmatrix} 1 \\ 2 \end{bmatrix}$

**E4** (a)

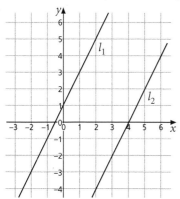

(b) (i) The lines are parallel.

(ii) The vectors $\begin{bmatrix} 1 \\ 2 \end{bmatrix}$ and $\begin{bmatrix} -2 \\ -4 \end{bmatrix}$ are parallel.

**E5** $L_2$

**E6** (a) Three points such as $(4, 3, 7)$, $(5, 3, 4)$, $(6, 3, 1)$, $(7, 3, -2)$, ...

(b) $\lambda = 5$

(c) If the point does lie on the line then there must exist a number $\lambda$ such that

$\begin{bmatrix} 7 \\ 3 \\ -1 \end{bmatrix} = \begin{bmatrix} 4 \\ 3 \\ 7 \end{bmatrix} + \lambda\begin{bmatrix} 1 \\ 0 \\ -3 \end{bmatrix}$. The value $\lambda = 3$ gives the

point with position vector $\begin{bmatrix} 7 \\ 3 \\ -2 \end{bmatrix}$ whose $x$- and

$y$-components match those of $\begin{bmatrix} 7 \\ 3 \\ -1 \end{bmatrix}$ but whose

$z$-component does not match. Hence no value

of $\lambda$ exists so that $\begin{bmatrix} 7 \\ 3 \\ -1 \end{bmatrix} = \begin{bmatrix} 4 \\ 3 \\ 7 \end{bmatrix} + \lambda\begin{bmatrix} 1 \\ 0 \\ -3 \end{bmatrix}$ and so

the point with position vector $\begin{bmatrix} 7 \\ 3 \\ -1 \end{bmatrix}$ does not

lie on the line.

**E7** (a) $7\mathbf{i} - 10\mathbf{j}$  (b) $\lambda = -1$

(c) If the point does lie on the line then there must exist a number $\lambda$ such that
$3\mathbf{i} - 3\mathbf{j} - 2\mathbf{k} = \mathbf{i} + 2\mathbf{j} - 3\mathbf{k} + \lambda(2\mathbf{i} - 4\mathbf{j} + \mathbf{k})$.
The value $\lambda = 1$ gives the point with position vector $3\mathbf{i} - 2\mathbf{j} - 2\mathbf{k}$ whose $x$- and $z$-components match those of $3\mathbf{i} - 3\mathbf{j} - 2\mathbf{k}$ but whose $y$-component does not match.
Hence no value of $\lambda$ exists so that
$3\mathbf{i} - 3\mathbf{j} - 2\mathbf{k} = \mathbf{i} + 2\mathbf{j} - 3\mathbf{k} + \lambda(2\mathbf{i} - 4\mathbf{j} + \mathbf{k})$ and so the point with position vector $3\mathbf{i} - 3\mathbf{j} - 2\mathbf{k}$ does not lie on the line.

**Exercise E** (p 120)

Each vector equation given in these answers is not unique but one of an infinite number of suitable equations.

**1** (a) $\mathbf{r} = \begin{bmatrix} 0 \\ 5 \end{bmatrix} + \lambda \begin{bmatrix} 1 \\ 4 \end{bmatrix}$    (b) $\mathbf{r} = \lambda \begin{bmatrix} 1 \\ 0 \end{bmatrix}$

(c) $\mathbf{r} = \begin{bmatrix} 5 \\ -2 \end{bmatrix} + \lambda \begin{bmatrix} 1 \\ -5 \end{bmatrix}$

**2** (a) $\mathbf{r} = \begin{bmatrix} -1 \\ 3 \\ 5 \end{bmatrix} + \lambda \begin{bmatrix} -1 \\ 1 \\ -3 \end{bmatrix}$    (b) $\mathbf{r} = \begin{bmatrix} 2 \\ 1 \\ 0 \end{bmatrix} + \lambda \begin{bmatrix} 1 \\ 3 \\ 4 \end{bmatrix}$

(c) $\mathbf{r} = \lambda \begin{bmatrix} 0 \\ 0 \\ 1 \end{bmatrix}$

(d) $\mathbf{r} = 2\mathbf{i} - 4\mathbf{j} + 7\mathbf{k} + \lambda(-3\mathbf{i} + 6\mathbf{j} - 8\mathbf{k})$

**3** When $\lambda = \frac{1}{2}$, $\mathbf{r} = \mathbf{i} - 3\mathbf{j} + 2\mathbf{k} + \frac{1}{2}(2\mathbf{i} + 4\mathbf{j} - 6\mathbf{k})$
$= \mathbf{i} - 3\mathbf{j} + 2\mathbf{k} + \mathbf{i} + 2\mathbf{j} - 3\mathbf{k} = 2\mathbf{i} - \mathbf{j} - \mathbf{k}$.
So the point with position vector $2\mathbf{i} - \mathbf{j} - \mathbf{k}$ lies on the line.

**4** (a) $\mathbf{r} = \begin{bmatrix} 3 \\ 1 \\ 2 \end{bmatrix} + \lambda \begin{bmatrix} 8 \\ -2 \\ -4 \end{bmatrix}$

(b) For the equation above, when $\lambda = \frac{1}{2}$,

$\mathbf{r} = \begin{bmatrix} 7 \\ 0 \\ 0 \end{bmatrix}$, which is the position vector of a point

on the $x$-axis. So the line intersects the $x$-axis.

**5** (a) $\mathbf{r} = -2\mathbf{i} + \mathbf{j} + \lambda(6\mathbf{i} - \mathbf{j} + 4\mathbf{k})$

(b) If the line did intersect the $y$-axis then there would exist numbers $\lambda$ and $a$ such that $-2\mathbf{i} + \mathbf{j} + \lambda(6\mathbf{i} - \mathbf{j} + 4\mathbf{k}) = a\mathbf{j}$. Equating coefficients for the $x$- and $z$-components gives $6\lambda - 2 = 0$ and $4\lambda = 0$. The first equation gives $\lambda = \frac{1}{3}$ but the second equation gives $\lambda = 0$. Hence no such value for $\lambda$ exists and the line does not intersect the $y$-axis.

**6** (a) $\begin{bmatrix} 10 \\ 50 \\ 8 \end{bmatrix}$    (b) 16.3 km    (c) 1.3 km

(d) 0 km, which means the planes collide

**7** $p = -17, q = 4$

**8** $(5, 5), (7, 1)$

**9** $(2, -1, 2), (1, -2, 2)$

**F Intersecting lines** (p 121)

**F1** (a) For the first line we have $\begin{bmatrix} x \\ y \end{bmatrix} = \begin{bmatrix} 1 + \lambda \\ -3 + \lambda \end{bmatrix}$ and

for the second we have $\begin{bmatrix} x \\ y \end{bmatrix} = \begin{bmatrix} 11 + \mu \\ 1 - 2\mu \end{bmatrix}$.

Equating $x$-components gives $1 + \lambda = 11 + \mu$ and equating $y$-components gives $-3 + \lambda = 1 - 2\mu$.

(b) $\lambda = 8, \mu = -2$

(c) $\begin{bmatrix} 9 \\ 5 \end{bmatrix}$

(d) Using the same parameter and equating the $x$- and $y$-components would only work if the parameter for each vector equation is the same at the point of intersection. Since the parameters are very likely to have different values at the point of intersection, we need to use different parameters to end up with the two different values.

**F2** (a) For the first line we have $\mathbf{r} = \begin{bmatrix} 2\lambda \\ 2 + \lambda \end{bmatrix}$ and

for the second we have $\mathbf{r} = \begin{bmatrix} 3 + 4\mu \\ 1 + 2\mu \end{bmatrix}$.

Equating $x$-components gives $2\lambda = 3 + 4\mu$ and equating $y$-components gives $2 + \lambda = 1 + 2\mu$.

(b) There is no solution so the lines are parallel and do not intersect. This can be seen from

the equations as the vector $\begin{bmatrix} 2 \\ 1 \end{bmatrix}$ is parallel to $\begin{bmatrix} 4 \\ 2 \end{bmatrix}$.

**F3** $(1, 7)$

**F4** There are an infinite number of solutions for $\lambda$ and $\mu$ that are of the form $\lambda = -2 - 2\mu$. This means that the two lines are actually the same.

**F5** (a) Parallel    (b) Intersecting    (c) Skew
(d) Skew    (e) Parallel    (f) Skew

**F6** For the first line we have $\mathbf{r} = \begin{bmatrix} 1+2\lambda \\ 2+3\lambda \\ 4-\lambda \end{bmatrix}$ and for the

second we have $\mathbf{r} = \begin{bmatrix} 3+4\mu \\ 6+5\mu \\ -2 \end{bmatrix}$.

Equating $x$-, $y$- and $z$-components gives the
equations $1 + 2\lambda = 3 + 4\mu$
$\qquad 2 + 3\lambda = 6 + 5\mu$
$\qquad 4 - \lambda = -2$

Solving simultaneously the first and third
equations gives $\lambda = 6$ and $\mu = 2\frac{1}{2}$ but this pair of
values gives $2 + 3\lambda = 20$ and $6 + 5\mu = 18\frac{1}{2}$ and so
does not satisfy the second equation. Hence the
lines do not intersect. Since they are not parallel,
they must be skew.

**Exercise F** (p 124)

**1** If the two lines intersect then there must be values
of $\lambda$ and $\mu$ such that $\begin{bmatrix} 5 \\ 4 \\ 3 \end{bmatrix} + \lambda \begin{bmatrix} 1 \\ 0 \\ -3 \end{bmatrix} = \begin{bmatrix} 7 \\ 10 \\ 9 \end{bmatrix} + \mu \begin{bmatrix} 0 \\ 2 \\ 4 \end{bmatrix}$

This gives the equations
$\qquad 5 + \lambda = 7$
$\qquad 4 = 10 + 2\mu$
$\qquad 3 - 3\lambda = 9 + 4\mu$

The first and second equations give $\lambda = 2$ and
$\mu = -3$ and this pair of values gives $3 - 3\lambda = -3$
and $9 + 4\mu = -3$ too and so the values satisfy the
third equation. Hence the lines intersect.
The point of intersection is $(7, 4, -3)$.

**2** If the two lines intersect then there must be values
of $t$ and $s$ such that $\begin{bmatrix} 2 \\ 0 \\ -1 \end{bmatrix} + t \begin{bmatrix} 0 \\ 2 \\ 3 \end{bmatrix} = \begin{bmatrix} -3 \\ 0 \\ 2 \end{bmatrix} + s \begin{bmatrix} 5 \\ 4 \\ -1 \end{bmatrix}$.

This gives the equations
$\qquad 2 = -3 + 5s$
$\qquad 2t = 4s$
$\qquad -1 + 3t = 2 - s$

The first and second equations give $s = 1$ and
$t = 2$ but this pair of values gives $-1 + 3t = 5$ and
$2 - s = 1$ and so the values do not satisfy the third
equation. Hence the lines do not intersect. Since
their direction vectors are not scalar multiples of
each other, the lines are not parallel and so they
must be skew.

**3** If the two lines intersect then there must be values
of $\lambda$ and $\mu$ such that $4\mathbf{i} + 3\mathbf{j} + \lambda(-\mathbf{i} - \mathbf{j} + \mathbf{k})$
$= 4\mathbf{i} - 3\mathbf{j} + \mu(-\mathbf{i} + \mathbf{j} + \mathbf{k})$. This gives the equations
$\qquad 4 - \lambda = 4 - \mu$
$\qquad 3 - \lambda = -3 + \mu$
$\qquad \lambda = \mu$

The first and second equations give $\lambda = 3$ and
$\mu = 3$ and clearly this pair of values satisfies the
third equation. Hence the lines intersect.
The point of intersection is $(1, 0, 3)$.

**4** (a) Intersect at $(5, 3, 11)$

(b) Parallel

(c) Skew

(d) Intersect at $(6, 3, -2)$

(e) Skew

**5** (a) 2 $\qquad\qquad$ (b) $(2, 0, 2)$

**6** (a) 1 $\qquad\qquad$ (b) $(5, 4, 4)$

## G Angles and the scalar product (p 125)

**G1** (a) 90° $\qquad$ (b) 45° $\qquad$ (c) 135°

**G2** (a) Vectors **a** and **b** can be drawn in any position
and could be shown placed 'head to head'.

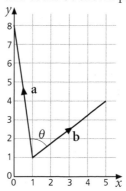

(b) $|\mathbf{a}| = \sqrt{50}$ or $5\sqrt{2}$, $|\mathbf{b}| = 5$

(c) $\sqrt{41}$

(d) 61.3° (to 1 d.p.)

**G3** (a) $|\mathbf{p}| = 3$, $|\mathbf{q}| = \sqrt{41}$

(b) $\sqrt{14}$

(c) 20.4° (to 1 d.p.)

**G4** (a) −5

(b) $|\mathbf{a}| = \sqrt{14}$, $|\mathbf{b}| = \sqrt{50}$ or $5\sqrt{2}$

(c) $\cos\theta = -\dfrac{1}{2\sqrt{7}}$, $\theta = 100.9°$ (to 1 d.p.)

**G5** $\mathbf{a.b} = (2\times 1) + (1\times -1) + (4\times 1) = 2 - 1 + 4 = 5$

**G6** $\overrightarrow{OA}.\overrightarrow{OB} = |\overrightarrow{OA}||\overrightarrow{OB}|\cos\angle AOB$
$= 5\times 5\times \cos 35 = 20.48$ (to 2 d.p.)

**G7** (a) 0                    (b) $\cos\theta = 0$

(c) They are at right angles to each other, that is they are perpendicular.

**G8** The scalar product of the two vectors is
$(2\times 4) + (-3\times 1) + (1\times -5) = 8 - 3 - 5 = 0$ so the two vectors are perpendicular.

**Exercise G** (p 127)

**1** (a) $\mathbf{a.b} = 0$, $\mathbf{b.c} = 0$, $\mathbf{a.c} = 20$

(b) $\mathbf{a}$ and $\mathbf{b}$, $\mathbf{b}$ and $\mathbf{c}$

**2** To 1 d.p., unless exact, the angles are

(a) $73.9°$          (b) $132.8°$          (c) $90°$

**3** $79.3°$ (to 1 d.p.)

**4** $\angle QPR = 90°$, $\angle PQR = 45°$, $\angle QRP = 45°$

**5** Using the formula for the scalar product gives
$\mathbf{a.a} = (a_1\times a_1) + (a_2\times a_2) + (a_3\times a_3)$
$= a_1{}^2 + a_2{}^2 + a_3{}^2$
Using the formula for the length of a vector gives
$|\mathbf{a}|^2 = a_1{}^2 + a_2{}^2 + a_3{}^2$ too so $\mathbf{a.a} = |\mathbf{a}|^2$.
Another way to show this is to note that the angle between a vector and itself is 0 so
$\mathbf{a.a} = |\mathbf{a}||\mathbf{a}|\cos 0 = |\mathbf{a}||\mathbf{a}|\times 1 = |\mathbf{a}|^2$.

**6** Using the formula $\mathbf{a.b} = |\mathbf{a}||\mathbf{b}|\cos\theta$ with the values $\mathbf{a.b} = 12$, $|\mathbf{a}| = 3$ and $|\mathbf{b}| = 4$ gives
$12 = 3\times 4\times \cos\theta$ which implies that $\theta = 0°$ or $180°$. Hence $\mathbf{a}$ and $\mathbf{b}$ are parallel.

**7** Labelling the points $O$ $(0, 0, 0)$, $A$ $(4, -2, 5)$, $B$ $(3, 6, 0)$ and $C$ $(7, 4, 5)$ we obtain these vectors.

$$\overrightarrow{OA} = \begin{bmatrix} 4 \\ -2 \\ 5 \end{bmatrix} \qquad \overrightarrow{OB} = \begin{bmatrix} 3 \\ 6 \\ 0 \end{bmatrix} \qquad \overrightarrow{OC} = \begin{bmatrix} 7 \\ 4 \\ 5 \end{bmatrix}$$

$$\overrightarrow{AB} = \begin{bmatrix} -1 \\ 8 \\ -5 \end{bmatrix} \qquad \overrightarrow{AC} = \begin{bmatrix} 3 \\ 6 \\ 0 \end{bmatrix} \qquad \overrightarrow{BC} = \begin{bmatrix} 4 \\ -2 \\ 5 \end{bmatrix}$$

We can see that $\overrightarrow{OA} = \overrightarrow{BC}$ and $\overrightarrow{OB} = \overrightarrow{AC}$ so we know that $OBCA$ is a parallelogram.
$|\overrightarrow{OA}| = \sqrt{4^2 + (-2)^2 + 5^2} = \sqrt{45}$ and
$|\overrightarrow{OB}| = \sqrt{3^2 + 6^2 + 0^2} = \sqrt{45}$ so $OBCA$ is a rhombus.

Finally, to show that $OBCA$ is a square we need to show that one of its angles is a right angle (which implies here that all the angles are right angles).
$\overrightarrow{OB}.\overrightarrow{OA} = (3\times 4) + (6\times -2) + (0\times 5) = 0$ so $\angle BOA = 90°$ and so the vertices form a square.

**H  The angle between two straight lines** (p 128)

**H1** (a) No

(b) You could move the line through $AC$ vertically upwards till it meets $HB$ and measure the angle between them.

**H2** $90°$

**H3** (a) $90°$          (b) $45°$          (c) $90°$          (d) $60°$

**H4** The angle between the lines is the angle between the direction vectors $\begin{bmatrix} 3 \\ 5 \\ -1 \end{bmatrix}$ and $\begin{bmatrix} 1 \\ 2 \\ 13 \end{bmatrix}$. So to show that the lines are perpendicular you can show that
$\begin{bmatrix} 3 \\ 5 \\ -1 \end{bmatrix}.\begin{bmatrix} 1 \\ 2 \\ 13 \end{bmatrix} = 0$

**Exercise H** (p 130)

**1** (a) $60°$          (b) $60°$          (c) $45°$          (d) $90°$

**2** $30.6°$ (to 1 d.p.)

**3** The scalar product of the direction vectors is

$$\begin{bmatrix} 3 \\ -6 \\ 0 \end{bmatrix} \cdot \begin{bmatrix} 2 \\ 1 \\ -3 \end{bmatrix} = (3 \times 2) + (-6 \times 1) + (0 \times -3)$$

$= 6 - 6 + 0 = 0$ so the two lines are perpendicular.

**4** $81.6°$ (to 1 d.p.)

**5** $88.2°$ (to 1 d.p.)

## I Shortest distance (p 131)

**I1** $\theta$ is $90°$.

### Exercise I (p 133)

**1** $(5.7, 1.9)$

**2** $(-2, 5)$

**3** $\sqrt{40}$, or $2\sqrt{10}$

**4** $(4, \frac{1}{2}, -\frac{5}{2})$

**5** $\sqrt{126}$, or $3\sqrt{14}$

**6** $(1, 1, 3)$

**7 (a)** One possible equation is $\mathbf{r} = \begin{bmatrix} 2 \\ 0 \\ -3 \end{bmatrix} + \lambda \begin{bmatrix} 1 \\ 1 \\ 2 \end{bmatrix}$.

**(b)** $\sqrt{54}$ or $3\sqrt{6}$

**(c)** The shortest distance is $\sqrt{3}$ and the area is

$\dfrac{\sqrt{162}}{2}$ or $\dfrac{3\sqrt{18}}{2}$ or $\dfrac{9\sqrt{2}}{2}$ or $\dfrac{9}{\sqrt{2}}$.

## Mixed questions (p 136)

Each vector equation given in these answers is not unique but one of an infinite number of suitable equations.

**1 (a)** If the two lines intersect then there must be

values of $\lambda$ and $\mu$ such that $\begin{bmatrix} 2 \\ 1 \\ 0 \end{bmatrix} + \lambda \begin{bmatrix} 1 \\ 1 \\ -2 \end{bmatrix}$

$= \begin{bmatrix} 5 \\ 2 \\ -1 \end{bmatrix} + \mu \begin{bmatrix} 2 \\ 0 \\ 1 \end{bmatrix}$. This gives the equations

$2 + \lambda = 5 + 2\mu$
$1 + \lambda = 2$
$-2\lambda = -1 + \mu$

The first and second equations give $\lambda = 1$ and $\mu = -1$ and this pair of values gives $-2\lambda = -2$ and $-1 + \mu = -2$ too and so the values satisfy the third equation. Hence the lines intersect. The point of intersection is $B$ $(3, 2, -2)$.

**(b)** The scalar product of the direction vectors is

$$\begin{bmatrix} 1 \\ 1 \\ -2 \end{bmatrix} \cdot \begin{bmatrix} 2 \\ 0 \\ 1 \end{bmatrix} = (1 \times 2) + (1 \times 0) + (-2 \times 1)$$

$= 2 + 0 - 2 = 0$ so the lines are perpendicular.

**(c)** When $\lambda = -1$, $\mathbf{r} = \begin{bmatrix} 2 \\ 1 \\ 0 \end{bmatrix} + -1 \begin{bmatrix} 1 \\ 1 \\ -2 \end{bmatrix} = \begin{bmatrix} 2 \\ 1 \\ 0 \end{bmatrix} + \begin{bmatrix} -1 \\ -1 \\ 2 \end{bmatrix}$

$= \begin{bmatrix} 1 \\ 0 \\ 2 \end{bmatrix}$. So point $A$ $(1, 0, 2)$ lies on the line.

**(d)** $p = 2$, $q = -3$

**(e)** $\sqrt{30}$

**2 (a)** $\mathbf{r} = \begin{bmatrix} 1 \\ 1 \\ -2 \end{bmatrix} + \lambda \begin{bmatrix} 1 \\ -4 \\ 2 \end{bmatrix}$

**(b)** $\mathbf{r} = \mu \begin{bmatrix} 7 \\ -3 \\ 8 \end{bmatrix}$

**(c)** A direction vector for $l_1$ is $\begin{bmatrix} 1 \\ -4 \\ 2 \end{bmatrix}$ and a

direction vector for $l_2$ is $\begin{bmatrix} 7 \\ -3 \\ 8 \end{bmatrix}$. They are not

scalar multiples of each other, so the lines are not parallel.

If the two lines intersect then there must be values of $\lambda$ and $\mu$ such that

$$\begin{bmatrix} 1 \\ 1 \\ -2 \end{bmatrix} + \lambda \begin{bmatrix} 1 \\ -4 \\ 2 \end{bmatrix} = \mu \begin{bmatrix} 7 \\ -3 \\ 8 \end{bmatrix}.$$

This gives the equations

$$1 + \lambda = 7\mu$$
$$1 - 4\lambda = -3\mu$$
$$-2 + 2\lambda = 8\mu$$

The first and second equations give $\lambda = \frac{2}{5}$ and $\mu = \frac{1}{5}$ but this pair of values gives $-2 + 2\lambda = -$  and $8\mu =$  and so the values do not satisfy the third equation. Hence the lines do not intersect.

Hence the lines are skew.

(d) $\sqrt{68}$, or $2\sqrt{17}$

**3 (a)** $\mathbf{r} = 5\mathbf{i} + 4\mathbf{k} + \lambda(3\mathbf{i} + \mathbf{j} - \mathbf{k})$

(b) $p = 8, q = 3$

(c) $39.5°$ (to 1 d.p.)

(d) $2\mathbf{i} - \mathbf{j} + 5\mathbf{k}$

**4 (a)** $\mathbf{r} = \begin{bmatrix} 2 \\ 1 \\ 1 \end{bmatrix} + \lambda \begin{bmatrix} 1 \\ 0 \\ -1 \end{bmatrix}$

(b) If lines intersect then there must be values of $\lambda$ and $\mu$ such that

$$\begin{bmatrix} 2 \\ 1 \\ 1 \end{bmatrix} + \lambda \begin{bmatrix} 1 \\ 0 \\ -1 \end{bmatrix} = \begin{bmatrix} 0 \\ 3 \\ -1 \end{bmatrix} + \mu \begin{bmatrix} -2 \\ 1 \\ 0 \end{bmatrix}.$$

This gives the equations

$$2 + \lambda = -2\mu$$
$$1 = 3 + \mu$$
$$1 - \lambda = -1$$

The first and second equations give $\lambda = 2$ and $\mu = -2$ and the value for $\lambda$ gives $1 - \lambda = -1$ and so the values satisfy the third equation. Hence the lines intersect.
The point of intersection is $(4, 1, -1)$.

(c) When $\mu = 4$, $\mathbf{r} = \begin{bmatrix} 0 \\ 3 \\ -1 \end{bmatrix} + 4 \begin{bmatrix} -2 \\ 1 \\ 0 \end{bmatrix} = \begin{bmatrix} 0 \\ 3 \\ -1 \end{bmatrix} + \begin{bmatrix} -8 \\ 4 \\ 0 \end{bmatrix}$

$= \begin{bmatrix} -8 \\ 7 \\ -1 \end{bmatrix}$. So point $C$ $(-8, 7, -1)$ lies on the line.

(d) $(-2, 1, 5)$

**5** $88.5°$ (to 1 d.p.)

**1 (a)** If the two lines intersect then there must be values of $\lambda$ and $\mu$ such that

$$\begin{bmatrix} 1 \\ 0 \\ -2 \end{bmatrix} + \lambda \begin{bmatrix} 1 \\ 4 \\ 3 \end{bmatrix} = \begin{bmatrix} 5 \\ 5 \\ 10 \end{bmatrix} + \mu \begin{bmatrix} 2 \\ -3 \\ 6 \end{bmatrix}.$$

This gives the equations

$$1 + \lambda = 5 + 2\mu$$
$$4\lambda = 5 - 3\mu$$
$$-2 + 3\lambda = 10 + 6\mu$$

The first and second equations give $\lambda = 2$ and $\mu = -1$ and this pair of values gives $-2 + 3\lambda = 4$ and $10 + 6\mu = 4$ too and so the values satisfy the third equation. Hence the lines intersect.
The point of intersection $P$ has position

vector $\begin{bmatrix} 3 \\ 8 \\ 4 \end{bmatrix}$.

(b) $77°$

(c) A direction vector for $l_3$ is $\begin{bmatrix} 2 \\ 8 \\ 6 \end{bmatrix}$ and a direction

vector for $l_1$ is $\begin{bmatrix} 1 \\ 4 \\ 3 \end{bmatrix}$.

$\begin{bmatrix} 2 \\ 8 \\ 6 \end{bmatrix} = 2 \begin{bmatrix} 1 \\ 4 \\ 3 \end{bmatrix}$ so the direction vectors are

parallel. Hence the lines are parallel.

**2 (a)** One way to argue is as follows.
$\overrightarrow{AB} = (4\mathbf{i} + 3\mathbf{j} + 3\mathbf{k}) - (2\mathbf{i} - \mathbf{j} + \mathbf{k})$
$= 2\mathbf{i} + 4\mathbf{j} + 2\mathbf{k} = 2(\mathbf{i} + 2\mathbf{j} + \mathbf{k})$ and
$\overrightarrow{BC} = (\mathbf{i} - 3\mathbf{j}) - (4\mathbf{i} + 3\mathbf{j} + 3\mathbf{k}) = -3\mathbf{i} - 6\mathbf{j} - 3\mathbf{k}$
$= -3(\mathbf{i} + 2\mathbf{j} + \mathbf{k})$. Hence $BC$ is parallel to $AB$.
So points $A$, $B$ and $C$ are in a straight line.

(b) A direction vector for $l$ is $\mathbf{i} + 2\mathbf{j} + \mathbf{k}$ and a direction vector for $OD$ is $\mathbf{i} + \mathbf{j} - 5\mathbf{k}$.
$(\mathbf{i} + 2\mathbf{j} + \mathbf{k}).(\mathbf{i} + \mathbf{j} - 5\mathbf{k}) = 1 + 2 - 5 = -2$.
$|\mathbf{i} + 2\mathbf{j} + \mathbf{k}| = \sqrt{1 + 4 + 1} = \sqrt{6}$ and
$|\mathbf{i} + \mathbf{j} - 5\mathbf{k}| = \sqrt{1 + 1 + 25} = \sqrt{27} = 3\sqrt{3}$.
Hence, if $\theta$ is the angle between the vectors $\mathbf{i} + 2\mathbf{j} + \mathbf{k}$ and $\mathbf{i} + \mathbf{j} - 5\mathbf{k}$ then

$$\cos\theta = \frac{-2}{\sqrt{6} \times 3\sqrt{3}} = -\frac{2}{3\sqrt{18}}$$
$$= -\frac{2}{9\sqrt{2}}$$
$$= -\frac{\sqrt{2}}{9}$$

So the cosine of the acute angle $(180 - \theta)$ is
$\frac{\sqrt{2}}{9}$ or $\frac{1}{9}\sqrt{2}$.

(c) A vector equation for $l$ is
$\mathbf{r} = 2\mathbf{i} - \mathbf{j} + \mathbf{k} + \lambda(\mathbf{i} + 2\mathbf{j} + \mathbf{k})$.
When $\lambda = -2$, $\mathbf{r} = 2\mathbf{i} - \mathbf{j} + \mathbf{k} - 2(\mathbf{i} + 2\mathbf{j} + \mathbf{k})$
$= 2\mathbf{i} - \mathbf{j} + \mathbf{k} - 2\mathbf{i} - 4\mathbf{j} - 2\mathbf{k} = -5\mathbf{j} - \mathbf{k}$ so $E$ lies on $l$.
$\overrightarrow{OE}.\overrightarrow{OD} = (-5\mathbf{j} - \mathbf{k}).(\mathbf{i} + \mathbf{j} - 5\mathbf{k}) = 0 - 5 + 5 = 0$
so $OE$ is perpendicular to $OD$.

**3 (a)** $\mathbf{r} = \begin{bmatrix} 3 \\ 1 \\ -2 \end{bmatrix} + \lambda \begin{bmatrix} 8 \\ 1 \\ -3 \end{bmatrix}$

(b) Let $P$ be the point on the line $l$ that is closest to $Q$ $(6, 5, -5)$ and let $O$ be the origin $(0, 0, 0)$. As $P$ is on the line, there must be some value of $\lambda$ for which $\overrightarrow{OP} = \begin{bmatrix} 3 \\ 1 \\ -2 \end{bmatrix} + \lambda \begin{bmatrix} 8 \\ 1 \\ -3 \end{bmatrix} = \begin{bmatrix} 3 + 8\lambda \\ 1 + \lambda \\ -2 - 3\lambda \end{bmatrix}$.

$\overrightarrow{QP} = \overrightarrow{OP} - \overrightarrow{OQ} = \begin{bmatrix} 3 + 8\lambda \\ 1 + \lambda \\ -2 - 3\lambda \end{bmatrix} - \begin{bmatrix} 6 \\ 5 \\ -5 \end{bmatrix} = \begin{bmatrix} -3 + 8\lambda \\ -4 + \lambda \\ 3 - 3\lambda \end{bmatrix}$

The direction of $l$ is given by the vector $\begin{bmatrix} 8 \\ 1 \\ -3 \end{bmatrix}$
and we know that $\overrightarrow{QP}$ must be perpendicular to this vector. So their scalar product must be 0.

Hence

$\begin{bmatrix} -3 + 8\lambda \\ -4 + \lambda \\ 3 - 3\lambda \end{bmatrix} . \begin{bmatrix} 8 \\ 1 \\ -3 \end{bmatrix} = 0$

$\Rightarrow 8(-3 + 8\lambda) + (-4 + \lambda) - 3(3 - 3\lambda) = 0$
$\Rightarrow -24 + 64\lambda - 4 + \lambda - 9 + 9\lambda = 0$
$\Rightarrow 74\lambda - 37 = 0$
$\Rightarrow \lambda = \frac{1}{2}$

So $\overrightarrow{QP} = \begin{bmatrix} -3 + 8 \times \frac{1}{2} \\ -4 + \frac{1}{2} \\ 3 - 3 \times \frac{1}{2} \end{bmatrix} = \begin{bmatrix} 1 \\ -\frac{7}{2} \\ \frac{3}{2} \end{bmatrix}$

The shortest distance is

$|\overrightarrow{QP}| = \sqrt{1^2 + \left(-\frac{7}{2}\right)^2 + \left(\frac{3}{2}\right)^2}$
$= \sqrt{1 + \frac{49}{4} + \frac{9}{4}}$
$= \sqrt{\frac{62}{4}} = \frac{\sqrt{62}}{2} = \frac{1}{2}\sqrt{62}$ as required.

**4 (a) (i)** $\frac{-4}{21}$

(ii) $\cos\angle PQR$ is negative but since the angle $PQR$ is part of a triangle then it must be less than $180°$ and so $\sin\angle PQR$ must be positive. Hence
$\sin\angle PQR = \sqrt{1 - (\cos\angle PQR)^2}$
$= \sqrt{1 - \left(\frac{-4}{21}\right)^2} = \sqrt{1 - \frac{16}{441}} = \sqrt{\frac{425}{441}} = \frac{5\sqrt{17}}{21}$
as required.

(b) $\frac{5\sqrt{17}}{2}$

**5 (a)** If the two lines intersect then there must be values of $t$ and $s$ such that
$\begin{bmatrix} 5 \\ 1 \\ -1 \end{bmatrix} + t \begin{bmatrix} 2 \\ 1 \\ 5 \end{bmatrix} = \begin{bmatrix} 13 \\ -6 \\ 2 \end{bmatrix} + s \begin{bmatrix} -3 \\ 4 \\ 1 \end{bmatrix}$.

This gives the equations
$5 + 2t = 13 - 3s$
$1 + t = -6 + 4s$
$-1 + 5t = 2 + s$

The first and second equations give $t = 1$ and $s = 2$ and this pair of values gives $-1 + 5t = 4$ and $2 + s = 4$ too and so the values satisfy the third equation. Hence the lines intersect. The point of intersection has coordinates $(7, 2, 4)$.

(b) $(9, 3, 9)$

# Index